THE WHEELWRIGHT'S SHOP

THE
WHEELWRIGHT'S SHOP

BY

GEORGE STURT
'GEORGE BOURNE'

CAMBRIDGE UNIVERSITY PRESS

CAMBRIDGE

LONDON   NEW YORK   NEW ROCHELLE

MELBOURNE   SYDNEY

Published by the Press Syndicate of the University of Cambridge
The Pitt Building, Trumpington Street, Cambridge CB2 IRP
32 East 57th Street, New York, NY 10022, USA
296 Beaconsfield Parade, Middle Park, Melbourne 3206, Australia

ISBN 0 521 06570 4 hard covers
ISBN 0 521 09195 0 paperback

First published 1923
Reprinted (by photography) 1934 1942 1943 1948 1958
First paperback edition 1963
Reprinted 1974 1976 1980

First printed in Great Britain at the University Press, Cambridge
Reprinted in Great Britain by
REDWOOD BURN LIMITED
Trowbridge & Esher

PREFACE

IN a vague way, no aim to that end having guided the writing of it, this book has become an autobiography for the years 1884 to 1891. For a long time after that my wheelwright business went on with no important change in technical matters although I had started some machinery; but there were great changes, for me personally, in the management of it; for it was in 1891 that I engaged a foreman-manager, William Goatcher, who after a few years became my partner. Incidentally his coming necessitated more careful book-keeping and "costing"; but my chief aim was to secure more freedom for myself; and in that respect the change was indeed a success. I was able to move into a village near Farnham, and to find leisure for playing at authorship at last. The authorship was hidden behind a pseudonym, to be sure, seeing that business still claimed most of my time and that some of my customers had no use for me as a literary man. They wanted a wheelwright, and my living depended as before on being that wheelwright.

But the new partnership involved one difference I had hardly foreseen. Goatcher—a Sussex man and an excellent "tradesman" (that is to say, a skilful man at his trade or craft)—was not only as acceptable as I had hoped to my customers, who soon and naturally put more confidence in him than in me; he also, and that too was not distressing, replaced me not a little with the workmen. Someone as practical as themselves had come between them and me. At the core my friendship with them was as true as it had ever been; yet some of the intimacies I had enjoyed in it were exchanged now for another intimacy—the helpful fellowship of a genial Sussex countryman.

The inner value of this fresh type of helpfulness did not at once impress itself on me. But after many years Goatcher, on whom I had laid so many burdens, died; and I began to know what he had been to me. I was by now, however, no longer young enough, or ignorant enough, to face a second time such a risky position as that described in this book. I had grown lazy. Authorship seemed easier than genuine work. In short it was with extreme reluctance that I took up again the never-ending burdens of business. I sought for someone to replace my lost partner, and in due course the very man was found in Mr William Arnold. Of the happiness for me in this new fellowship all that must be told here is how, upon my being paralysed in 1916, Mr Arnold carried on for me, never sparing himself but sparing me all he could, during the two or three years while the war still lasted. They would have been difficult years at the best; but, apart from the war, they were momentous years for wheel-wrights and coach-builders. The long-impending change from horses to petrol had come at last. An entirely new era had begun in my ancient business, needing an active man to face the root-and-branch adjustments called for; and being nowise active my-self, I stood aside to make way for Mr Arnold; and Mr Arnold, not eagerly, at last yielded to my persuasions to buy me out. By 1920 therefore I found myself for the first time a free man. My strength truly was gone, but at least all the leisure a man could wish for was mine now. Henceforward I had nothing to do but to "pacify the time," as a friend said.

I "pacified" it partly by writing one or two short books, and at last I turned to this. Was not the former experience wholly done at last? One thing, I found, was not ended at all. In 1884 true friends—they are named in these chapters—had stood by me in my great need; and now other friends were ready to help me, in shaping this account of the old wheelwright adventure into a book and getting it published. I do not refer to my sisters, who lent hands and feet and at last the voice I wanted. Without them, typing, sorting, indexing, this book could not have been done at all. Nor do I refer to my brother, with his unfailing encouragement and his remembrance of details I had forgotten. But after these three, I think of Mr Charles Young, who now joyfully took on all the business arrangements for me as if he were another self; and, next to him, Doctor Brown who was helpful with the proofs, and Miss Eleanor Dutton who spent days of her holidays helping my sister with the index.

Then also acknowledgement should be made to Miss Robins, and to Miss West, for preparing diagrams from my sketches. These two were indefatigable. Mr Douglas Benger found ways of his own to help me. Mr Arnold had provided some of the photographs: Mrs Barling took others. Mr Tester found and instructed a photographer to get three more. Mr Lunn put his farm tackle at my disposal; Mr Charles West helped with the index; Mr and Mrs Alfred Prior gave hours to it. And to say nothing of others, whose ready interest was encouraging from time to time, there are various men connected with the Cambridge University Press who have earned not a little of my gratitude, by their eagerness to meet my suggestions. One of them only perhaps may be named now—the late Mr J. B. Peace. Though I never met Mr Peace, his sudden death seemed to me like losing a friend. Only a day or two earlier he had contributed a useful suggestion for the glossary; and already he had taken special pains to get one of the insets properly re-drawn. But true craftsmen are like that. They love to be helpful, as this book may further show.

G. S.

6 *February* 1923

CONTENTS

ORIGINS

TIMBER

GENERAL WORK

WHEELS

TYRING

SMITHING AND SUNDRIES

THE OLD ORDER CHANGING

ILLUSTRATIONS

PLATES (*between pages* 100–101)

TEXT-FIGURES

ORIGINS

I

BEGINNINGS

THE title-deeds to the property referred to in this book begin with an indenture of the 17th October, 1706, on which date Robert Hewitt, yeoman, and his wife Joan, in consideration of five shillings paid to them in hand, agree to sell fifteen rods of hop-ground to George Draper, wheel-maker.

The property is described as part of six acres of hop-ground purchased of "one John fforder, late of ffarnham, Gentleman," and is indicated as being three rods wide adjoining the highway leading to Guildford, and five rods in length, to the north. On the following day the sale was completed, the Hewitts conveying the land to George Draper and his wife Elizabeth for twelve pounds.

Here I stop a minute to reflect that Farnham was no longer at that time, if it had ever been, quite the sleepy rustic village one is tempted to imagine. If the Castle looked across more thatched roofs even than tiles, and over a wider spread of meadows than now, and if many of those roofs covered barns or little farmsteads, still the place had its towny features. What sort of street life did George Draper see when he glanced up from his wheel-making in his new shop? And what sort of business did he expect? Besides strangers coming to the Castle or to the Grammar School and sometimes wanting their coach wheels mended, or travellers along the roads out of London—now through Bagshot Heath, now through Guildford, but in either case passing through the one and only street of Farnham— besides these, and wayfarers from off the sea at Southampton, and the well-known figures of native townsfolk, native crafts- men, often in smock frocks—besides these, and hop-planters, and yeomen of the town such as Robert Hewitt, there would be drovers and waggoners, and, every market day, farmers from outlying farms coming to the corn-market for which Farnham was already almost famous throughout the south of England.

These last—these farmers—I surmise were the customers to whom Draper was mainly looking for trade. For these he was prepared to build the dung-carts and waggons, the ploughs and harrows, that must have been wanted on the land. The farmers may be pictured, as they entered from that end of the town, pulling up at the "Seven Stars," just past the wheel-maker's new shop, and bargaining with him there about their tackle.

Of course they had hardly left the country behind. Hop-grounds then came down to the very road just before Draper's was reached—a steep lane (with five-bar gate—which I remember—across it at the top, to keep out cattle or pigs) led up amongst the hops and divided Draper's place from the "Seven Stars." An elm-tree (now pollarded and dying) was a sort of rustic sign to the new premises; and in short everything must have been what we should call most countrified. Yet it is pretty safe to guess that Farnham folk were not of that opinion. More likely they said, as I lately heard one of their successors say, "It gets more like London every day."

Certainly things were moving. Many handsome houses in Farnham that now look antique yet substantial were new houses at that period and show that it was a time of prosperity and growth. In the more modest style of a working tradesman George Draper did his share in the little town's advancement. Precisely what he built I can hardly even surmise; but build he must have done—some cheap workshop perhaps; for after fifteen years, namely in 1721, he sold the whole property, of which £12 had been the purchase price, for £90. The buyer was Edward Wheeler, of Badshot, a blacksmith. The conveyance is signed also by a bricklayer and a tallow chandler.

A mortgage of the property, for £60, redeemed in January, 1724, possibly points to further building; but I have nothing to prove this. Wheeler died intestate: the property came to his son John, also a blacksmith; and eventually passed into the hands of John's two nieces. In 1792 these two sold it to John Tarrett or Jarrett; and he, in 1795, to William Grover, wheelwright. The price, then, was £200.

At this point the history begins to be of great personal interest to me. Within a few months Grover was mortgaging the premises for the full amount he had given for them; and I incline to think he was raising money for building. This would give 1795 as about the date, which also was the date an architect on other grounds surmised, of the existing shop and the adjoining dwelling-house. That is to say, "the shop" of these chapters—the shop I came to know so well—was erected about 1795 by William Grover.

Something he had done, at any rate, to heighten the value of the place before he in his turn sold it. From £200 it rose to £700, when, in June, 1810, it was bought by my own grandfather, George Sturt. From that date until 1920, when at last I sold it, the property was uninterruptedly in the possession of my family.

II

THE STURTS

George Sturt, my grandfather, was not a stranger to the shop when he bought it. He had been leading man there for some time; and he seems to have introduced sundry improvements in the work as well as in the premises. That he put up a new workshop for Grover appears from an indorsement of the conveyance (7 June, 1810) in which Grover acknowledges £50 paid by Sturt for building a new workshop. This, I fancy, was the building afterwards called "The Lathe House," where stood the antique lathe described on p. 56, which I have always understood was set up by my grandfather. It seems almost certain to me, first, that he only made a lathe on condition that a proper "house" for it should be built, and second, that Grover was not very well able to refuse what his leading man wanted. But perhaps he was already under a promise to sell him the place.

Be that as it may, George Sturt was a strong man at his trade. For some time he had worked in London, where he only escaped being taken by a press-gang by hiding in a barrel. His London work was the making of wheels, for stage-coaches probably; and this was on piece-work terms, the task being, if it can be believed, a wheel a day. So I have been told, but it seems incredible. Without machinery, to mortice a stock, foot and shave and drive and tongue the spokes, bore and perhaps mortice and shave and wedge on the felloes, for one wheel, all in a single day, was (I should guess) utterly beyond any man, even in those days. True, the customary hours were from five in the morning until eight at night: true, George Sturt used to get back to his inn so tired that he was obliged to lie down for half an hour before he could eat any supper. It is also true that he was a very quick workman—he was always the second in the shop to have finished the day's task, the first being a man named Keen, of whom more presently. But, in spite of all these considerations, I still find it hard to believe the statement I had more than once from one of his daughters, that George Sturt, when a young man working on task-work in London, was wont as his task to make a wheel a day.

The man Keen just mentioned must now be spoken of. Probably his comradeship with George Sturt in the same London shop sprang from a childhood friendship in a village, for while there was a large family of Sturts at Liphook, in the neighbouring parish of Headley dwelt the Keens.

The chief of these was Edward Keen, a yeoman, presumably father of George Sturt's comrade in London. This Edward Keen seems to have backed George Sturt in his purchase of the shop in Farnham about Midsummer, 1810, having already in February given his daughter in marriage to the young man. The marriage was at St Mary's, Whitechapel, and I think it possible that the purchase of the Farnham business was a part of the marriage arrangement. The dwelling-house, much as it is to-day, was already in existence. I have an inventory of the household furniture (a quantity of which was still in being in my childhood) taken over at a valuation on the 1st August, 1810. That was presumably the date of my grandfather's settling into that house—so familiar to me. There he brought up his family, making wheelwrights of his five sons, of whom my father was the youngest.

But Edward Keen, the Headley yeoman, had another interest in the business, besides his daughter's. That son of his, the quick wheel-maker in London, came into partnership with George Sturt, and he also came to live in Farnham, a few doors away. This much I have been told. The first notice I have of him in writing however is a bond of the 3rd of August, 1826, dissolving the partnership and restraining "William Keen" from wheel-wright's work for twelve years. He practised coach-building—almost a distinct art—and was the founder of the business now carried on as motor-works by Messrs Heath and Wiltshire. I just remember being taken to see William Keen's widow—"Aunt Keen," my own aunt called her—an old lady in black silk and with no charm for a child. As I have since heard, she and George Sturt's wife (whom I never saw) were the cause of the ultimate dissolution of the partnership. The two wives, living so close to the workshops, quarrelled over the spoils—the waste refuse of the timber, so useful for firing—and the husbands parted.

The rest is pretty nearly all hear-say. George Sturt, carrying on business alone, secured, after renting it for some years, another small piece of hop-ground for a timber-yard; but I cannot now determine where it was; and he also, in 1828, raised £550 by mortgaging the original property, probably for further building. This, however, would rather have been for some adjacent cottages than for the wheelwright's shop.

Meanwhile—I wonder for how long?—the back part of the premises, afterwards occupied by smithy and timber-shed, was given over to kitchen garden and pigsties, some of the garden trees being still alive in 1884. There was no smithy. Such iron-work as was wanted for the business was made at Frensham, three miles away, where George Sturt had acquired a smithy and was soon to start a branch of his wheelwright business. He was wont to fetch the iron-work to Farnham himself, bringing it back from Frensham on his own shoulders—a circumstance very indicative of how little encroachment iron-work had made upon wood-work at that period. Well might my friend, Harry Hole, tell me lately (1920) that he had always liked making dung-carts in the old shop, because he could get so far with them without troubling the blacksmith. The iron-work still did not amount to much. Hole was talking of a time not more than forty years ago or so, but it was probably one of the advantages of dung-carts that the village wheelwright could build them without going often to the smith. These carts were, I suspect, one of my grandfather's staple products. Was it not in a dung-cart of his build that a certain well-to-do Frensham farmer was in the habit of driving to Farnham market? At that time part of the road he would traverse was an uncertain heath-track, and farmers had not risen to the grandeur of a dog-cart or the respectability of a gig. Even in the matter of wheel-tyres their tackle required but little smithing. At least it is likely that the wheelwrights at Farnham were able to put on the "strakes" without blacksmiths' help; for I think the apparatus for that job, as I found it in 1884, was much older than the smithy. Anyhow, smithy there was not, any nearer than Frensham, to work for this old shop at the time referred to now.

A little before the day of railways my grandfather had a contract to keep the "road-waggons" in order for his district. He used to go to his front gate, on the main Farnham street, to listen for their coming across "The Downs," that is to say, along the Hog's Back. When the waggons were coming down the incline by the "Victory" Inn, though still three miles away, they were audible to my grandfather at his gate. He could go indoors then—have some supper probably. The waggons got to Farnham, where it was his duty to look to them, about ten o'clock at night. The place where they put up is now Messrs Mardon & Ball's "Wagon Yard Joinery."

In connection with this same business one Johnny Gunner has been named to me, as the only workman my grandfather could find in the neighbourhood able to deal with road-waggon wheels. Those large and cumbersome vehicles, meant to carry the sort of goods now loaded on railway-trucks, had hind wheels six feet high or more, and very wide. And since Master[1] Gunner

---

[1] This is the way that men in the shop were spoken of by the aunt mentioned above. Again and again in her chatter she told, as if with esteem, of "Old Master Whiten," his position being that of a skilled craftsman. A comparatively unskilled labourer was spoken of as Old Henry.

was singular in his skill to handle them, it is not surprising if he took advantage of his position. Several times he was discharged, but each time he had to be re-engaged. He lived at Hale, on the opposite side of Farnham Park. In order to get home the more quickly he used to climb the fence about a furlong away from the shop and strike across the Park. 'A track through the turf there was pointed out to me by my aunt as "Johnny Gunner's Path."

In 1865 the business, with the stock-in-trade, was made over to my father, the shop and dwelling-house being conveyed to his sister and to his brother John, who had worked in the shop but was paralysed at about that time. But all this was merely a precaution. Wishing to spare his children the legal expense of legacies, the old man chose to distribute his property amongst them during his life-time. I don't think it made much difference to him or to them. Years afterwards I saw him (John too) in the old house. He kept the accounts for my father—I remember him putting his pen across between his lips, so as to have two hands for turning over his ledger. I thought it fussy of him to complain if I happened to shake his table.

But, at some time before this transfer, he had taken another step in the development of his business, building smithy and timber-shed at the back of the premises, where the pigsties used to be. The smithy was the one I remember and sometimes worked in—the one that was burnt down about twenty years ago; and the first smith there was probably Will Hammond, who had already worked at Frensham for my father's brother Richard. All that is told about Will Hammond in the following chapters supposes this smithy my grandfather built to be the scene of his lofty-souled though lowly-minded labours. Let me give here a sketch-map (not to scale, but from memory) of the premises at this time, when I was but a child.

From the bench under the smithy window, where he "tapped" his nuts or did his painstaking filing—from this bench or from the open upper half of the door beside it, Will Hammond had view some thirty feet down the sloping yard to the back door of the wheel-shop below. Or, if any job was brought up the lane outside from the street, that too he could not fail to see, for there

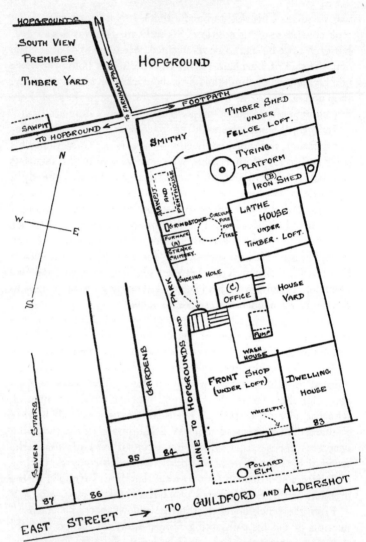

GROUND PLAN (NOT TO SCALE) OF THE WHEELWRIGHT'S SHOP
IN 1884.

was no other way to the smithy, unless you went through the wheelwright's shop itself—the original site fixed on in 1706—and up the steps at back of it. "Up," observe. Everything was on a steep incline. The floor of the smithy was up the hill, well above the level of anybody's head in the street. And behind the premises the ground continued rising, through hop-gardens, until Farnham Park was reached; and still in 'the Park it rose as far again—a fine and very peaceful acclivity.

In the succeeding years, while I was growing up, a number of changes in the premises and neighbourhood left the general quietness little if at all disturbed. At the spot marked (A) in the plan a "furnace" for hoop-tyres was built, superseding the old circle in the middle of the yard; at (B) a shed was put up for holding iron bars, bundles of hooping, plough-castings, drug-bats, and other odds and ends in iron; while at (C) my father had an office erected, doubtless when his own father at last gave up keeping the books for him. This diminutive place, with a smaller "nail-loft" up some steep stairs, became my own private refuge for years and I remember it with affection.

The biggest change, however, was the beginning of building in Farnham—one of the first moves towards modern conditions in fact, in all the recent growth of that town; and it was my father who opened the door for it. With dreams of going into the timber-trade, for which indeed he had knowledge enough if not enough capital, he was on the look-out for a timber-yard; and an opportunity came, when a strip of hop-ground stretching from the back of East Street right up to Farnham Park palings was sold to him. The greater part of this he laid out as the "South View Building Estate," reserving to himself one corner, near to his shop, for the desired timber-yard. Here he made a saw-pit, and put up various sheds and a temporary workshop; here he projected who knows what other developments? It was too late. The year was 1883. In 1884 he died; and I, for my part, did not know how to carry on even the ordinary business. I had no more than a month, if as much as that, of my father's guidance in it. He was, in fact, sickening for his last illness, when I entered the business in 1884.

III

MY OWN START

Ruskin's *Fors Clavigera* had made me think meanly, if not meanly enough, of the school teaching which had been my work since 1878; and under the same influence of Ruskin's book I felt that man's only decent occupation was in handicraft. I shudder yet smile to think now what raw ideas swayed me then; yet the enthusiasm so ill-reflected in them were the sweetness of life to me in every disillusionment that was to come. They saved me from the worst sordidness of business. Finishing my school work with the first term of 1884, namely the day before Good Friday, I took four days of rest (I was to have no more vacations for many years) and began work at the shop on Easter Tuesday.

I don't remember what I did that day; but I do remember the grey and searching east wind that faced me in the street at six o'clock in the morning. There was a little over a furlong of street for me to travel, familiar enough, but I had never before seen it at that early hour. I have a vague idea that my brother went with me those first few mornings, to protect me. It is what he would have done. But I did not realise that. With everything to learn I was not much good; but I could at least deputise for my father, who seemed so poorly, to the extent of unlocking the shop at six o'clock in the morning and locking up again at six at night.

This was a rather more complicated affair than it need have been[1]. My grandfather, when living in the adjoining house, had quite naturally got into his shop from the back. He had not needed to enter the street at all. My father, also living in the same house until he was married, had never altered the arrangement. But, for me, it was awkward. I couldn't go through the dwelling-house, which was let. But the front doors of the shop had never been made to be unfastened from outside—from the

[1] See p. 209.

street. So, every morning I had to walk up the lane and unlock the side gate, unlock and remove the padlock from the back door of the shop and grope my way down through the litter of chips and shavings to the front doors. This too, in the dark; for the gas meter, lately fixed, was at the wrong end of the shop near the front doors. There, in the dark, I had to unpin and unchain a bar, and pull out bolts, just as men of my name had been doing for three-quarters of a century, before the double doors in front could be opened. Of course it didn't take long, but it should not have been so at all. Usually the front doors were then thrown back for the rest of the day; but in very bad weather—in driving snow or rain—they were drawn together again, the one of them bolted as for night, the other latched to it inside, with a wooden latch. The only way of lifting this latch from the outside was to put your finger under it, through a hole in the door provided for that purpose.

The shop was still but half opened when the two front doors had been unfastened. On either hand was a window, shuttered at night with two shutters put up from within and then fixed with a wooden bar. When the shutters had been taken down from the windows there was nothing to take their place. Snow, freezing wind, had a clear run. With so much chopping to do one could keep fairly warm; but I have stood all aglow yet resenting the open windows, feeling my feet cold as ice though covered with chips. To supply some glass shutters for day-time was one of the first changes I made in the shop. Nowadays, when all the heavy work is done by machinery, men would not and probably could not work at all in such a place; yet it must have sufficed for several generations. My grandfather and my father had put up with it, and so did I until the winter came round again and the men began to ask me for sundry small indulgences, of which this was one.

Six o'clock in the morning was well enough in the summer; none the less I liked the dark winter mornings better. Truly they were dark! At that time the Farnham Local Board, caring nothing for working-class convenience and caring much to save money, had all the street lamps in the town put out at midnight.

The result was that, in the depth of winter, every man who went
to work at six in the morning, and most artisans did, had to find
his way without any light. To be sure, there were moonlight
mornings. Sometimes, too, snowy roofs showed clear enough
under glittering starlight. But, on the other hand, there was
freezing fog, there was the blackness of dense rain. One foggy
morning I lost my whereabouts in the familiar street; no building
could be seen nor any sky distinguished; nothing but a slight
difference in the feel of the pavement under my feet told me
that I was passing So and So's shop. Another time a little
glimmering light that met and passed me proved to be a lighted
candle-end between the fingers of a chimney sweep, against
whom one might otherwise have uncomfortably blundered. And
one black morning I walked through and was conscious of what
I took to be the aura of a man on the pavement whom I never
saw—probably a motionless policeman.

Yet these dark mornings pleased me, as I have said, better
than the summer mornings. For, when at last I had got to my
office and made up a fire in my little stove, I could usually be
sure of an uninterrupted hour for my own pursuits. No man
came asking me to look out nails before daylight; there was
small need to wander across the dark yards and into the ill-lit
shops at that hour. Under the naked gas jet—burning "horny"
because full of dust—my office desk was a sort of heaven for
me. Sometimes, like a good boy, I spent that precious hour at
accounts; oftener, it was given to literary exercises—imitations
of Thoreau or Emerson or Carlyle—anything that seemed to
uplift me above the sordid cares (as I thought them) that would
come with daylight, so pale and chilly too.

There was another reason for preferring dark mornings.
With my mind so priggishly puffed up, I was glad to miss the
"Good mornings" of other wayfarers not recognisable in the
unlit street. I wanted to be alone. Nay, so great was my passion for
solitude that sometimes, if I had time and the weather allowed,
I digressed into a lonelier though slightly longer route. From the
sticky hop-ground footpath at the back of East Street I might
hear (if I could not see, across the night) the trees in Farnham

Park, keeping up their everlasting noise in the wind. Then I felt nice and poetical I thoroughly enjoyed getting afterwards into my gas-lit office and flattering myself that I was writing like Thoreau.

Getting up in the morning was not my strong point, for my evenings were too interesting and I could not bring myself to go to bed quite soon enough. Indeed, there was no other way of securing a little time. Every night I wound up an alarum, and saw to it that some coffee had been put ready for warming up while I was dressing the next morning; yet often I lay too long after the alarum, skipped into my clothes without waiting for the coffee, and swung out into the street, late again and cross. But tobacco was a help. Coffee or none, I always lit a pipe for that four minutes' walk; and I have never again since that was given up enjoyed a smoke so much. At that early hour whiffs from other men's pipes were good to smell. Often, on getting to the shop, I found one man there. He had walked from Wrecclesham—two miles; and he was always the first and always punctual. Several times, when he stepped into the newly opened door and met the sudden gas-light, it was startling to see (what had been invisible in the darkness until then) a white beard coming into the shop instead of a black one; only, pricklings in my own moustache had warned me what to expect. Ten or twelve degrees of frost would make little icicles from my breath even in that short walk of mine; and naturally after his two miles the blacksmith looked frosty.

He was so regular and so true he would have been a first-rate "knocker-up" for me; but seniority gave the claim for that to Will Hammond. It was Will's duty, as he passed my door, to ascertain if I had left a bit of string on the knob of the bell: if not, he would know I was not gone and would ring for me. A horrible thing it was, to be wakened out of sleep by that peal; but it happened sometimes, the very alarum having failed to arouse me. I grew to hate that alarum. On Saturday nights, instead of winding it up, I used to shake my fist at it, as it were tauntingly, because it would not be able to disturb my Sunday morning.

This early morning work I kept up for seven years, with little but week-end holidays besides the Bank Holidays. Longer indulgences were not for the working-classes or anybody who aped them. But there were times—too many of them—when heavy bronchial catarrh made me almost unable to cross the room; and at such times my brother—as if he had no exacting days of his own—would deputise for me at six o'clock in the morning. He had one odd experience. It should have been explained that, as we had at home but one door into the street and no latch-key to it, the custom was to lock the door behind one and put the key back through the letter-box for those inside. My brother did this one freezing dark morning, and then heard the town-clock, up in the dark, strike four. He had locked himself out two hours too soon. If you think he woke the household to be readmitted you don't know the sort of man he is. Other people's convenience was never sacrificed for his own. He went for a walk to Caesar's Camp, three miles away, where he found the silence and darkness almost uncanny. There must be few if any other men who have ever been there at all on a dark winter morning.

It was probably in 1885 that we left off on Saturdays at one o'clock instead of at four; and it may have been about the same time (but I have no recollection of it) that half-past five was substituted for six as the normal closing time. If the shop was "making over-time" we took half an hour for tea and then went on again from six to eight. Including meal-times, this gave us a fourteen-hour day. The meal-times were, for breakfast half an hour (from eight to half past); for dinner, from one to two. The ringing of Heath's bell across the street (Sturt had none) was the signal. To see the shop empty at the first stroke for dinner was to know the source of that metaphor for quickness, To Go Like One O'clock.

Though the normal hours were too long, the men were glad of over-time. In this connection it should be pointed out that in those days a man's work, though more laborious to his muscles, was not nearly so exhausting yet tedious as machinery and "speeding-up" have since made it for his mind and temper.

"Eight hours" to-day is less interesting and probably more toilsome than "twelve hours" then. But when men welcomed over-time it was because with their 24s. for an ordinary week they were underpaid and were glad to add to the money. The addition was at the rate of 6d. an hour, I think. One odd thing, which I never could understand, was that jealousy which caused the men to regard it almost as a right for all to have over-time if one did; so that however pressed the smiths might be I hardly dared ask them to work longer without giving the same treatment to the woodmen. A pack of children, I sometimes thought these grown men, all older than myself.

IV

THE WHEELWRIGHT'S SHOP

To say that the business I started into in 1884 was old-fashioned is to understate the case: it was a "folk" industry, carried on in a "folk" method. And circumstances made it perhaps more intensely so to me than it need have been. My father might just possibly, though I don't think he would, have shown me more modern aspects of it; but within my first month he took ill of the illness he died of five months later. Consequently I was left to pick up the business as best I could from "the men." There were never any "hands" with us. Eight skilled workmen or apprentices, eight friends of the family, put me up to all they could: and since some of them had been born and trained in little old country shops, while this of my father's was not much better, the lore I got from them was of the country through and through.

The objects of the work too were provincial. There was no looking far afield for customers. Farmers rarely more than five miles away; millers, brewers, a local grocer or builder or timber-merchant or hop-grower—for such and no others did the ancient shop still cater, as it had done for nearly two centuries. And so we got curiously intimate with the peculiar needs of the neighbourhood. In farm-waggon or dung-cart, barley-roller, plough, water-barrel, or what not, the dimensions we chose, the curves we followed (and almost every piece of timber was curved) were imposed upon us by the nature of the soil in this or that farm, the gradient of this or that hill, the temper of this or that customer or his choice perhaps in horseflesh. The carters told us their needs. To satisfy the carter, we gave another half-inch of curve to the waggon-bottom, altered the hooks for harness on the shafts, hung the water-barrel an inch nearer to the horse or an inch farther away, according to requirements.

One important point, which it's true was not always important (for hard roads, for instance) but was sometimes very important indeed, was to make the wheels of waggon or dung-cart "take the routs[1]," as we said. A variant of this was to get the wheels of a waggon to "follow," the hind wheels cutting the same ruts as the front. One inch of variation was allowed, no more. The track of new dung-cart or waggon might measure 5 ft. 10½ ins. or 5 ft. 11½ ins. "over," that is, from outside to outside. A miry lane at a farm revealed to me the importance of keeping to this measurement. Two parallel ruts went all down the lane, deep as the hub of a cart wheel. Many carts, for many years perhaps, had followed there; and plainly the lane would be impassable for any cart or waggon with wheels too wide asunder or too narrow. So, the wheel-spaces were standardised.

This was but one of the endless details the complete wheelwright had to know all about. For the complete wheelwright, acquiring skill of eyes and hands to make a wheel, was good enough workman then for the job of building a waggon throughout and painting it too; and all this was expected of him. There was a tale (of another shop than mine) of an aged man who, having built and painted a waggon, set about "writing" (lettering) the owner's name and address on the small name-board fixed to the off front side. He managed all right until he came to the address, "Swafham" or "Swayle," but this word puzzled him. He scratched his head, at last had to own himself baffled; and appealed to his mate. "Let's see, Gearge," he said, "blest if I ain't forgot how you makes a Sway!"

Gearge showed him.

Truly there were mysteries enough, without the mystery of "writing," for an unlettered man. Even the mixing and putting on of the paint called for experience. The first two coats, of Venetian-red for the underworks and shafts and "lid colour" (lead colour) for the "body," prepared the way for the putty, which couldn't be "knocked-up" by instinct; and then came the last coat, of red-lead for the wheels and Prussian-blue for the body, to make all look smart and showy.

Not any of this could be left wholly to an apprentice. Apprentices, after a year or two, might be equal to making and painting a wheelbarrow. But it was a painful process with them learning the whole trade. Seven years was thought not too long. After seven years, a young man, newly "out of his time" was held likely to pick up more of his craft in the next twelve months than he had dreamt of before. By then too he should have won the skill that came from wounds. For it was a saying of my grandfather's that nobody could learn to make a wheel without chopping his knee half-a-dozen times[1].

There was nothing for it but practice and experience of every difficulty. Reasoned science for us did not exist. "Theirs not to reason why." What we had to do was to live up to the local wisdom of our kind; to follow the customs, and work to the measurements, which had been tested and corrected long before our time in every village shop all across the country. A wheelwright's brain had to fit itself to this by dint of growing into it, just as his back had to fit into the supplenesses needed on the saw-pit, or his hands into the movements that would plane a felloe "true out o' wind." Science? Our two-foot rules took us no nearer to exactness than the sixteenth of an inch: we used to make or adjust special gauges for the nicer work; but very soon a stage was reached when eye and hand were left to their own cleverness, with no guide to help them. So the work was more of an art—a very fascinating art—than a science; and in this art, as I say, the brain had its share. A good wheelwright knew by art but not by reasoning the proportion to keep between

[1] Note B, p. 206.

spokes and felloes; and so too a good smith knew how tight a
two-and-a-half inch tyre should be made for a five-foot wheel
and how tight for a four-foot, and so on. He felt it, in his
bones. It was a perception with him. But there was no science
in it; no reasoning. Every detail stood by itself, and had to be
learnt either by trial and error or by tradition.

This was the case with all dimensions. I knew how to "line
out" a pair of shafts on a plank, and had in fact lined and helped
saw on the saw-pit hundreds of them, years before I understood,
thinking it over, why this method came right. So too it was years
before I understood why a cart wheel needed a certain convexity
although I had seen wheels fall to pieces for want of it. It was
a detail most carefully attended to by the men in my shop; but
I think none of them, any more than myself, could have explained why it had to be so.

Some things I never learnt at all, they being all but obsolete
even in that primitive shop. To say nothing of square-tongued
wheels—a mystery I still think of with some awe—there was
the placing of the "tines" in a wooden harrow that remained an
unknown secret to me. The opportunities of investigating it
had been too few when cast-iron harrows, ready-made, banished
the whole subject from our attention. I just learnt how the
harrow was put together to be hauled over the field by one
corner; but the trick of mortising the teeth—the "tines"—into
it so that no two cut the same track—this was known to one
elderly man but never to me. The same man also failed to teach
me how to "line out" a wooden axle. Indeed, he forgot it
himself at last. So it happened that when an ancient dung-cart
arrived, needing a wooden axle for its still serviceable wheels,
nobody was quite sure how to mark out the axle on the bone-hard
bit of beech that was found for it. It was then that my rather
useless schooling came in handy for once. With a little geometry
I was able to pencil out on the beech the outlines of an axle to
serve (in its clumsier dimensions) the better-known purposes of
iron. Yet I have no doubt that the elderly wheelwright's tradition
would have been better, if only he could have remembered it.

TIMBER

V

BUYING

ONE aspect of the death of Old England and of the replacement of the more primitive nation by an "organised" modern state was brought out forcibly and very disagreeably by the War against Germany. It was not only that one saw the beautiful fir-woods going down, though that was bad. The trees, cut into lengths, stripped of their bark and stacked in piles, gave to many an erst secluded hill-side a staring publicity. This or that quiet place, the home of peace, was turned into a ghastly battle-field, with the naked and maimed corpses of trees lying about. Bad enough, all this was. Still, trees might grow again; the hollows might recover their woodland privacy and peace for other generations to enjoy. But what would never be recovered, because in fact War had found it already all but dead, was the earlier English understanding of timber, the local knowledge of it, the patriarchal traditions of handling it. Of old there had been a close relationship between the tree-clad country-side and the English who dwelt there. But now, the affection and the reverence bred of this—for it had been with something near to reverence that a true provincial beheld his native trees—was all but gone. A sort of greedy prostitution desecrated the ancient woods. All round me I saw and heard of things being done with a light heart that had always seemed to me wicked—things as painful to my sympathies as harnessing a carriage-horse to a heavy dray, or as pulling down a cathedral to get building-stone. I resented it; resented seeing the fair timber callously felled at the wrong time of year, cut up too soon, not "seasoned" at all. Perhaps the German sin had made all this imperative; yet it was none the less hateful. Not as waste only was it hateful: it was an outrage on the wisdom of our forefathers—a wanton insult put upon Old England, in her woods and forests.

The new needs were so different from the old. What had been prized once was prized no more. The newer vehicles, motor-drawn, were not expected to last longer than eight or ten years at the most; five years, oftener, found them obsolete, and therefore durability was hardly considered in the timber used for their construction. But it was otherwise in the earlier time, in the old-fashioned wheelwright's shop. Any piece of work had to last for years. Fashion, or invention, didn't affect it. So it was held a shame to have to do work twice over because the original material had been faulty; and I have known old-fashioned workmen refuse to use likely-looking timber because they held it to be unfit for the job.

And they knew. The skilled workman was the final judge. Under the plane (it is little used now) or under the axe (it is all but obsolete) timber disclosed qualities hardly to be found otherwise. My own eyes know because my own hands have felt, but I cannot teach an outsider, the difference between ash that is "tough as whipcord," and ash that is "frow as a carrot," or "doaty," or "biscuity." In oak, in beech, these differences are equally plain, yet only to those who have been initiated by practical work. These know how "green timber" (that is, timber with some sap left in it, imperfectly "seasoned") does not look like properly dried timber, after planing. With axe or chisel or draw-shave they learn to distinguish between the heart of a plank and the "sap." And again, after years of attention, but nohow else, timber-users can tell what "shakes" are good and what bad. For not all shakes, all natural splits, in seasoned timber are injurious. On the contrary it was an axiom in my shop that good timber in drying was bound to "open" (care had to be taken to prevent it from opening too far) and that timber must be bad, must have lost all its youthful toughness, if the process of drying developed no shakes in it.

A wheelwright had to be quite familiar with little truths like these in buying his timber, and then not forget other considerations. In my shop we bought trees "in the round"—as they lay in the wood or the hedgerow where they had been felled or "thrown." And, immediately, the season of throwing came into question. Some oak, cut down in the dead of the winter, was called "winter-cut." It dried into excellent material, the sap almost as hard, though nothing like so durable, as the heart. Winter-cut oak always had the bark on it. And for this reason it was scarce, and "spring-cut" was commoner, the bark having a high market-value for tanning. Most oak therefore was thrown early in spring, when the running of the sap allowed the bark to be stripped off easily. A further advantage was that this spring-cut oak lent itself so well to the craft of "cleaving" spokes and laths.

It followed that the expeditions to buy oak were always in the late spring or the summer. The bark had been stripped then—it stood in big brown stacks beside the shining butter-coloured "sticks" or butts of timber, where they lay in the brambles and newly springing fern. The "lop and top"—the branches and twigs—had also been stacked, the bigger branches into cordwood, good for fires, the smaller—the twiggy boughs—into "bavins" or "sprays" such as bakers want for their ovens or potters for their kilns. So, the ground was clear enough for the wheelwright to examine his trees, and to measure them if he bought. And a delightful outing he had of it.

For his quest took him into sunny woodland solitudes, amongst unusual things and with country men of a shy type good to meet. It was while looking at some oak (near the Hog's Back) that I first heard the word "puckeridge," when a startled bird flitted away into a shady thicket. "Nasty p'isonous birds," said the man with me. Another time, as I pushed through some brambles in "Alice Holt" and came to a patch of spurge (or it may have been a mist of blue-bells), the tall young forester who was showing me the oak-trees suddenly dropped forward his full length without bending; and when he stood up he had got a rabbit in his hands.

Other timber than oak (always, of whatever sort, felled in winter) invited the timber-buyer into the winter woods or along leafless hedgerows. It was in stodging from hedge to hedge across wet water-meadows in February to look at some ash that my father took the chill which started his last illness. Elm was rather a haphazard crop with us: it would keep so long in the round that the season of throwing was not much if at all regarded

—though I have seen it "perished" by its own sap imprisoned in the unopened log. With beech it is just the reverse. During the war vast quantities of beech were spoiled, in the prevailing ignorance when to throw it and open the timber. Spoiled, I mean, for old-fashioned wheelwright work, chiefly in axle-trees. For this purpose beech should be hard as bone, and should therefore be cut down in November (they used to say in my shop) and opened into quarters by Christmas.

Another matter the wheelwright buyer had to know about was the soil the timber grew on. Age-long tradition helped him here. I, for instance, knew from my father's telling, and he perhaps from his father's, that the best beech in the district came from such and such a quarter: that the very limbs from the elm in one park would yield good "stocks" (hubs for wheels); and that in a certain luxuriant valley the beautiful-looking oaks had grown too fast and when opened were too shaky to be used. Yet I didn't know (and paid for not knowing) that on the clay, in one hollow of Alice Holt, the oak had a nasty trick of going "foxy-hearted." I bought a small "parcel" of trees there. They looked well enough too in the yard until the winter, when the sawyers began to saw them open. But then—tree after tree, sound at the butt, began about two feet up to disclose the "foxy" middle, the rusty-looking pith like rotten string or rope running far up. I don't think my father or grandfather would have bought timber from that hollow. They knew "England" in a more intimate way.

One point further concerned the timber-buyer. The best of trees, thrown at the right time, was after all useless if it could not for any reason be hauled up on to timber-carriage, or swung under "nib" or "timber-bob" (the same thing), for bringing home to the saw-pit. So it behoved the wheelwright buyer to refuse if, as sometimes happened, a tree had fallen in an inaccessible place. In steep hanger, or over shelving stream-banks, it might be impossible to place the skids from ground to wheel-top for rolling the tree up on to the "carriage." Running-chains and horse-power availed nothing then. The tree must rot where it lay. A slighter difficulty was a very miry road. The broadest wheels were not always broad enough to save the heavily-laden timber-carriage from sinking inextricably into a very soft surface. If the buyer of the tree could wait for dry weather, well and good. But what if the sawyers should have finished for him and gone away while his trees were stuck in the mud? These things had to be considered.

When the bargain was settled it remained to measure the timber—a pleasant and interesting job. To get the string between tree and ground (I never found a "tape" measure of any use) I had a "needle" or "sword"—a slender and curved rod of iron—to push under the tree. At its end the needle was forged into a small hook like a button hook, and the looped string was then easily drawn back and so the circumference of the tree was taken. From that, to the "girt," allowing for the thickness of the bark, and then (with slide-rule) calculating how many cubic feet of timber the tree held, was child's play. I liked it well, clambering over the prone tree-stems, amongst foxgloves and ferns perhaps. To guess the "misure" of a tree, before actually taking its "misure"—that in itself was a game. And, afterwards, the timber-carter liked to be told what the "meetins" were—what was the average size of the trees he was sending his horses out to bring home.

VI

CARTING AND "CONVERTING"

I never saw it, but I judge it must have been a noble sight— the loading of a timber-carriage in the woods. For the trees had been criss-cross, anyhow, as they fell; yet when they were brought home they lay evenly on the carriage—butt-end foremost always; and it must have involved no end of patient skill in the carters, and of well-applied strength in the straining horses, to get them there. Often clay covering the wheels betokened difficult forest ways; often there had been a six or seven mile journey after the loading was finished; but I don't remember timber ever being brought to my yard too late to be unloaded before dark, though sometimes of a winter evening the dusk would be deepening before all had gone and the yard was quiet again.

And anyhow the unloading—what a display of sense and skill and patience and good-temper it was! The carters laid their skids from wheel to ground or to trees previously thrown down there—laid them and chained them to the wheels; and then one by one the trees were rolled or slid down the skids to the stack until the carriage was cleared. Levers were needed for all this —an old waggon-shaft or so—and one or two wheelwrights came out from the shop, or may be a blacksmith from the smithy, to lend a hand. Truly it was worth while to get away from bench or forge. The wheelwrights had a sort of connoisseurs' interest in the timber; besides, some ingenuity was often called for in the unloading: the horses stood about, to be spoken to or patted; and always it was good to be with the carters. These men, old acquaintances from a near village, had rustic talk and anecdotes, rustic manners. I never saw them other than quietly wise. To watch them at work, unhurried, understanding one another and seeing with keen-glancing eyes what to do, was to watch (unawares, and that is best) the traditional behaviour of a whole country-side of strong and good-tempered Englishmen. With the timber and the horses they seemed to bring the lonely woodlands, the far-off roads, into the little town.

Having been got home if possible in summer, when the forest tracks were dry enough to bear a load, the trees were better left until winter before being sawn up. Even then—and in hotter weather it would have been worse—the planks of oak or ash were liable to "spring," that is to say to split all up, with the too-quick loss of sap. They needed to be handled gingerly. I have seen a freshly-cut plank—falling over sideways on the saw-pit or dropped, "bang," too carelessly on its fellows—fly almost asunder from end to end. Elm, so crooked in the grain, was not liable to this disaster; but a far more ruinous one, known as "casting," made it advisable to keep the elm longer in the round—two years or so—and with the bark on too, so that the timber should dry a little more, but more steadily, before the weather was let in upon its grain. For it would warp here and shrink there, would bend, would twist, so much and so incalculably as to be useless if opened too soon. It was no uncommon thing to see an elm-tree in the timber-yard try to put out leaves two seasons after it had been thrown.

The coming of the sawyers at last—I think all the summer they worked in the woods, where the temporary saw-pits were without shelter, and where the men worked at cutting posts and rails and so on for land-owners—the coming of the sawyers, towards winter time, when a roof over their heads became desirable, woke up the master-wheelwright to a new interest in the timber he had bought. The proof was beginning, personal to himself. His judgment in buying those trees was put to its first test now. Its last was yet far ahead. Not until the seasoned timber was proven on the workman's bench in five or six years' time would the final verdict be given; but the first test began on the saw-pit, when the sawyers "opened" the yet "green" or sap-filled tree. What did it look like? The wheelwright was most eager to know how it looked, that heart of ash or oak or elm, of so many decades standing, which no eye had ever seen before. Lovely was the first glimpse of the white ash-grain, the close-knit oak, the pale-brown and butter-coloured elm. Lovely, yet would it dry into hard tough timber? Was the grain as straight as had been hoped? And that knot—right through one plank, how far did it go into the next? Every fresh tree, as the sawyers cut out and turned over the planks, at last gave rise to questions like these.

The oaks under the saw had the fresh scent of the forest, nameless as their colour. Elm didn't smell nice—an unclean smell. Sometimes from the ash came fumes as of wood burning. Had the saw—it often grew too hot to touch—actually set something afire? But no. That penetrating odour, so disquieting in a woodshop until you knew its source, merely told that the ash-tree on the pit would probably turn out to be "black-hearted." A narrow band as if of ink-stain ran along the very core of the central planks. It was supposed to reduce their value slightly; but the wheelwright was thinking of use in his shop; and I, for my part, never grieved to see or to smell black-hearted ash. The texture of the grain told me more than the colour did.

Before ever the sawyers could begin, there was much for the owner of the timber to do, in deciding what they should cut it into. No doubt a builder or a shipwright would want different sizes and shapes, but no needs can have been more exacting or diverse than the old-fashioned wheelwright's. Length, thickness, "turn" or curve, were all more or less fixed by traditions ever renewed, and even the sort of timber for different parts of waggon or cart or even wheelbarrow was not wholly a matter of indifference. Those portions which could not be easily replaced but might have to last for forty years or so had to be heart of oak. Nothing less durable would serve. Yet this limitation gave a sure guidance. It almost ear-marked the pick of the oak—the clean-run butts without bad knot or flaw—for the bottom framework of waggon or cart. And this gave the dimensions of the plank to be sawn, waggons taking the preference because the lengths required for them were none too easy to get.

Outside these limits there was indeed much opportunity for substituting one kind of timber for another (excepting in wheel-stuff). Tapering thicknesses of plank, to be sure, were set out for shafts ("sharps" we called them) usually in ash. But oak would do very well for this use, or even good elm, if some length or thickness or curve not prepared for in ash happened to be wanted.

Bearing in mind all the possibilities thus open, the wheelwright dealt carefully with each tree, deciding first the lengths it should be cut into, and perhaps altering his plans altogether if a bad knot after all turned out to be in the wrong place, or if the original intention would have involved too great waste in the total length. With a little pinching the measure here, and a little stretching there, it was usually possible to rescue odd and otherwise wasted inches and get them all together at the top into the two feet or so required for a "felloe-block." Lastly, the various points for cross-cutting the tree were scratched with a "race"—

a sort of knife with point turned back and sharpened at the bend for this especial purpose—and this done the wheelwright might pass on to the next tree. If he was really master of his timber, if he knew what he had already got in stock and also what was likely to be wanted in years to come, he kept a watch always for timber with special curve, suitable for hames, or shaft-braces, or waggon-heads, or hounds, or tailboard rails, or whatever else the tree-shape might suggest.

And when the sawyers had been instructed, still it was well to be near their work. Besides, the felloe-blocks, sawn down the middle, could often be profitably sawn again; and to pencil out the shapes on them gave the wheelwright much scope to exercise his ingenuity and his knowledge. It was in fact a fascinating task. I have spent hours at it beside the saw-pit. It must have been a cold job too. For it was always winter work; and sometimes snow lay on the felloe-blocks. It was cold, to handle them; cold, to stand hour after hour trying the varying felloe-patterns on them. At least so I should suppose now; yet I have no recollection of feeling the cold at the time. The work was too interesting. The winter, the timber, the wheelwright's continuous tussle, the traditional adaptation, by skill and know-ledge—all these factors, not thought of but felt, to the accompaniment of wood-scents and saw-pit sounds, kept me from thinking of the cold—unless to appreciate that too. Delightful? It was somehow better than that. It was England's very life one became a part of, in the timber-yard. The settling of this Island had only started about fifteen hundred years earlier and was still going on. It was no picnic. I was often tired to death at it. For I by no means perceived what a big thing I was taking so obscure a part in. In fact, more than once I tried to get clear of the business altogether, it was so fatiguing and it bored me so. Only now have I realised how I ought to have felt privileged to be taking part at all in the century-old colonisation of England.

VII

THE SAWYERS

For a reason to be told presently the ultimate disappearance
of sawyers from my trade was not an unmixed evil; yet there
was much to regret in it. Such a venerable craft theirs was; so
full of skill; so rich in associations with English village, English
woodland; so suggestive of summer forests or of bleak winter
timber-yards. The men, unlettered, often taciturn, sure of themselves, muscular, not easily tired, were in many ways a sort of
epitome of the indomitable adaptation of our breed to land and
climate. As a wild animal species to its habitat, so these workmen had fitted themselves to the local conditions of life and
death. Individually they had no special claim to notice; but as
members of old-world communities they exemplified well how
the South English tribes, traversing their fertile valleys, their
shaggy hills, had matched themselves against problems without
number, and had handed on, from father to son, the accumulated
lore of experience. If one could know enough, one might see,
in ancient village crafts like that of the sawyers, the reflection
as it were of the peculiarities of the country-side—the difficulties
and dangers, the daily conditions—to which those crafts were
the answer.

The special problem the sawyers knew how to tackle looks
simple enough at the outset. What was it, save to get the timber
—the oak, the ash, the elm, the beech—slit or slithered into
sizes that experts might handle afterwards? Experts already had
thrown the timber; others had carted it to the yard; another
still—the master-wheelwright—had marked it into lengths and
was at hand to direct the sawyers throughout; and what else was
there for them to do, except supply mere brute strength? That
looked about all they were fit for, with their stupid brains and
brawny arms.

Yet, in point of fact, they themselves, you found, were
specialists of no mean order when it came to the problem of

getting a heavy tree—half a ton or so of timber—on a saw-pit and splitting it longitudinally into specified thicknesses, no more and no less. What though the individuals looked stupid? That lore of the English tribes as it were embodied in them was not stupid any more than an animal's shape is stupid. It was an organic thing, very different from the organised effects of commerce.

Some skill was involved, even at the start, in cross-cutting a tree into lengths—nay, it took experience, if nothing else, to prop the tree up properly for cross-cutting. If it didn't lie right it might sag down and "pinch" the saw (though a wedge might help here); or else the two ends, parting before the cut was done, might rip asunder with their own weight and tear open a nasty shake in the sound timber. For the actual cross-cutting—no joke through eighteen inches or so of hard wood—it was needful to keep the cut at the proper angle, that is, at right angles with the tree.

Given all this as a preliminary, the sawyers' more recondite work began—usually under the wheelwright's eye. Trees were rarely crooked in more ways than one; and the object was so to open them that this one curve, this one crookedness, was preserved. To save it for longforeseen uses was probably the wheelwright's object: he had arranged the cross-cutting of the tree to take advantage of this curve. Thus, if a butt of ash had the shape of a waggon-shaft, it was marked off the right length for that and then split from end to end so that there were two curved pieces, one on either side of the saw, suitable for shafts. Fortunately, the wide saw lent itself to this. To keep it in one plane (as Euclid might say) for the whole length of a tree did indeed call for skill and strength; but no man on earth could have done anything at all with it in any other way. The steel saw might have broken, or else the man's own back; or his arms might have come out from the shoulders; but the saw would not have gone down the tree, excepting in a tolerably straight line.

So there was the problem set for the sawyers—in a curved tree (butt or top it didn't matter) to find that one aspect of it which was not curved—that one direction in which it could be sawn into two practically equal and similar halves from end to end. This direction having been settled upon indicated the upper surface of the tree, which had to be specially treated for two purposes.

For as it was on this surface that the "top-sawyer" would have to stand when the tree was on the saw-pit, so it had to be made reasonably smooth and flat, for him to keep his balance. The second purpose, soon seen when the tree was at last in place on the pit, was to mark, more plainly than the bark would have shown, the lines desired for the saw-cuts.

So the tree was thrown over to its side, and, standing on it, with their two-handed long-shafted axes, the sawyers hewed down below them, to get the surface they required. The great chips flew; the sound of the axe-blows echoed across the yard; soon the tree was ready. Then began a straining and levering and pushing, until at last, on two rollers besides another beam or two, the tree was coaxed into place over the pit. With a "ring-dog" one man would generally turn it over with the chopped side up: and while he held it there his mate could fix it with another sort of "dog," whose spiked ends were meant for just this and could be tapped in with the back of the axe.

And now the tree could be "lined out" for sawing. A "line," a long cord on a reel, was chalked—or rubbed with charcoal off a burnt stick, if the axe had left the timber too pale to show chalk lines—and was carefully "snapped" along the very centre of the tree. That, at least, was always the way in my shop. We liked to split the heart—not to let it come out whole in one central plank, but to have one middle cut and a plank on either side of it. So, the danger of "ring-shakes" was minimised. From this central line the planks or boards could be easily marked off. What was done on the underside of the tree, or what guide the bottom-sawyer had, I cannot remember. The reel of the chalk line served as a plumb-bob for "trueing" the end of the timber for the first opening cuts.

After a good opening, indeed, the bottom man might slacken his attention a little. To lift the saw strongly and strongly pull it down, keeping the teeth of it close to the work—this was his chief duty. Laborious it was in the extreme; and the sawdust poured down on his sweating face and bare arms, and down his back; but at least he was spared the trouble of thinking much. To be sure, he might not go quite off to sleep, although his view went no farther than the end of the saw-pit, and his body and arms were working laboriously up and down for hours. But there were short breaks. Now his mate would call down to him to oil the saw. For this purpose he had a rag tied on a stick, kept in a tin of linseed oil in a crevice of the saw-pit. And now roller or beam in front of the advancing saw had to be pulled out and set in again at the back of it, lest the teeth should tear into it.

But the top-sawyer had no such easy time. He, master of the saw, not only had to keep pace (and more toilsomely, I was assured) with the other's rythmical lift and pull. It fell also to the top-sawyer to keep constant watch on the work, with a special eye on the saw's action. The least deviation from the straight line might spoil the timber, besides bringing the work to a standstill. And it was likely to be his saw's fault in bad sharpening.

Something of an art by itself was involved here. A special half-round file and a "set" were the instruments, with a "sharpening horse" to rest the saw on. The sharpening horse was a trestle about three feet from the ground and five feet long. From the horizontal top piece stood up three pegs slotted so as to hold the saw on its back, teeth upwards. Laying the saw in the slots, the sawyer could attend to every tooth, bevelling it off at its proper angle, filing out the front curve of it, and so on. With the palm of his hand passed lightly along he could feel if there was sufficient "cut" in the blade. If any tooth was a shade too high, it would cause a painful "jump" in the sawing by and by; and a tooth too low was almost as bad. The whole row of teeth therefore had to be on a dead level. And as there was no gauge the sawyer's hand needed to be sensitive and his eye true.

Levelness, however, was only half the battle. If you squint along the top of the teeth of any saw you will see not one but two rows of serration, with a sort of valley between, producing a right and left side to the saw. The truth is, the teeth are bent out a little on either side, so that the rest of the saw is thinner than its own cut and slides easily up and down without "pinching." No oil, no wedges, would suffice if the saw didn't thus "clear herself." Further difficulties, however, arise out of this device. Unless the two sides of the saw match one another, the side that cuts the faster will get ahead of the other and try to run round it, just as two legs of unequal stride walk in a circle. This circular effect may sometimes be seen, when perhaps some inexpert farmer helped by his cowman has cut down a road-side tree with an old cross-cut saw. At great cost of arm-ache and sweat such a thing can just be managed, because after all it requires only one short cut to cut down a tree. But it would not do for parallel cuts all down the tree. That is work for skilled sawyers armed with centuries of country tradition. So the top-sawyer watches his blade and exercises his skill, I think, more when he is solemnly progressing with the file along the saw—up one side and down the other—than when he is stepping backwards along the tree to keep pace with the advancing cut.

The triumph of saw-sharpening appeared when a tree was being cut into boards. The least deviation then would have brought all to nought; but I never knew it happen. I have watched the work with admiration. As the cut grew longer and longer the half-cut boards, still united in the log at one end, would vibrate together with the up-and-down motion of the saw. Ropes had to be twisted round them at last to preserve some steadiness, and then, to spread them asunder and to prevent an intolerable jarring on the saw, wedges were driven in. As the thing proceeded, so true, so nice, the sight became fascinating. I speak not of the men only, bending up and down hour after hour, silent, intent. Somehow—I don't know why—there was fascination in the ever-lengthening parallel cuts down the tree. To see them growing, growing, quarter-inch by quarter-inch, nothing shirking (every speck of sawdust had to be cut out), yet so relentlessly—oh, it was like watching Fate at work. There is no need to picture "The Mills of God" to anyone who has seen sawyers converting a big elm-tree into boards.

For reasons too technical to go into here, elm was the timber chosen. The biggest elm-trees, two or three feet in diameter, would have a few one-inch boards taken out of the middle, for the sake of the width. (The wheelwright wanted this width for his dung-carts[1].) But towards the outside, where the tree narrowed down, three-quarters of an inch sufficed for the boards. A good thing to see, while the boards were a-sawing, was the shifting of the saw. To avoid moving the tree it was well to do a whole section of parallel cuts—a dozen or twenty—before altering the roller, to get it behind the saw instead of in front of it in order to get at the next section. This meant that the top-sawyer must lift the saw right out of one cut and slip it down into the next. He never fumbled; yet, as his hands were shaky after such heavy work, so a tremble came into the end of the flexible five-foot saw too. Like a live thing it quivered; hovered over the opening, then sunk in and through, where the bottom-sawyer could imprison it again in his "box." The "box" was a pair of handles that could be easily slipped on and wedged to the bottom end of the saw. After many years the box in my saw-pit was dark and shiny with oil from the saw and from the man's hands.

A narrower saw, tightened at both ends into a light wooden frame, had to be used for "turning" the curved felloe-blocks. The rollers on the pit were bored at the end for putting in a stout crowbar and rolling the whole tree forward on them if need be. Moreover, to make this movement easier, the two sides of a permanent saw-pit were lined with sills, for the rollers to turn on smoothly. And when all was done, when the new planks or boards were at last carried from the pit, again it was the top-sawyer who measured them. As it was "the thing" to do—as there was held to be room for suspicion—I was wont to measure for myself after the sawyers; but I never had reason to think they had tried to cheat me. On the contrary they had cheated themselves once or twice, and I had to point out to them

---

[1] Undertakers were always alleged to want one-inch elm boards for making coffins. This is probably true. At any rate it gives point to a circumstance I heard of during the war. A big elm-tree was being hauled along the street. On the end of it was chalked "Coffin for Kaiser Bill."

that their measure was insufficient. It's worth noting that the measurements, scratched with a "race" on board or end of plank, needed to be in straight lines, since the "race" would hardly mark rounded figures. A sort of Roman notation[1] was used therefore, ancient enough, yet perhaps not so ancient as the craft itself, which seemed to continue the original colonisation of this country. In this notation the half of a superficial foot was expressed by a half-length notch; and if there was also a five or ten in the number, this half-length was scratched in the angle of the V or X, this way. I suggest that an American or an Australian might find antiquities of this sort in his own country, for they are probably far-travelled as well as ancient. In English timber-yards (not mine alone) were not these marks a continuation of the work of clearing the forests and building the first towns and carts?

What was it that at last caused the disappearance of the sawing craft? For although there may be a few sawyers left, I do not personally know of one, where of old there were several couple. Of old you might catch sight of a sawyer—perhaps at a winter night-fall on a Saturday—trailing off with his saws and axes for some remote village. Long before he could get home he would be benighted—the country lanes would be dark; yet sawyers never hurried. They dragged their legs ponderously, and they looked melancholy—I do not remember seeing a sawyer laugh. A sort of apathy was their usual expression. They behaved as if they felt they were growing obsolete.

And no doubt they were right. Their race had all but finished their colonisation of England. New adventures beckoned—adventures in Steam, in Electricity, in Cosmopolitan cities of Men. Steel was taking the place of timber. The sawyers were being crowded out; and they seemed as if they knew it.

Certainly they took no pains to keep up to date, or to be even tolerable in the new conditions which were already confronting every provincial trader who employed sawyers. In my experience they were drunken to a man. And the worst of it was that they

[1] And that, too, was probably prehistoric. See also p. 86 and Note F, p. 207.

worked in pairs. One sawyer was no good without his mate—
he was as useless as one scissor would be. So, on a Monday
morning, the one who reached his work first would loaf about
waiting for the other, and then, sick of waiting, drift off to a
public-house—his home perhaps for a few days or weeks. His
mate, coming at last, would presently find that his predecessor
had begun boosing; and was likely enough to end a disgusted and
wasted day by following suit. He might be, himself, in the thick
of a great drink by the time that the first man was ready. And
so it would go on. I have known sawyers unable to get together
and start their week's work until Thursday morning.

Sometimes a fit of bad temper started the trouble. I think it
was usually the top-sawyer who began their quarrels. Owner
of the saws and leader too, responsible for all things, some little
thing would go wrong, and then he would begin to swear down
at the man sweating in the saw-pit. Of course in a swearing
bout he had all the advantages—the under man can't even look
up easily, because of the sawdust. If blackguard oaths came
pouring down on him too, what more natural thàn that he should
chuck up his job, come up out of the saw-pit and adjourn
sullenly to the public-house? I have known many a good day's
work spoilt in this way. Now and then, in a fit of repentance,
the two mates would try to work on cold tea, keeping bottles of
it tucked away in corners. But it must have been a dismal
beverage, unsuitable for men really overworked. It had no
sting to feel refreshing in the throat, and was always abandoned
after a day or so.

Sharpening times were bad times for the bottom-sawyer. The
temporary rest left him at a loose end for an hour or so. None
could blame him if he slouched off for a drink, where he might
find a fire to sit by and somebody to talk to. Unfortunately he
was not always in a hurry to go back to work. To the top-
sawyer, sharpening was none the more welcome on this account.
To know that the other fellow was in the bliss of a tap-room,
while he himself was tied to a job, earning no money and using
up a sixpenny file—to know all this made sharpening a nuisance
at the best. At the worst—

Sometimes the placid snoring sound of the up-and-down sawing was suddenly stopped by a sort of shriek, telling all across the timber-yard that the worst had happened. The delicate saw-teeth had been ripped hard into an unsuspected nail, and it might cost half a day to repair the mischief. Then came swearing, a torrent of discussion, the sound of painfully sawing on through the nail—if nail it was—and finally taking out the saw to inspect the damage. Hedgerow timber—especially elm—was most subject to this trouble, and therefore park timber was preferred. For in hedge timber (apt to be knotty too) a nail—always in the best part of the tree, worse luck—betrayed where some farmer had nailed his fence to the tree instead of to a post. Usually these obstructions were discovered by the axe before the tree was rolled on to the pit; and then they could be chopped out. An elm butt I once had was chopped half asunder in this way, because, grown over by the bark, a chain was found twisted all round. It suggests, now, some idle carter or ploughman hanging it there, some lonely field with horses and sky—for the sawyers' work was always suggestive of the open; but at the time it was pure vexation. Sawyers once found stones in the heart of an elm-tree I had bought. Boys had doubtless tossed them there generations earlier. This would be higher up in the tree, when a hole was already there. Not good timber, evidently. But a customer with a tree for sale expected the wheelwright to buy it of him.

The sawyers were on the whole so erratic I was always glad to see the back of them. Yet the real trouble was that, as competition grew, a less costly way of getting timber had to be found. At any rate, when planks could be bought in London nearly fit to use, it would no longer do to buy local timber and pay for sawing it, thereby locking up one's money for years while the timber dried. Timber-merchants might do some of that. It was for them to employ the sawyers—or to set up the steam-saws.

VIII

SEASONING

From the first it was needful for the wheelwright to bear in mind the ultimate uses of his timber, in dung-cart, in harvest-waggon. The field, the farm-yard, the roads and hills, the stress of weather, the strength and shape of horses, the lifting power of men, all were factors which had determined in the old villages how the farm tackle must be made, of what timber and shape and of what dimensions, often to the sixteenth of an inch. Already, when the tree was on the saw-pit, these details had to be provided for. If, for instance, one-inch boards would be needed, it was a mistake to prepare for seven-eighths only; and first the sawyers had to see to this. A six-inch thickness of elm would not make six one-inch boards. Some of it would be ripped out and wasted as sawdust, so that in fact not more than five boards could be cut from it, to "hold-up" one inch "good."

Nor was this all. No care on earth could prevent the elm from drying "curly" as we said, that is to say, with a sort of ripple in the grain, making narrow and shallow cross waves from one end of the board to the other. And seeing that, in getting rid of these ripple marks, the wheelwright's plane made the board thinner still, a very generous inch had to be allowed for it while it was "green," or as yet unseasoned. Do what he would no wheelwright could wholly guard against this sort of trouble. The elm boards insisted on going curly; the oak and ash planks stubbornly bent all along the centre into a kind of shallow trough on the one side with corresponding lumpiness on the other. The better the timber the likelier it was to develop these defects in seasoning. And worse still might happen, if this last operation was not done with care. It was the next thing for the master-wheelwright to be busy about. As soon as the sawyers had cut the planks and boards the seasoning of them had to be set about before they began to "cast"—to warp.

So, with a strongish man or two to help (and mind not get

the fingers pinched! 'Tis easily done. Unless you are quick, before you know it two boards, heavy with sap, may have nipped between them a quarter of an inch of your skin lovingly, and then you have a small black "woodlouse" of a pinch!) with a strongish helper or two, straining, heaving, gingerly placing, you raise the newly-cut stuff in orderly stacks. It needs care, or over the stacks go. The very first thing of all is the "bearing," to keep the lowest plank a few inches off the ground so that the air may play freely under it. Anything will serve for a bearing— old shafts, axle-beds, anything; but the several pieces of it must be near enough together to prevent any sagging of the planks piled on it. And lest these planks should twist, the bearers below them needed to be all quite level—"true out of wind" or of twist. Besides, any unsteadiness at the base would jeopardise the whole erection. Afterwards, similar care had to be bestowed on the whole stack to the very top, in the case of every fresh plank or board added to it; and, atop of all, heavy weights were advisable to keep the casting and twisting of the grain within bounds. Nothing would quite prevent it, but with care in the stacking it could be held within reasonable limits. No two planks might touch; the sap slowly escaping would have rotted them. It had to be dried off by the air. To secure this, narrow strips of board were laid between plank and plank, board and board. Even so, elm boards were liable to "sweat." For steadiness it was well to build two stacks at a time, side by side, so that here and there a longer strip might be laid in, tying them together.

A prudent man, handling a plank, took care not to be the first nor yet the last in letting go his end of the plank, unless due warning was given. For either he might jar the other fellow's hands, in which case he was likely to hear of it; or else his own would be jarred—and there were pleasanter ways of warming them. As the stacks were best built out of doors, to get all the air they could, a sort of roof was extemporised over them. Nothing clinging would do—no old rick-cloth to lie too close; but any old bit of fencing to keep off the rain or the summer sun. A shady place was best for the stack, but March winds did it good. Before those winds began every plank should have had a strip nailed across each end to keep it from splitting as the weather grew dry and warm. For these strips—bits of old board chopped out—I found clout nails the best. When all these things had been attended to the timber might be left with an occasional glance to see that all was well, until the autumn or early winter brought the time for putting it away permanently. In its permanent quarters it was stacked again, but without strips. The slow years—a year for every inch of thickness was none too much—gradually finished the seasoning and the timber was fit for use.

I never heard of the timber, well managed in this old, deliberate, village way, being "too dry." That fault appeared in later times, when attempts were made to hurry the process. Certainly, a capitalist cannot nowadays afford to have his money lying idle so long. Moreover, modern vehicles are not wanted to last like the ancient waggons and dung-carts, built for a life-time. But in the old shop, men thought nothing of timber eight or ten years old, albeit it meant money locked up all that time.

Clearing up after the sawyers included dealing with the "slabs"—the thin outside pieces, two from each tree. The ash slabs, truly, could be used to the last inch and were properly seasoned therefore. But the oak slabs—mostly useless sap—and the elm slabs—thin and "casting"—were thrown into a heap, or sold for firing or for building a pigsty or what not. A penny a foot "run"—a foot of length—was the selling price. I forget what was done with the green sawdust, to clear the pit; I think it was sold for bacon-drying at fourpence the sack.

Winter work and out-door work, all this, and that was a fortunate thing in more ways than one. As the farmers could not be persuaded to have their tackle looked to until they actually wanted it in the spring or the summer[1], the wheelwright's yard was nearly empty in the dark days. There was plenty of room for the sawyers therefore, while young men to stack the planks and boards could easily be spared from the shops or from the smithies. You couldn't begin stacking timber much

[1] See also p. 178 and Note L, p. 210.

before eight o'clock breakfast. Then, with a welcome hour's rest at dinner time, there was a warmish job (save for your feet) until dark, at half-past four or so. It wasn't bad fun either. Rain might stop it, or heavy snow; on the other hand, you grew as intimate as any shepherd with frosts that covered the planks in thin coating of ice, with still silence of fog, with cutting winter winds all across the yard. The work called for too much attention to be dull; only, as the monotonous afternoon began to grow darker, arms ached a little and brains felt drowsy. The day had been pleasant; yet it was a good thing to knock off. Already a star or two was showing. Against the on-coming night the sparks from the blacksmith's chimney were suggestive of in-doors and warmth.

IX

WHEEL-STUFF

In the same winter weeks, while the wheelwright's trade was quiet and the master was superintending the sawyers and helping the less skilled men stack the boards and planks out-o'-doors for seasoning—in those same weeks, within doors, the older and trustier men, who needed no supervision, were busy with the new spokes and felloes. (In this word leave out the o. Make the word rhyme to bellies.) Well experienced in all wheels, and understanding what was sure to be wanted for waggon or cart in years to come, these men required no telling what to do. They knew well enough. All the wheel-making lore of the country-side for generations guided their judgment.

The felloe-blocks from the saw-pit required roughly shaping while still green, before they too could be stacked up for seasoning; for although hard enough in all conscience they would be far harder years hence, when the sap had dried out of them and they came to be used. Now was the time. And much remained to be done to them. The sawyers had but halved the smaller blocks, putting a longitudinal cut down the middle, so that now there were two pieces, each piece half cylindrical It was the wheelwright's business to chop each of these pieces into a felloe, as large and long as the timber would make. Or if, as sometimes happened, there had been material enough in either half to make two felloes, still the sawyers (following a line pencilled for them by the master out in the yard) had but cut this one curved line. It was left to the men in the shop to trim the felloes down sideways and to shape out the rounded back to the outer piece, the hollow belly to the inner.

The tools were axe and adze and sometimes hand-saw, and the implements (besides a square) a chopping block and a felloe-horse. Yet it is in vain to go into details at this point; for when the simple apparatus had all been got together for one simple-looking process, a never-ending series of variations was introduced by the material. What though two felloes might seem much alike when finished? It was the wheelwright himself who had to make them so. He it was who hewed out that resemblance from quite dissimilar blocks, for no two felloe-blocks were ever alike. Knots here, shakes there, rind-galls, waney edges (edges with more or less of the bark in them), thicknesses, thinnesses, were for ever affording new chances or forbidding previous solutions, whereby a fresh problem confronted the workman's ingenuity every few minutes. He had no band-saw (as now) to drive, with ruthless unintelligence, through every resistance. The timber was far from being a prey, a helpless victim, to a machine. Rather it would lend its own subtle virtues to the man who knew how to humour it: with him, as with an understanding friend, it would co-operate. So, twisting it, turning it "end for end," trying it for an inch or two this way and then an inch or two that, a skilful wheel-maker was able to get the best possible product from his timber every time. I don't think I ever afterwards, in the days of band-saws, handled such a large proportion of superlatively good felloes as used to pass through my hands in those days of the axe and adze. Perhaps the sawn-out felloes look better—to a theorist from an office. But at the bench you learn where a hard knot may be even helpful and a wind-shake a source of strength in a felloe; and this was the sort of knowledge that guided the old-fashioned wheelwright's chopping.

The felloes for seasoning were piled up in rows of five, "athirt and across." If care was taken to keep the thickest felloes always outside, all was well. If not, in a high wind the rocking stack might blow over; and what was worse, a too thick bearing in the middle might give a bend to every felloe that rested on it. And felloes were easily enough "cast" without that encouragement. Ash, elm, oak, beech were all useful for them, and they could all warp. There was no such diversity in spokes. These were invariably oak, chiefly because oak alone, of the suitable English hard-woods, could be cleft instead of sawn. It mattered, with spokes. A cut across the grain, on a saw-bench, might have produced a cross-grained spoke that would be liable to snap shamefully. Therefore spokes were never sawn. And since only oak would cleave, or unsuitable beech, properly cleft oak was always used. But the cleaving had to be done in the summer, while the oak was full of sap and would "run" from end to end. Cleaving was a job for the woods therefore; woodmen with beetle (pronounced bittle) and wedges usually had first handling of the beautiful yellowish parallel grain for spokes, that split so easily yet was tough as wire the other way. So the spokes were bought, by the hundred or the long hundred, in their native woods. Yet the wheelwright had a little to do to them in the winter, before they were finally stored away for drying. They could be "dressed," that is to say chopped, a little nearer to their ultimate size. Then they were stacked in layers of five, with just the same precautions as felloes. For want of such precautions my first stack of spokes blew down the night my father died. I found it a wreck the next morning and remember building it up again, feeling very forlorn.

Warm work, all this winter chopping of wheel-stuff was, and a good thing too. At six o'clock on a December morning the shop was raw cold. Men coming in out of the dark were glad of heavy work to warm them up before opening the shop to the winter day. As already explained, the windows were not glazed. As soon as the shutters were taken down—a little before breakfast at eight o'clock—the wintry air was free to come in, unless a piercing east wind or a driving snow were screened by putting up one of the shutters again. But of course this could not be effectively done during day-light; until it was dark once more the cold had to be countered by vigorous work. By half-past four or so the winter night allowed a more snug shuttering. The men kept on until six o'clock by artificial light.

'Twasn't much of a light. True, the cracks between the shutters or under the doors looked cosy enough to anyone passing outside, in the dark; but within....

Fortunately men didn't want a very good light for felloe-chopping or spoke-dressing, for a good artificial light was not to be had in those far-off times. We worked by little hand-lamps of colsa oil. Flat wooden pegs made handles for these lamps. The pegs could be stuck into a movable stand—a "dummy" as we called it; and the lamp set down close to the work shed a dim but sufficient light on it. Otherwise the shop was not lit up. A "dummy" was the simplest thing imaginable. From a low three-legged stool a slender centre-piece stood up, about three or four feet high. Auger-holes about six inches apart, bored through the centre-piece, allowed the lamp-peg to be put in fairly safely and at a convenient height.

With so much chopping—it went on for weeks sometimes, as I fancy—it will be easily understood that chips accumulated. So did the pennies received by the sale of them. Neighbours—decrepit old men and women, shy children—were always coming with sack or basket to buy chips. Indeed, the big splintery choppings from spokes could not be surpassed for fire lighting, while the more flaky waste from felloes was often thick enough for a lasting fire. Ash, big or little, would burn "like a candle," we used to say.

But now, what of the hubs—the "stocks" as they were called locally? The workmen in the shop were hardly troubled with these until the time for using them came. Comparatively few in number, and of no excessive weight, they were the employer's own affair; for indeed they wanted next to no preparation, but much watchful care while drying. The main thing was to buy the right quality of trees for them, and to get them sawn off the right length. A slant in the saw-cut was to be avoided, for slanting stocks could not have been piled atop of one another for drying, and would have been a bother in the lathe when dry. So a square cut was demanded. And even this little trouble was spared if, as often happened, a good consignment of stocks—a waggon load or so—could be bought from a timber-merchant. The advantages of this plan lay in the chance it gave to be sure of sound timber throughout. It did not exonerate the wheel-wright from the cares of seasoning. In my experience it was never possible to buy dry stocks, though they might be called that.

For the process of seasoning a stock took years. And seeing that one wanted it well done, the only way was to do it one's self. I know some people sought to expedite it by boring a big auger-hole through the centre of the stock, and perhaps this did gain some time—a year or two, may be. But this device was not favoured in my shop, for the gain was dearly bought at the cost of quality in the ultimate product. At least it always seemed to me that there was a loss. Once they were really dry, the unbored stocks could not be beaten.

But, as I said, they needed constant watching. The elm—it was almost always elm, though a few oak stocks had to be kept —the elm was for ever going white with mildew, as the sap slowly exuded: and if this mildew was not brushed off (it took a hard brush) every three or four months, fungus came next, and under the fungus the timber began to decay. Of course the earliest months were the worst, while the stocks were still juicy. After the piles of them had been pulled down again in the winter for a thorough brushing, the stocks might be put away in a dry shed. They were laid down on their sides too, with their ends exposed for any further brushing they needed. If the date was chalked on each end, it served to identify them in four or five years time, should they be then mingled with others for use.

And in that dry shed it was very pleasant to spend an hour sometimes amongst the stocks. A stage came in their drying when it was worth while to dress them down a little if they were unshapely, or at any rate to chop off the bark. I have passed pleasant afternoons this way. The time of year didn't matter. From the shed I could catch glimpses of a sunny harvest-field and fir-woods: the quiet was just broken—or emphasised—by tinking from the near smithy or by mallet strokes from the wood shop. And within—oh, as the axe forced its way through the elm bark (now and again sundering some fat wretched maggot)—oh, then one's eyes were unsealed to meanings of grain and texture only reached by actual work with timber.

Some time ago I was told that a satisfactory way had been found for drying timber in a few months, by steam or perhaps by hot air. It may be. Yet I should as soon believe that a quick process for maturing wine had rendered bottling and cellars unnecessary. I never came upon a quick substitute for the seasons in drying timber. My first experience of steamed Canadian ash made me very sceptical. It looked nice; but it seemed a little "frow" or "biscuity" under the workmen's tools; and after some three years of use it crumbled into touch-wood.

I once kept half-a-dozen oak felloes under water, to see what would happen. The water turned an inky blue—even as the edge of the axe used in chopping the felloes had turned blue—with stain. In fact, it looked as if the water was driving out the sap. Yet I think March wind and the warm air of June would have done as well.

GENERAL WORK

X

KINDLY FEELING

I SHOULD soon have been bankrupt in business in 1884 if the public temper then had been like it is now—grasping, hustling, competitive. But then no competitor seems to have tried to hurt me. To the best of my remembrance people took a sort of benevolent interest in my doings, put no difficulties in my way, were slow to take advantage of my ignorance. Nobody asked for an estimate—indeed there was a fixed price for all the new work that was done. The only chance for me to make more profit would have been by lowering the quality of the output; and this the temper of the men made out of the question. But of profits I understood nothing. My great difficulty was to find out the customary price. The men didn't know. I worked out long lists of prices from the old ledgers, as far as I could understand their technical terms.

Commercial travellers treated me well—Sanders from Auster & Co., Bryant from Simpson's, Dyball from Nobles & Hoare. The last-named, I remember, fearing that I was in danger of over-stocking, could hardly be persuaded to book an order for four gallons of varnish, when he was expecting it to be for only two gallons. It was not until customers had learnt to be shy of my book-learned ignorance, my simplicity, my Ruskinian absurdities, that they began to ask for estimates, or to send their work elsewhere.

The steadiness of the men was doubtless what saved me from ruin. Through them I felt the weight of the traditional public attitude towards industry. They possibly (and properly) exaggerated the respect for good workmanship and material; and I cannot blame them if they slowed down in pace. Workmen even to-day do not understand what a difference this may make to an employer. The main thing after all (and the men in my shop were faithful to it) was to keep the business up to a high level, preserving the reputation my father and grandfather had won for it. To make it pay—that was not their affair. Certainly they taught me how to be economical, in "lining-out" the timber and so on; but the time came when I found it needful to curb their own extravagance, scheming all sorts of ways, for instance, to get three shafts out of a plank, where a too fastidious workman would have cut only two. It rarely happened the other way about, rarely happened that the condemnation of a piece of timber came from me; but it did happen, not infrequently, that a disgusted workman would refuse to use what I had supplied to him.

In this temper the shop, I feel sure, turned out good work. Especially the wheels which George Cook used to make were, I am bound to think, as good as any that had been built under the eyes of two experts like my father and his father. Cook, it is pretty sure, took his own time; but what a workman he was! There was another wheelwright in the shop whose wife used to take out garden produce in a little van: and when the van wanted new wheels, this man would not make them himself but asked that George Cook might make them. Truly, it was a liberal education to work under Cook's guidance. I never could get axe or plane or chisel sharp enough to satisfy him; but I never doubted, then or since, that his tiresome fastidiousness over tools and handiwork sprang from a knowledge as valid as any artist's. He knew, not by theory, but more delicately, in his eyes and fingers. Yet there were others almost his match—men who could make the wheels, and saw out on the saw-pit the other timbers for a dung-cart, and build the cart and paint it— preparing the paint first; or, if need be, help the blacksmith tyring the wheels. And two things are notable about these men. Of the first, indeed, I have already given some hint: it is, that in them was stored all the local lore of what good wheelwright's work should be like. The century-old tradition was still vigorous in them. They knew each customer and his needs; understood his carters and his horses and the nature of his land; and finally took a pride in providing exactly what was wanted in every case. So, unawares, they lived as integral parts in the rural community of the English. Overworked and underpaid, they

none the less enjoyed life, I am sure. They were friends, as only
a craftsman can be, with timber and iron. The grain of the wood
told secrets to them.

The other point is, that these men had a special bond of
comfort in the regard they felt for my own family. This was of
old standing. Consideration had been shown to them—a sort of
human thoughtfulness—for very long. My grandfather, I heard
more than once, wanting to arrange his wayzgoose[1] for
Christmas, had been careful not to fix it for the same day as the
wayzgoose at Mason's, the carpenter's, but to have it so that
the sawyers, who worked for both firms, could attend both
feasts. My father had been habitually considerate. "The men"
sought his advice as if they were his trusting children. He and
his brothers had all mastered the trade: they were looked up to
as able workmen; they always chose the hardest work for themselves. It was my father who was furnaceman at "shoeing"
(putting the iron tyres on the wheels); who sharpened the pit-
saws, acted as "striker" to the smiths for special jobs, stacked
the timber—never spared himself. Thanks largely to him a sort
of devotion to the whole family had grown up in the shop, and
in time was of incalculable help to me, all inexperienced. For
some years I was called familiarly by my Christian name; and
when at last it was more usual to hear myself called "the guv'ner,"
still something like affection followed me; not because I was
an able workman (I had had no apprenticeship for that), but
because I was heir to a tradition of friendly behaviour to "the
men." Older than myself though most of them were, while all
were abler, they seemed to me often like a lot of children—
tiresome children sometimes. And still they came to me for help
and advice, in their own small business difficulties.

[1] Note C, p. 206.

XI

HAND-WORK

There was no machinery, or at any rate there was no steam or other "power," in my father's shop in 1884. Everything had to be done by hand, though we had implements to serve machine-uses in their feeble way. I myself have spent hours turning the grindstone. It stood under a walnut tree; and in sunny weather there might have been worse jobs. Only, sometimes the grinding lasted too long—especially for a new tool, or for an axe. Cook was a terror in this respect. Time seemed no object with him; he must get his edge. And he had a word I used to wonder at. For when a new plane or chisel proved over-brittle, so that a nick chinked out of it and needed grinding wholly away, Cook used to look disapprovingly at the broken edge and mutter "Crips." What was that word? I never asked. Besides, Cook was too deaf. But after some years it dawned upon me that he had meant crisp.

Another implement to be turned with a handle was a drill, for drilling tyres for the blacksmiths. To put this round, under its horizontal crank, was harder work than turning the grind-stone. The shaft of it went up through the ceiling to a loft, where a circular weight—a heavy iron wheel in fact—gave the pressure on the drill. Men took turns at drilling, for it was often a long job. I don't remember doing much of this; yet I well remember the battered old oil-tin, and the little narrow spoon, and the smell of the linseed oil, as we fed it to the drill to prevent over-heating.

More interesting—but I was never man enough to use it—was a lathe, for turning the hubs of waggon and cart wheels. I suspect it was too clumsy for smaller work. Whenever I think of this, shame flushes over me that I did not treasure up this ancient thing, when at last it was removed. My grandfather had made it—so I was told. Before his time the hubs or stocks of wheels had been merely rounded up with an axe in that shop,

because there was no lathe there, or man who could use one.
But my grandfather had introduced this improvement when he
came to the shop as foreman; and there the lathe remained until
my day. I had seen my father covered with the tiny chips from
it (the floor of the "lathe-house" it stood in was a foot deep in such
chips), and too late I realised that it was a curiosity in its way.

On a stout post from floor to ceiling was swung a large wheel
—the hind wheel for a waggon—to serve for pulley. All round
the rim of this slats were nailed, or perhaps screwed on. They
stood up on both sides of the felloes so as to form a run or channel
for the leather belting that was carried over the pulley-wheel,
across to the stock to be turned. A big handle, which years of
use had polished smooth and shiny, stood out from the spokes
of this wheel, just within the rim. Gripping this handle two
men (but it took two) could put the wheel round fast enough
for the turner with his gouge. They supplied the needful
"power." Thanks to them a fourteen-inch stock could be kept
spinning in the lathe. And had I but realised it in time, near at
hand was a most interesting proof of the advantages of this
implement. For the stock of the waggon wheel—that very
wheel now used for turning other stocks—had not itself been
turned. It had only been rounded up very neatly with an axe,
in the old-fashioned way. It puzzles me now how they could
ever have built a wheel at all on so inexact a foundation.

But the want of machinery was most evident in the daily task
of cutting up plank or board for other work, and of planing and
mortising afterwards. We had neither band-saw nor circular
saw. Most of the felloes were shaped out by adze and axe: the
pieces for barrow-wheel felloes were clamped to a woodman's
bench (for they were too short and small for an axe), and sawed
out there by a boy with a frame-saw (I hated the job—it was
at once lonely and laborious); the heavy boards were cut out
(and edged up) with a hand-saw, being held down on the trestles
with your knee (it was no joke to cut a set of one-inch elm
boards—for a waggon-bottom—your arm knew about it); but
all the timbers for framework of waggon or cart, or harrow or
plough or wheelbarrow, were cut out by two men on a saw-pit.

From my childhood I had liked this saw-pit. It lay under a penthouse—just beyond the grindstone already mentioned; and in summer the walnut-tree over the grindstone sent a cool and dappled shadow down on the tiles of the saw-pit roof. The sill at the farther end was cumbered up with lengths of timber standing on end—timber "in cut," as we said, meaning that widths had been already cut off from it. But if you merely jumped across the saw-pit to the opposite side you were brought up short by a tier of plank stacked there to get the shelter of the roof. When this plank came to be moved (but that was not often) it disclosed tarred weather-boarding, closing in that side of the saw-pit penthouse from the public lane outside.

A short old piece of ladder enabled one to get down the five or six feet into the saw-pit. On either hand was brickwork— two bricks having been left out, each side, to hold an oil-cup, and wedges for the "saw-box" which clutched the bottom-end of the saw. But the "box" itself, and the little oily club for knocking it on, might be tossed down anywhere on to the layer of sawdust at the bottom. Sometimes a frog was hopping about in this sawdust, sometimes one saw a black beetle there. The sight of this quiet fauna gave me, as a child, a sense of great peace. The aged-looking brickwork—greyish pink and very dusty—helped the impression, and so did the planks stacked on the sill at the side. The daylight seemed to float in a sort of dusty ease amongst the planks and the sawdust, as if nothing noisier than a frog or a black beetle need be thought of there.

And there I found the same settled peace when, as a young man, at last I began to go down into the saw-pit to work. Certainly peace was beneficial; for sawing was hard work and often lasted a whole day—or more than that, if the timbers for a new waggon were to be sawed out. One got a queer glimpse of the top-sawyer, as one glanced up (with puckered eyelids) through the falling sawdust. Gradually the dust accumulated about one's feet, and eventually it had to be shovelled up into sacks. Being from dry timber, and mostly oak, it was useful for bacon-curing, and I used to sell it for that purpose at fourpence the sack.

Excepting that the timber was harder yet thinner (for it was dry plank instead of green round timber) and also that the work was far more varied—excepting for these reasons this pit-sawing I took part in was not very different from a professional sawyer's. I never had confidence enough, or muscle enough, to choose the top-sawyer's arduous post: I was only bottom-sawyer. And truly the work was hard enough there, though I suspect I didn't do my share. I suspect so, judging by the frequency of the top-sawyer's exhortations to "Chuck her up." (Pit-saws were always feminine.) How was a man to chuck her up when his back was one ache and all he could do for rest was to lean his weight on the handles of the saw-box for the down-pull? When the down-streaming sawdust caked on his sweaty arms and face? And thirst too! After those parched hours I have always felt that there were excuses for the notorious drunkenness of sawyers, who had not hours but years of this exhausting drudgery to endure.

Not but there were compensations, at least for the bottom man. He might not, indeed, quite go to sleep. He had to keep the saw perpendicular, to watch "the cut" as best he could through the ever-descending sawdust, and now and again he halted (straightening his back) to carry out the blessed command from the top-sawyer to drive in a wedge or to "oil-up." But with these exceptions the bottom-sawyer's lot was placid in the extreme. The work was hard enough to prevent thought, there was nothing to see beyond the brick walls of the saw-pit, and the up-and-down sway of arms and body was frequent enough and regular enough to induce a restful drowsiness.

Yet, fatiguing though it was, the work was full of interest—for me, who owned the timber, and for the skilled man who was going to work it up. We both were anxious to see how it looked after sawing—if any knot or shake or rind-gall or other unsuspected flaw should make it necessary to condemn this or that piece and to start again. On the other hand we were sometimes rewarded by the sight of really beautiful "stuff"—beautiful, that is to say, in the qualities only an expert could discern.

Of course before the sawing could begin we had taken much

pains to find the right timber and to mark it out. As I made a practice of doing this for every job, whereby nothing was used without my knowledge (it was my father's way), so my acquaintance with the individual pieces (planks and "flitches," to say nothing of spokes and felloes and hubs) became intimate and exhaustive. I spent hours, often by myself, hunting for just the exact piece that would be wanted, perhaps, to-morrow. Or, was any man about to begin on new cart, or waggon, or wheelbarrow, he looked to me to find him the material for the whole.

Truly interesting this was. Most of the timbers required a slight curve in them, the exact curves being preserved in patterns, some of them dating from my grandfather's time, no doubt. Thus there was a pattern for the bottom-timbers of a waggon, and another for a dung-cart, and yet another for a "raved" cart. Waggon-shafts "off" and "near," cart-shafts, "hounds," "hames," tailboard rails, and a dozen other things, having to be cut to pattern, were first marked-out or "lined-out" on their respective planks, before the sawing could begin.

Tricky work it was, very often. Especially tricky, until you knew how, was lining-out the shafts for a cart. The pattern was not enough here. It gave the curve; but the outside width of the shafts at the back end where they fitted the cart, and the inside width the horse needed between them in front, introduced complications which had to be allowed for, before one shaft could be sawed out. So the lines had to be completed with chalk line and two-foot rule. I learnt how to do this years before I saw the reason for what was done. "Rule-of-thumb" was my guide, and as I suspect that this was all that the men had to go by, it may be supposed that it was a sort of folk tradition we were following each time we lined-out a pair of shafts.

There was a choice of two saws, but after a long time they both grew so dull that the men began to give broad hints of the need of the file. But not one of the staff offered to do the sharpening, probably because it was a mystery to them all. Indeed, sharpening the pit-saws had been my father's care. Accordingly, eager to fill his place wherever I could, I took on this job. To be sure, I had a little dim theory of what was wanted; I had watched the professional sawyer too; conceivably I was as likely to succeed at it as any of the wheelwrights. And at least I got a little "cut" into the saw. "She" felt right, when I passed my hand gently along the teeth, as I had seen the real sawyer do; yes, one felt a sort of bite from the newly filed teeth. And she looked right too, when I squinted along to see if the teeth stood out evenly in their two rows, this side and that. It is true, in the act of sawing afterwards an occasional jump of the saw almost jarred one's arms out and probably the top-sawyer swore a little, yet I do not recall any complaints. Only a facetious wheelwright took to calling one of the saws "Old Raspberry," in allusion to her scratching character. He also hinted that the teeth were "all uncles and aunts," they were so uneven.

If the one o'clock bell sounded before we had done, this same man was wont to say wearily: "Well, let's go and have some dinner. Perhaps we shall be stronger then." I wonder now— was that "just a thing to say"? or was he gibing at my physical weakness?

XII

BOTTOM-TIMBERS

The wheelwright's first job, when he had got his "stuff" from saw-pit to bench, was to plane it all—this, not so much for the sake of getting it smooth, as to be sure that he was working with squared angles, or with a known bevel. Bevels had to be taken, so as to make the cross-timbers—the fore and hind shutlock, and the various "heads"—fit the slant of cart or waggon. But while these were bevelled all the other timbers were exactly squared, or there could have been no certainty in the work. Each woodman, each smith, was most careful on this point. A "square" was an indispensable part of every workman's outfit.

When it came to laying down the bottom-timbers still the principle of squareness governed all, although, for carts (two wheels) at least, there was a slight apparent departure from it. For a cart was made a little wider at the "tail" end than at the fore end, so that when it was tipped up the load might loosen and slip out easily. Dung-carts, lime-carts, gravel-carts were alike in this, they were wider by two inches at the back than at the front. Accordingly, in laying down the bottom of any cart the main-timbers—the "sides" as we called them—converged a little and the corners of the cart were therefore not actually

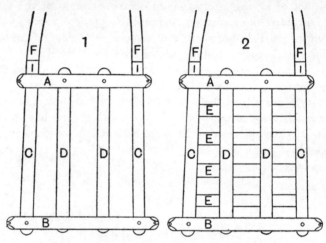

BOTTOM FRAME-WORK OF TWO-WHEELED CARTS

1. A cart for cross-boarding, in which the boards were nailed across on top of the sides and summers. 2. A cart for long-boarding, in which the boards lay on the keys, being fitted down lengthwise between sides and summers.

A, fore shutlock; B, hind shutlock; C, sides; D, summers; E, cross keys; F, shafts.

square. Yet great care was taken not to get either side forward of the other; the two had to be exactly opposite, so that the finished cart might be symmetrical. The method of testing this symmetry with a long stick across from corner to corner was probably a folk knack of great antiquity.

For reasons to be discussed (I hope) in a separate chapter a waggon—that triumph of the folk art of wheelwrighting—was not laid down on quite the same principles as a tip-cart; though here too the symmetry of the "sides" was as important as ever. But leaving the peculiarity of waggons, I wish to speak of another feature they had in common with some (not all) carts, when the main-timbers came to be laid down. Soon after I went into the business, this peculiarity indeed went quite out of use; yet just before that time it had been almost general.

It was another case of use dominating construction. Just as all tip-carts were made wider at the back than in front so that the load might fall easily, so, for carts and waggons alike, it was most desirable that the bottom-boards should be laid longwise, not crosswise. Wherever a shovel had to be used for clearing the floor this was desirable—that is to say, always with waggons which could never be tipped at all, and often with tip-carts—as when the load was to go up into a loft or over a wall. In such cases tipping had to give way to shovelling, and then the bottom-boards were better longwise—from head to tail—than crosswise —from side to side.

For plainly what the carter wants is a smooth surface for his shovel to slide along. If the boards go across there may be difficulties. One board a shade thicker than the one next it will lift a low but exasperating ridge all across the cart. Or stones may get wedged in between two cross-boards; or a small stone may force one of the boards up a little; or the edge of an elm board (and they were all elm at that time) may curl up right in the way of the shovel. It was most desirable, therefore, for any or all of these reasons, to have no joint, no sudden change of thickness, no lodgment for stones, no curled-up edge, to stand up against the shovel. It should slither along the cart-floor, the waggon-floor, from front to back, as if the floor were greased. In fact, why should not the floor go shiny with shovelling? It sometimes did. Plainly, the boards should be laid longways, from front to back.

But, to secure this advantage, a great modification of the bottom framework was necessary. Consider again that framework. The two main "sides" were held together, at both ends, by bevelled "shutlocks." But the three or four feet between the sides needed some filling up to serve as joists serve on the floor of a room. There must be something for the boards to be nailed to.

Now, in waggons and most carts, this "something" was furnished by lighter timbers, roughly parallel with the "sides." These lighter timbers, serving the purpose of floor-joists, were called "summers." Two summers ran all down the waggon, two down the cart, from front to back. Between them, also from front to back, were three spaces to be boarded up.

It was easy (or rather, it was simple—I never found it "easy") to saw out the elm boards that were to fill these spaces. Only, what were they to rest on, between the summers though not on them? This problem had been met, probably for many ages, by mortising "keys"—thin slats of oak—right through the summers and into the main sides, so that the whole bottom framework, before the boards were put in, was a sort of lattice-work—sides and longitudinal summers crossed by keys. The boards, when they were in place, lay down between the summers —parallel to them and level with them—but were nailed over and hid the keys. The nails were "wrought" nails, "rose" nails, which could be clenched. Often I held an iron bar butted against them, while the woodman clenched them on the other side. And so the main purpose was fulfilled. The bottom was boarded over with boards, which, lying in the same direction as the sides and summers, offered no obstruction to a shovel through the whole length from head to tail[1].

Why was this excellent plan ever abandoned, as in fact it was early in 1884 if not sooner? To the best of my recollection I never in any way took part in making a new cart or waggon with keyed bottom, although I have helped renew the boards in them many a time and have sighed despairingly over the long business of sawing out those boards. But new one I never saw made, the reason being probably that it was so costly a job, mortising-in all those keys and fitting the boards neatly between the summers. In later days a man might half build a cart in the time that was spent in this tedious preparation of the floor. Soon too, though not just at first, elm was superseded by deals

[1] Note D, p. 206.

—all equal in thickness, not liable to curl up, as elm had been, and practically ready, as they were fit, to lay across cart or waggon (but they wanted fitting at the ends) on top of the summers, instead of between them. And thanks to this change of material—this replacement of English elm by Norwegian deal—the old method of long-boarding was really unnecessary, as it was also too costly.

Yet, looking into the matter with the respect due to ancient crafts, one may see in it some of the spirit in which the older work was done. No sentiment governed it, no commercial greed affected it much. The spirit was simply utilitarian. The flooring of the cart or waggon had to be adapted to the use of the shovel; that was all. Because Farmer So-and-So would expect his waggoner to shovel the lime or the clay or what not cleanly from the waggon, the provincial waggon-builder made his waggon-bottom in this way rather than that, choosing and mortising his timbers accordingly. It was rather a long business, but in country places that didn't matter so much as getting the job effectively done. This was still the governing idea in that seemingly far-off time.

It should have been said that dung-carts, specially designed for field work, were built in an entirely different and much simpler way, so that the same problem did not arise with them.

XIII

WAGGONS

Long after the peaceful period these chapters deal with, I was really pained at the sight of an old farm-waggon being trundled along with a load of bricks towards what had been a quiet country place on the Surrey and Hampshire border. It was bad enough for bricks to be going there at all—to desecrate some ancient heath or woodland or field. Too plainly Old England was passing away; villas were coming, the day of farm-waggons was done. Here was this stately implement forced, like the victim of an implacable conqueror, to carry the materials for its own undoing. No circumstance of tyranny was omitted. Ignominy was piled upon ignominy. I felt as if I were watching a slave subjected to insult and humiliation. It was not so much that bricks were out of place. True, the delicate lines of the waggon-timbers had been shaped for other uses—for hay or for corn-sheaves, or flour-sacks or roots—but waggons have been used for "brick-cart" often enough, and no wrong done. But here the shame seemed emphasised by the tractor. Instead of quiet beautiful cart-horses, a little puffing steam-engine was hurrying this captive along, faster than ever farm-waggon was designed to go. The shafts had been removed—as when Samson was mutilated to serve the ends of his masters—and although I couldn't see it, I knew only too well how the timbers would be trembling and the axles fretting at the speed of this unwonted toil. I felt as if pain was being inflicted; as if some quiet old cottager had been captured by savages and was being driven to work on the public road.

Very likely it was silly to feel so keenly as I felt then for a dead thing, and yet—the truth is, farm-waggons had been adapted, through ages, so very closely to their own environment that, to understanding eyes, they really looked almost like living organisms. They were so exact. Just as a biologist may see, in any limpet, signs of the rocky shore, the smashing breakers, so the provincial wheelwright could hardly help reading, from the waggon-lines, tales of haymaking and upland fields, of hilly roads and lonely woods and noble horses, and so on. The age-long effort of Englishmen to fit themselves close and ever closer into England was betokened in my old farm-waggon; and this the little puffing steam-tractor seemed to flout.

But where begin to describe so efficient an organism, in which all the parts interacted until it is hard to say which was modified first, to meet which other? Was it to suit the horses or the ruts, the loading or the turning, that the front wheels had to have a diameter of about four feet? Or was there something in the average height of a carter, or in the skill of wheel-makers, that fixed these dimensions? One only knew that, by a wonderful compromise, all these points had been provided for in the country tradition of fore-wheels for a waggon. And so all through. Was it to suit these same wheels that the front of a waggon was slightly curved up, or was that done in consideration of the loads, and the circumstance merely taken advantage of for the wheels? I could not tell. I cannot tell. I only know that in these and a hundred details every well-built farm-waggon (of whatever variety) was like an organism, reflecting in every curve and dimension some special need of its own country-side, or, perhaps, some special difficulty attending wheelwrights with the local timber.

Already, indeed, when I entered the business, the heyday of waggon-building was over and that decline had set in from which the old craft is now wellnigh dead. In details to be discussed in another chapter, the new wheels of 1884 were made more cheaply than of old: for the countryman was growing so commercial that he would not—perhaps could not—afford to have work done with a single eye to its effectiveness. So with the waggon-bottoms. Just before my time a change for the worse had been introduced. The floors were now cross-boarded, although (as pointed out in the last chapter) the costlier long-boarding had been a more useful if not a stronger device. This, as I say, was giving way to something cheaper. The earlier adjustments, which in fact had given the beauty as of an organism, were being neglected. Yet this neglect did not, could not, spread far. For years the old country traditions of waggon-building continued to be faithfully followed. Details which might not be cheapened still achieved the superb adjustments, and waggons grew into beauty, not to please artists who gushed about them, but to satisfy carters and to suit the exigencies of field and crop and road[1].

* * * * * *

Apart from the shafts (or sharps as we often called them) a waggon, though it looked one and indivisible, was made up of three main parts. First, on the fore-wheels, was the fore-carriage.

[1] Note E, p. 207.

The hind-carriage, on the hind-wheels, came next, carrying a "pole" (like a long arm) to hold on to the fore-carriage centrally so as to be drawn along obediently behind it.

With a special and simple apparatus these two "carriages" could be, and often were, used without the third portion. For, when put together, they made a sort of trundling framework, as high in front as behind, very useful for loading hop-poles for the Farnham hop-grounds. This was every way an advantage. The hop-poles packed better than they would have done had the third portion—"the body"—been on the waggon; further it was worth while, for the sake of the horses, to dispense with the weight of the body if possible, seeing that the complete waggon, empty, weighed eighteen hundredweight or so. I am talking of a "three-ton waggon"—to carry three tons, that is.

The body, too often spoken of as the bed, had its head, tail, waist; it lay on pillows (we called them "pillars") and bolsters. When, new-made, it was at last hoisted on to its wheels, we spoke of "gettin' her on to her legs"—using the feminine gender, perhaps in allusion to the complexity of the structure. Two "pins" held the body in its place; a "round-pin," of $1\frac{1}{4}$ inches diameter or so, fixing the head down to the fore-carriage; and a tail-pin (about five-eighths of an inch) sufficing to keep the tail from jolting up off the hind-carriage.

On recalling it I find myself wondering that a waggon was ever got together at all in my shop and under my management. Without pulleys or sling, strong arms alone had to raise the body from the ground and secure it to its two carriages; moreover, there needed to be a boy inside, to plunge the round-pin down into its place just at the critical moment—namely, when the pole from the hind-carriage was inserted into the fore-carriage and the body too was lying atop of them all right. Fewer than four men—to shift the wheels and so on—could hardly have done the necessary lifting—body and boy and all; and, as I was too ignorant, there was for the first months at any rate nobody to take command. Yet this seems not to have mattered. Waggons were constantly being "taken down" for painting or mending, and then being lifted up again; and, as I

remember no quarrel or disagreement over this work, I gladly
believe that the workmen themselves liked to get it done effici-
ently and that their own friendly good temper taught them how
to pull and lift together. Certainly it was an occasion for gruff
jokes. Good humour saw us through. In one case, the round-
pin having got jammed, a sledge hammer was called for to knock
it down; whereupon the puny apprentice inside said "Shan't I
knock it down with my fist?" It's strange, how well I remember
his smile after all these years.

XIV

WAGGON-LOCKING

A pleasant story lingered in the shop, and was now and then
told again, about an estate carpenter employed by Bishop Sumner
at Farnham Castle. This man had built a new waggon in a
workshop there, only to find that it was too wide to be got out
of the door. And when the waggon, having been taken to
pieces in the shop, was put together again in the yard, there now
proved to be too little room in the yard for turning it round,
and it had to be got into Farnham Park for more room.

This story, I will admit, had probably been invented by a
wheelwright to pour contempt upon the craft of carpenters.
Certainly an idea prevailed—not wholly without justification
perhaps—that while any man able to make a wheel knew
enough to be a carpenter, on the other hand a carpenter could
not do wheelwright's work, for lack of apprenticeship. In this
connection a strong prejudice was felt against any casual who
claimed to be wheelwright and carpenter both. Such a pre-
tension was almost enough in itself to prevent the wretched
tramp from getting a job in my shop—would he not prove to be
Jack of all trades and Master of none? Unshapely cart-work by
carpenters sometimes forced its way under my notice, and served
as a warning against the employment of such men.

To return to the story of the waggon at Farnham Castle—it illustrates a difficulty that an inexperienced man would hardly fail to meet with. To build a farm-waggon that would turn round in reasonable space—something less than Farnham Park —was a problem that needed attention even in marking-out the main-timbers for the sawing. The trouble was that the front wheels would not "lock" (that is turn) full circle under the waggon. For reasons not to be discussed just here the said wheels were too high, so that about half-way round the upper edges of them clashed into the body and were stopped. If then the horse still went on turning he might have overset the waggon or else caused it to skid, but to turn it, even at right angles, was impossible.

How to prepare for this no carpenter could be expected to know; only by faithfully following a certain tradition could the wheelwright partially meet the difficulty. One detail, as I have said, had to be provided for on the very saw-pit. It's true, there were other reasons for sawing-out that gentle upward curve in the front of a waggon, that rise of the floor-timbers; but this also was one reason for it: if the floor stood up a little out of the way it allowed the foremost wheel to get an inch or two further round before being blocked. Accordingly, that beautiful boat-like lift of the front of the waggon was carefully prepared on the saw-pit, not for beauty but for use.

Of small avail would it have been, however, for the foremost wheel thus to gain an inch or two forwards, unless the opposite wheel, which pivoted against it on the other side, could also gain an equal inch or two, backwards. If it jammed into the waist of the waggon—well, it jammed, and the horse could do no more. So, to balance the advantage of lifting the floor in front and letting one wheel run under a little further on one side, a slight narrowing was effected at the waist, so that there the other wheel, twisting in the reverse way, might get a little further back on the opposite side. A well-trained waggon-builder knew to a nicety how to arrange this matter. He kept it in view and provided for it from the first, not by scientific calculation but by following the methods long ago learnt in his trade. It is quite conceivable that a carpenter, unaware of those methods, might indeed have got a waggon together so that all Farnham Park would not have been big enough for it to turn round in. In some districts waggons were specially formed at the waist, nay, oak-trees were specially planked out, to give the requisite shape for this. Sussex waggons were of singularly beautiful construction for this reason. The Surrey fashion followed in my shop was, I think, not so good. Yet it sufficed for a long time. Even when buying oak I used to look out for butts that would saw into plank fit for a waggon-bottom. And it was not any understanding of the Why and Wherefore that guided me, but the traditional good sense of Surrey waggon-builders for generations.

It would take me too deep into technicalities to tell how this same problem of turning round—the problem overlooked by the estate carpenter at Farnham Castle—affected other points of construction—how the "sweep" under the pole had to be ironed because of it, or how the side-timbers were protected by "locking-cletes" at the waist, where the wheels ground back against them. But one detail may be mentioned. After many years (and waggons were meant to last many years) the "pillar" of the fore-carriage was apt to wear down too flat for turning this way and that under the weight of the head. The easy middle rise that had been given to it at first was lost and the carriage, with never so much grease, could not be got round.

Then the "pillar" had to be seen to. It was taken off and "turned" as we used to say, that is, the original turn or convexity was restored to it, with wedges and by various devices known to the trade.

But why—for we must come to it at last—why were the two fore-wheels not made low enough to "lock" right under the waggon, as, at a later date, fore-wheels were made to lock under a brewer's dray, a miller's van? It would have been much better, surely? The farm-waggon could have been built straight-bottomed, there need have been no pinched-in waist to it; it would have turned round in much less space, with saving of time and trouble and horse-strength. In short, would it not have been better in every way to make this so simple and desirable alteration, and to have had the fore-wheels twelve inches or so lower in diameter, so as to lock right under the waggon?

One reason has been hinted at why this was not done. It was no easy job, wheelwrights knew, to make (with the old apparatus) a low wheel strong enough for the front of a waggon. But no doubt this difficulty could have been got over, had there been no others. There were others though outside the wheelwright's reach. And as he might not alter them he had to adjust his work to them. It is the only way. An organism must be adapted to its environment.

But consider for a moment the front waggon-wheels, four feet two inches high (that is, in diameter) at the most. There were a pair of them revolving on a straight axle between them. Now, in the most favourable case, this axle, being at the half diameter, could not clear the ground by more than two feet. In the old days of wooden axles it must have been an inch or two nearer the ground than that. So the wheelwright had to plan an axle for skimming along behind the horses at no more than two feet from the ground. The ground must be pictured therefore over which this organism was to pass to and fro. In fact the waggon dimensions become a sort of photographic negative, showing, to those who know what it means, the normal English farm land and the country lanes.

And what sort of land, or what lanes, do the four-foot-two waggon-wheels reflect? Not the smooth road—white with dust perhaps, or slimy with mud but always fairly even—not the made road traversed by commerce. The three-foot wheels of dray or van were very well on roads like that. But the farm-waggon had to go over a different surface. Horses had to pull it all about the meadows, the furrowed harvest-fields, the miry root-fields. It had to jolt along deep-rutted lanes; to bump into ditches on one side while it strained, perhaps, over a tussock of grass, or a mole-hill, on the other side. There were gateways trodden deep in mud by cattle; the "lands" left by the plough made the stubble-field wavy as the sea: now the waggon had to pass across a stream, now across the stumps of a newly-cut coppice.

And at any of these difficulties an axle-bed too low might have brought all to a standstill, or, being stopped with sudden jerk, involved breakage of timbers and perhaps death for waggoner or frightened horse. Certainly it would have been a mistake to build the front waggon-wheels any lower.

And, for similar reasons, the alternative of raising the body higher, out of the reach of the wheels altogether, was never contemplated so far as I know. An image of the waggoner, which comes into the mental farm picture just here and is perhaps a little out of place, shows a man from five to six feet tall, hard at work; and one sees how awkward for his stature a higher waggon-body might have been, whether for pitching hay into it or for lifting sacks from it on to his shoulders. Small heed, however, was paid to matters of mere human convenience, by farmers or labourers faced with the everlasting task of taming England's soil into new fertility every season. That was the central object of having a waggon at all, and there is no doubt that, convenience or none, the waggon-body would have been carried higher above the ground had there been any advantage therefrom. But in fact it would have been awkward—awkward and dangerous; seeing that on those uneven fields, those deep-rutted lanes, a load too high must have turned over. Such a contingency might not be risked. Necessity in fact fixed for waggons the lines between too high and too low; and in generations of experiment farm men found these invisible lines and wheelwrights learnt how to get every farm-waggon trundling along on them.

This illustrates, in one point, the conditions in which the waggon grew into a thing of beauty, comparable to a fiddle or a boat. Necessity gave the law at every detail, and in scores of ways insisted on conformity. The waggon-builder was obliged to be always faithful, to know always what was imposed on him, in wheels, shafts, axles, carriages, everything.

The nature of this knowledge should be noted. It was set out in no book. It was not scientific. I never met a man who professed any other than an empirical acquaintance with the waggon-builder's lore. My own case was typical. I knew that the hind-wheels had to be five feet two inches high and the fore-wheels four feet two; that the "sides" must be cut from the best four-inch heart of oak, and so on. This sort of thing I knew, and in vast detail in course of time; but I seldom knew why. And that is how most other men knew. The lore was a tangled network of country prejudices, whose reasons were known in some respects here, in others there, and so on. In farm-yard, in tap-room, at market, the details were discussed over and over again; they were gathered together for remembrance in village workshop; carters, smiths, farmers, wheel-makers, in thousands handed on each his own little bit of understanding, passing it to his son or to the wheelwright of the day, linking up the centuries. But for the most part the details were but dimly understood; the whole body of knowledge was a mystery, a piece of folk knowledge, residing in the folk collectively, but never wholly in any individual. "However much a man knows," old Bettesworth used to say, "there's sure to be somebody as knows more." And that is characteristic especially of all folk knowledge.

XV

CURVES

The change which all nations are going through in their ideas of environment, involving them in unrest everywhere, is curiously exemplified in the conversion of timber and the uses made of it. By the time that I had to give up my old shop practically all the stock of the older kind was obsolete. Not only were the planks not long enough; worse still, they were not straight enough. Timber was wanted for unexampled purposes, regardless of qualities thought essential heretofore. For, by 1920, the strength of oak and ash was insufficient; steel had to be used where strength mattered; and the fate of all timber was to be degraded into a sort of enslaved and humiliated padding for steel. Deal was often preferable to oak, because it could be obtained longer and straighter. "Wheel-stuff"—spokes, felloes, stocks—(to say nothing of the art of making wheels) gave place to stamped metal disks; and, horses being exchanged for motors, planks intended for ash shafts proved so wasteful for any other purpose as to be almost worthless.

The general change of outlook, illustrated thus in the timber-trade, followed upon the discovery by science of an environment unknown to our forefathers. It was more strange than emigration had ever afforded, and yet it came to those of us who stayed at home. The Pilgrim Fathers had not found so new a world. They, after all, had to practise the old arts, but our own unexplored environment of molecular forces, of steam and petrol and electricity, of steel, and of telegraphy and newspapers too, made nothing of hill and valley, of mountain and sea, or of national boundaries. Steam and steel were too powerful, and local needs were exchanged for cosmopolitan wishes. The new environment, into which we are still stumbling blind, awaits us everywhere, and rests in Universal Law, in laws of Strain and Stress, of Combustion, and so on. To meet it, workmen have to evolve new forms of skill. They must also discover new modes of farming the land and of working together, new principles of social life.

Incidentally, some of us are obliged to adopt entirely new tools and implements. Implements on wheels have already suffered a thorough change in their character. They are now required, not for a quiet half-century in this or that parish; they must travel hundreds of miles at a pace likely to rattle them to pieces in eight or ten years. It has followed that the wheelwright trade is being fast forgotten, while the old forms of timber are growing obsolete.

The older forms were almost all curved. Only the cross-pieces—the various "keys" and "bars," the "shutlocks," the "pillars" and axle-beds, the occasional "whippances," the bottom tailboard rails, the splinter-bar, were straight; the longest of them being the last-named—nearly six feet long. It would be a pleasant exercise in philosophical speculation to determine why transverse pieces generally are straight, what law of mechanics makes it so plainly right to keep slavishly to the rectilinear in so many crosswise things—railway sleepers, window-bars, schoolboy slate-frames, for instance. There must be some law, giving grandeur to this unanimity, and it would be well to get one's eye on it. But, for now, I prefer to recall how we obtained straightness in the few things where it was sought in the ancient wheelwright trade. It sets me smiling to myself. Does any young sawyer with a machine know what it is to "snap a chalk line"? It was considered the way to get straightness amongst my men, so much the way that one of them, telling of a march-past of the Guards at Aldershot, could find no better way to describe their flawless rank than to say "'Twas as if you'd snapped a chalk line along their noses." But what was this sovereign method? Simplicity itself. Two men held a line taut, while one of them rubbed a lump of chalk over it. Then (with aid of two-foot rule) it was placed on the plank where the mark was wanted, and, being drawn tight at both ends was snapped down on to the timber, leaving a white line there. A little cloud of dusty chalk rose above it when it struck the wood; the cord needed rubbing afresh every time, and soon the lump of chalk—as big as a walnut, say—was scored with convolutions deeper than in any walnut. Unless you were careful to find a new place, the cord cut it asunder. To climb up the ladder half-way out of the saw-pit, and hold the chalk line while the top-sawyer snapped a new or plainer mark, was often a welcome relief for the bottom-sawyer....In these days a steel gauge beside the circular saw makes all these devices unnecessary and speeds up the pace too.

But, as I was saying, there was not much straight timber used in the old days. Until "Scotch Carts" were introduced for builders, every longitudinal piece for cart or waggon was, I think, slightly curved; and every curve was justifiable, if reason had been asked for it. We never did ask. There were the patterns to go by—dozens of patterns left long ago by ancient craftsmen who knew what was wanted, and all we had to do was to be guided by those men's unwritten wisdom. And what was wanted was tough slender lengths of timber with just the right curve. Timber that had grown so was what we sought, for nothing was known about bending it by steam or otherwise.

It has been pointed out before how conditions of necessity— the nature of the land and the incidents of turning round— imprinted themselves, as it were, on the main-timbers of a waggon, so as to be almost perceptible there by anyone who knew enough. Much the same might be said about any of the other curved lines in waggon or two-wheeled cart. It was not for whim that the floor of a dung-cart was slightly hollowed from front to back; and if I learnt, when the sawyers were about, to look out for oak butts that would plank into seven-foot

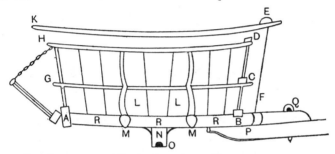

SIDE ELEVATION OF RAVED CART, WITH TAILBOARD LET DOWN

A, hind shutlock; B, fore shutlock; C, D, middle and top heads; E, F, shamble head and staff; G, H, K, "middle," "top," "out" raves; L, strouters, in sockets, M; N, axle-bed; O, arm; P, shafts; Q, keying iron; R, main "side."

lengths, with suitable curve, for "cart-sides," that also was no whim. The fact was that men dead long before my time— unlettered and therefore unfamed villagers—had felt as it were what shape a load of dung or of turnips would shake into in the bottom of a cart and had worked out that shape in heart of oak. The record was in the patterns my grandfather left behind him, and it would have been foolish to depart from those patterns. To match them with new planks was obvious common sense.

Many curved timbers might be told of—"heads" hollowed to throw the heaped-up loads together; "hounds" to lead through the fore-carriage from horse down to axle-tree; poles, reaching with curving tongue to receive the pull of the horses on the fore-carriage and to pass it along to the hind-carriage; but of all the curves perhaps the most beautiful as well as the most obvious was that which had to be given—and no man could escape it—to shafts or "sharps." It may be—I remember as I write these lines—that hames were even more obvious and more beautiful, yet they were not so essential and constant a part of every wheelwright's output. We made wooden hames now and then to oblige some fastidious customer; but shafts, for cart or waggon, were wanted every day all the year round. And the general pattern of them never varied.

A pair of shafts shows, approximately, a horizontal section of a horse in motion. It is a bird's-eye view. The driver of a hay-waggon, perched high on his load, would look down upon the shape of the horse for which wheelwrights were expected to provide. It was something the shape of a squat fiddle, or of a pear. In front the shafts were wide enough if they did not actually touch the horse's collar or shoulders, and more than that was too much; but rearwards more width was required. This, not only because horses are indeed wider at the back. Added to the increased size is a slight sway of the whole body, first this side and then that, with the alternate stepping of the hind-legs; and the area of this rhythmic movement also comes into the wheelwright's reckoning. He has to fit not the stationary horse but the horse in motion—to allow both for the unchanging width at shoulder and for the to-and-fro width behind. This latter consideration, perhaps, did not greatly affect the shafts for a two-wheel cart. They had to have the same width at the back as the cart had, where there was always room enough for any horse. For a cart therefore the main concern of the wheelwright was so to reduce the shaft-width as to bring it at the front end gradually up to the required narrowness by the collar. This was arranged at the saw-pit, with much solemn rule work and snapping of chalk line, according to a time-honoured formula. But waggon-shafts could be built more entirely for the horse, and, though I have forgotten the measurements, left a little less room at the rear than cart-shafts did. They followed the shape of the striding horse more closely.

In either case—waggon or cart-shafts—curve best served the ends of usefulness and strength. In the case of "double shafts" for a waggon, where a pair of horses worked side by side, in order to get them a little closer together the two inside shafts were sawn rather straighter. Yet the curve was never quite abandoned. It was specially looked for when the sawyers were planking the ash; and for myself—often I have seen trees growing with exactly the right shape for shafts and have chuckled inwardly, admiring how accurately woodland nature seemed to know the shape of moving horses.

XVI

TAPERING AND SHAVING

A certain Farmer Tupp "down country" (this is not the same thing as "down in the sheers," which means the Midlands, but refers vaguely to the West of England) a certain Farmer Tupp long ago, when ordering a new waggon, begged the wheelwright not to put any of "these 'postles" into it. It is supposed that he referred to the "shaving" of the timbers, seeing in its effects some attempt at ornament, like the apostles carved in church. Truly he was justified had this been so. Any farmer might well deprecate such extravagance on his tackle. Usefulness, not beauty, was wanted. I knew a farmer once who would not have the new dung-cart wheels painted. He wished to see for himself that spokes and felloes were free of knots and shakes, clear of putty. Afterwards he could tar them himself, for what cared he for appearances?

But Farmer Tupp, down country, was badly mistaken if he thought (as was supposed) that money would be saved by forbidding the wheelwright to spend time in shaving-up the waggon timbers. As is often the fate of stingy men, he was over-reaching himself. If indeed by his parsimony he saved a few pounds in his wheelwright's bill, it must eventually have cost him many times as much in horseflesh. For this "shaving" was one of the ways by which a wheelwright reduced the weight of his always too cumbersome product. Every time that a horse went out with a waggon the farmer ought to have blessed the skilful workman who had spent days with the draw-shave, cunningly lightening every future load. These considerations may be less important, with motor-traction. But with horse-traction the advantage was incalculable.

Not that the draw-shaving was the only way of reducing the weight of the farm tackle while preserving its strength. Much of the blacksmith's labour was spent, as I may presently show, on "drawing-down" the iron-work to tapering though strong slenderness. And then there was seasoning the timber. This, I own, was effected for other ends, for timber was neither tough nor durable until it had been properly dried. But, incidentally, a great deal of weight was got rid of in getting rid of the sap. Not at first, but in the course of years, I learnt to judge the dryness of a piece of timber partly by its weight. Without scales to go by—you could not confer such knowledge on anybody's intellect—one's arms learnt (in an artist's way) to recognise what mattered. In my muscles I knew. A piece of timber too light was immediately suspect, and on examination almost certainly turned out to have lost its toughness along with its weight: it was "doaty," or "biscuity," or "frow," or even "frow as a carrot." On the other hand suspicion fell on unwonted weight. One looked to see if the plank "opened" with any tint of pinkness—a fairly sure sign of sap; or perhaps one's nose might detect the sappy smell; or, lastly, a certain woolliness of texture —quite indescribable yet easily known to the man who planed the timbers—might betray why the wood had been so heavy. The test of weight was not in itself quite conclusive. For instance black-hearted ash was often unduly heavy, and still worse was ash where big "maggots" had left their dark borings. Different trees from different soils varied considerably in their weight, and due allowance had to be made for such variations. Yet, when all is said, it must be acknowledged that the proper seasoning of the timber was a large factor, perhaps the largest, in keeping down the weight finally to be reduced still further by the draw-shave.

Then too the work of the plane tended the same way, if it did not amount to much. Of course the prime object of planing cart timbers was to get them square for framing, and then, well planed, they were less liable to keep moisture standing harmfully on them. But certainly every stroke of the plane removed some weight—not a little either, if all the timbers of a farm-waggon are considered.

Moreover the wheelwright practised one other economy of weight, long before there could be even any planing. Sundry planks were cut thicker at one end than at the other. Thus cart sides "tapered" from three-and-a-half inches at the butt end to three inches at the fore end, where less strength was demanded. Something of the same sort was done for "hounds": and, most noticeably of all, for shafts. Beginning with three-and-a-half to four inches square near the body, where shafts had to be very strong, they "tapered" to three inches at the point. If they didn't, you knew it. To raise from the ground a pair of shafts that had not been duly "tapered" was to know what the poor horse might have been spared, but for ignorance or parsimony. It happened that properly tapered shafts looked graceful. But I am not aware that this appearance was ever deliberately sought. Yet doubtless it had a charm for the wheelwright none the less effective for being subconscious. He felt that it looked right.

None of these devices, however, exonerated him from the final duty of removing with his draw-shave every superfluous bit that could be pulled or nicked away from the timber, in waggon or dung-cart, wheelbarrow, timber-carriage, plough, harrow, whippance. One principle governed all this work. It was no decoration, as Farmer Tupp fancied. The object was to relieve the horses of every ounce possible. To this end the timbers were pared down, here and there, to a very skeleton thinness. But wherever strength was essential—where a mortice or a bolt-hole was made, or where a bearing was wanted for another timber, there nothing was shaved away; the squared timber was left square. The result was a frequent shaving out of short curves, which had indeed some look of being meant for beauty, but their usefulness came first. At a rough guess I should say the eighth part at least of the weight of squared waggon timbers was taken away with the draw-shave. Shafts were reduced even more than that, and so were "pillars." The corners even of axle-beds could be spared without weakening anything, and were therefore lightly "broken" down.

A man skilful with his draw-shave enjoyed this work, lingering over it like an artist. I often laughed to myself, seeing how the so feeble and scribbled pencillings which marked on the planed timber where the shaving was to be were translated into perfect curves as soon as the man got to work with the tool he knew.

A stiff blade seven or eight inches long was fitted with a handle at each end for drawing towards you. Strong arms could get a great pull on it. By a clever knack—

DRAW-SHAVE (about 12 inches long)

one handle being held under the left armpit while the right hand guided the blade—a carpenter's pencil could be sharpened with it, but there were finer uses of it. Hurry not being so great then as now, wheelwrights, delighting in their craft, would spend costly minutes "butterflying" here and there. A "butterfly" was a shallow design, nicked out at the middle of a timber-edge—an axle-bed or a shutlock. Quite useless, it refreshed the workman's temper. Can you not imagine a little the joyous sensations running up his wrists and calming his nerves as he feels the hard wood softly yielding to his wishes, taking the fine clean-edged shape under the faithful tool? But certainly this sort of thing took time. It was decoration, and I think modern Farmer Tupps do not want to pay for that nowadays. Truly, it was easily over-done. An elaborate shaving sometimes effected on millers' vans, on brewers' drays, was as ugly as it was useless. But to see this sort of thing at its worst one had to see a costly "gipsy-van" or "show-cart." There, the timbers were often decorated to an excess with useless shaving, which, being gilded or "picked-out" in crude colours by the painter, had a truly barbaric effect.

XVII

LEARNING THE TRADE

With the idea that I was going to learn everything from the beginning I put myself eagerly to boys' jobs, not at all dreaming that, at over twenty, the nerves and muscles are no longer able to put on the cell-growths, and so acquire the habits of perceiving and doing, which should have begun at fifteen. Could not Intellect achieve it? In fact, Intellect made but a fumbling imitation of real knowledge, yet hardly deigned to recognise how clumsy in fact it was. Beginning so late in life I know now I could never have earned my keep as a skilled workman. But, with the ambition to begin at the beginning, I set myself, as I have said, to act as boy to any of the men who might want a boy's help.

I recall one or two occasions when the men smiled to one another, not thinking I should see them smile; yet on the whole most kind they were, most helpful, putting me up to all sorts of useful dodges. The shriek of my saw against a hidden nail would bring the shop to a horrified standstill. When the saw jumped away from the cut I was trying to start, and jagged into my hand instead of into the timber, the men showed me where my hand ought to have been. Again, they taught me where to put my fingers, and how to steady my wrist against my knee, for chopping out wedges or "pins." Without this help, and if also my axe had been sharp enough (but that is unlikely), it would have been easy to chop off my fingers; with it I made better wedges than skilled men know how to make now, because with their machinery modern men are able to use material which anybody with an axe would know at a glance to be unfit. The men showed me how to drive in a nail without splitting the board yet without boring a hole for it to start. Wire nails had not then been introduced. "Rose-nails"—wrought iron, of slightly wedged shape—were the thing. By forcing it in the right direction a two-inch "cut-nail," as we called this kind, might be driven down to the very head, through inch elm into oak, with proper hammering. If sometimes a nail curled over instead of entering, or if it insisted on turning round so that the board was split after all, the fault was that the hammering was feeble or indirect. The men could not help that. They could not put into my wrist the knack that ought to have begun growing there five years earlier.

This same difficulty in hammering, which I never quite overcame, made me a poor hand at "knocking out dowels"— another job for boys. A dowel, with us, was a peg holding together the joints of a wheel-rim where the felloes meet. Heart of oak was not too tough for it; in fact, my father, superintending some spoke-cleaving, had carefully saved the very innermost cleft, all torn and ragged, for dowels. About the size and shape of a sausage, they were made by driving prepared lengths of oak through a "dowel cutter"—a sharp-edged ring of steel set in a block for that purpose, and a man with a heavy mallet could soon knock out a set of dowels. But, in my hand, the mallet was apt to fall a little sideways, so that the dowel, when finally slipping through on to the ground, proved crooked and useless.

Of course I had far too many irons in the fire—that was one part of the trouble. I was trying to learn four or five trades at once; and "intellect" fooled me by making them look simple. Indeed, so much of hand-work as intellect can understand does have that appearance, almost always to the undoing of the book-learned, who grow conceited. How simple is coal-hewing, fiddling, fishing, digging, to the student of books! I thought my business looked easy. Besides playing "boy" to the woodmen I went sometimes to help the blacksmith "shut" a tyre, and I always lent a hand at putting on tyres. Painters there were none, but as paint was used by the wheelwrights after they had finished a job, of course I came in for a little rough painting. I hadn't strength enough in my arm to grind up Prussian-blue for finishing a waggon-body. (Ah, the old muller and stone under the skylight in the loft, where in summer time one or two cabbage-butterflies would be fluttering! All the edges of the stone were thick-encrusted with dry paint, left behind by the flexible palette-knife and the shavings with which the middle of the stone was cleaned. The bench and the roof-beams all round were covered too with thick paint, where brushes had been "rubbed-out," for cleaning them, during many years.) I knew how to make putty, "knocking it up" with whiting and oil. I was familiar with "thinnings" of "turps," as we called turpentine. I kept watch on the kegs of dryers, Venetian-red, and so on, to see that paint was not drying on their sides but was kept properly scraped down into the covering puddle of water in the keg.

A number of duties fell on my shoulders in which nobody could guide me in my father's absence. During his illness and after his death I had to be master, as well as boy. Amongst other things was the work of store-keeper. Not only timber, iron and paint were wanted; axles and half-axles known as "arms" were kept in a corner of the body shop; and in my office, under lock and key, were the lighter kinds of hardware. Many times a day I was called away from my own job, whatever it might be, to get nails, screws, bolts, nuts, "ridgetie" chains, bolt-ends, "nut-heads," or what not. Sometimes, with hammer and "hard-chisel," I cut off lengths of chain for a tailboard, sometimes a longer length of a stouter chain for a "drag-bat," or of a slighter chain for a "roller." It was so small a shop that these interruptions were after all not too frequent. And anyhow I was proud to feel that I was doing what my father would have done. But of course I had to buy all the stores; to write orders for them or to interview commercial travellers; to overhaul invoices and pay the bills. As I said before, I do not remember that any commercial traveller ever tried to take advantage of my ignorance; but it is dreadful to think how much temptation I must have presented to them, running from saw-pit or smithy or paint-loft and aping the man of the world, in the hope that they might not notice anything odd about me.

Whenever a job was finished I went with slate to the men who had taken a hand in it, and wrote down what they had done to it, what materials they had used, and so on. Until I began to know the technical words, and the Surrey dialect of the men too, this was a great puzzle to me. How was I to know that when the old blacksmith spoke of a "roppin cleat" he had meant wrapping plate? or that a "shetlick" was the same thing that my father and grandfather spelt shutlock in the old ledger? The worst of it was that this gibberish (as it seemed to me) had to be charged up to customers. An uncle, long since dead, advised me to "charge enough and apologise"; but I have long known that I did not "charge enough." Hunting through the old ledger—my grandfather had started it—I was able to pick out and tabulate many customary prices. Not for many years did I introduce a proper system of "costing." In those old days there was a recognised price for much of the work. I believe that the figures were already antiquated and should have been bigger even at that far-away time; yet on the whole they served to keep things together while I was finding my feet. Customers seemed satisfied and continued sending work. Surely that meant that my charges were fair? It probably meant that they were found to be agreeably light. At any rate, the time came when I found out that most of the customers knew nothing about the meaning of the technical language of their wheelwright bills. Rather, they guessed what they would be called upon to pay and were pleased if I asked them for less—for they were surprisingly good judges of the price of things. Sometimes they complained—it was a principle with many—and enjoyed, I feel sure, the annoyance caused me. For I took it seriously, never dreaming that they were "pulling my leg." For my part I used to sigh, "How pleasant business might be were it not for customers!"

Of course I had no proper system of account-keeping, or the work could not have been done in the little time I gave to it. Not that I was quite primitive. I was at least a stage beyond the blacksmiths, who, weighing scrap-iron for sale (3s. 6d. the cwt. was the price), chalked up the hundred-

CHALK MARKS, IN PRIMITIVE NUMERATION

weights on the door until they came to five, and then made a fifth stroke across the other four[1]. I was not quite so bad as

[1] Note F, p. 207.

this; indeed, I used decimals in checking the invoiced weights of new iron; but for all that, my book-keeping was antiquated enough. It was hardly more elaborate than my grandfather's had been. In normal times, therefore, the office-work can hardly have occupied two hours of the day. The account-books were always at hand. It was quite easy to do all the writing in odd half-hours, so as not to feel office-work irksome at all. Bill-making times of course were busy; yet it was only at Christmas that all the bills were sent out. The idea was that farmers might have money at that season. And in Farnham especially it was worth while to ask for money then—so soon after the hop-fair at Weyhill in October.

WHEELS

XVIII

"DISH"

AFTER the last chapter it will be seen why I never learnt to make a wheel. In the course of many years many things became clear enough to me in theory, so that I could form a pretty good opinion whether or no a finished wheel had been well put together—I knew the signs to look for, the jointing of the felloes, the fit of them on the spokes, and so on—but there were mysteries about getting that finish which I never properly fathomed. Bookish training was too feeble to enter into these final secrets; evidently there was something more, only revealed to skilled hands and eyes after years of experiment. Precision eluded me; my eyes didn't see it. I was unable, up to the very last, to detect the exact angle at which, for instance, the tongues of spokes should be inserted into felloes, or the angle for dowels. Theory could tell near the matter, yet that was not near enough for the son and grandson of an expert. It could easily detect where a fault had been made; and yet fail after all to find exactly what the fault was. I feel sometimes too ignorant about wheel-making to say anything at all about it; but still, before the ancient art as practised in my shop is quite forgotten, some things should be told about it that have become known to me. The wheels I shall speak of are chiefly the wheels of waggons, drays, dung-carts, builders' carts, and so on—heavy wheels from four to six feet in diameter, and capable of carrying a load of three-quarters of a ton each. These are all but gone, but some remembrance may yet be saved of the art of making them.

Quite early in my time I realised that wheels for any horse-drawn vehicle must have more or less of "dish." A friend, hearing this word from me perhaps too often, jeered me into silence, pretending that I had said wheels should be like dishes. Perhaps he would have understood better if I had said they should resemble plates or saucers, with the hollow side outwards; for that indicates what the "dish" of a wheel was. A concavity.

It gave the shape of a Japanese umbrella seen from underneath, only it was shallower. A dished wheel was rather like a flattish limpet.

What was the use of "dish"? That question, I am ashamed to say, puzzled me for years, long after I had seen that this odd shape lent itself to many advantages and that a wheel lacking it could not be trusted to travel a mile safely. "Dish" was plainly necessary, but why? Why was a wheel without it so sure to turn inside out like an umbrella in a gale? Why should not the load, if really too heavy, sometimes crumple a wheel up the other way, instead of invariably the one way?

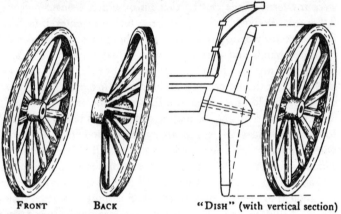

FRONT   BACK   "DISH" (with vertical section)

The advantages certainly were great. Consider the shape of a cart (in section) mounted between wheels with a proper dish. The inside of the cart could be wider along the top than at the floor. It could "spread" and yet not graze the wheels; and so a load could be bigger in size—appreciably bigger—if it was light stuff such as hay; and if it was close-lying stuff, like manure or sand, it could be easily shot out. Had the wheels been the other way about, this could not have been. Clearly it was convenient that they were farther apart in their higher curves, near the top, than they were at the ground.

Other advantages arose from the "dish" of the wheels; yet why dwell upon them? To explain them would involve an

explanation of technicalities which might be very tiresome, and
they never really satisfied me. For years I was careful to follow
the tradition, without fully seeing the sense of it. And all the
time it was staring me in the face. A number of familiar details
were pointing almost straight at it; only, as it chanced, one
other circumstance was causing me at the same time to look
another way.

Leaving the wheels for a minute, consider one apparently
irrelevant matter, which in fact is mixed up with this question
of "dish." It will be well remembered that, in the old days of
horse-traction, roads were worn down, crosswise, into a wave-
work of shallow hollows from one side to the other, about a yard
or so apart. This was not very visible in broad day-light, but at
night a lantern in a wayfarer's hand, or the low-hung head
lights of a motor-car, would show up the road, as far as the light
travelled, corrugated all across with bars of brilliant light and
pitchy darkness.

And one day I saw how this road-surface was produced. A
cart just before me was gently swaying from side to side with
every step of the horse. And as it swayed, the wheels—first the
off, then the near, in fine alternate rhythm—loosened a grain or
two of road-metal, ground the channel across the road a grain
or two deeper, now at this step, then at that. It was inevitable.
As long as horse-drawn vehicles used the road, and horses walked
or trotted one step after another from side to side slightly swaying,
so long the carts and waggons and carriages behind the horses
would gently grate into the road-surface and wear it into those
wavy channels.

But what has all this to do with the "dish" of wheels? This:
The loaded body of cart or waggon, swinging to the horse's
stride, becomes a sort of battering-ram into the wheels, this side
and then that. It slides to and fro, on well-greased arms, right
into the nave of each wheel. Now the off-side wheel gets a
ramming, and promptly throws the weight back to the near
side. And so it goes on with every horse, all day long. The wheels
have to stand not only the downward weight of the load; a
perpetual thrust against them at the centre is no less inevitable.

Motors pull straightforward and are wearing the roads differently, I am told, and certainly their wheels have little or no "dish"; but that was never the case with horse-traction, always slightly waddling. The sideways thrust was seldom great perhaps, but it continued all the time a cart or waggon was on the move—in hay meadow as much as on the high-road.

What it was that drew my attention for so long a time away from this so obvious circumstance will be explained later. Just at present it is more to the purpose to note how profoundly all wheel-traffic was affected in getting the shape of wheels adapted to the exigencies of horse-movement, and what a difference it made to the skill of many thousands of men. Not waggons and carts and timber-carriages and nebs alone, though the like of these alone will be dealt with here, but coaches and carriages, omnibuses and cabs of all kinds, were under the same necessity with regard to construction. All alike were modified in endless details, because their wheels had to be made to suit horses. And to meet all these exactions the wheel-maker and the blacksmith in the village, and the axle-makers at Birmingham or Wolverhampton, practised special forms of skill, which are at last being forgotten. For the "dish" of wheels came of no whim that might have been avoided: it was the answer country folk had to make everywhere to a law as inevitable as gravitation. Wheels were built to meet force in two directions, not in one only. Besides the downward weight of the load there was the sideways push right at the very middle of the wheel, all the time the horse was moving. I even heard it, and yet was too dense to comprehend.

(Here, it may be well to point out, was the "circumstance" to which allusion has already been made, which blinded me to the true reason for "dish" in wheels. As it was so inevitable that a wheel must yield to the tightening strain of a tyre, and so likely that it would become more convex or concave in the course of doing so, I long supposed that "dishing" was simply a preparation for this last movement, in order to regularise the contraction and know beforehand how to take advantage of it. It was evidently more convenient that a wheel, certain to "dish" one way or the other, should dish outwards; and it was evidently desirable, too, that the extent of this should be calculable. In view of these obvious advantages, though they did not quite satisfy me, I was contented to go on for years without grasping the true meaning of "dish." I saw wheels turned inside out—like an umbrella in a wind—where the "dish" was too feeble. I even noticed that this was always in one direction—the centre had invariably come forward. Yet it was not clear to me that this was the result of a central thrust outwards, due to an unalterable movement of the body.)

XIX

SPOKES AND FELLOES

The device of lightening the horse-load in a vehicle by shaving away every superfluous hair's thickness of timber was carried to its highest in wheels, and especially in their spokes. Here, least of all, was any concession made to ornament. It is true I once saw, perhaps at South Kensington Museum, a pair of Chinese wheels the spokes of which had been turned in a lathe, to look as pretty as stair banisters, but this would not have done for English waggons and dung-carts on English farms. In the wheels for a use so rough, often in rough weather, it was needful to save every possible grain of strength, while shaving ruthlessly away every grain of mere weight. The draw-shave by itself was not enough. A more delicate tool followed it, significantly called a spoke-shave. In later years spokes were even finished off with sandpaper. But this was rather to please the painters, who by then were specialising in wheelwright's work as they had long done in coach-building—it was to please the painters rather than to lighten the wheel. Sandpaper was used also by clumsy boys, who had not learnt how to finish with a spoke-shave. Of course it was not the spokes alone that came in for this attention. The felloes had their share. A well-finished wheel, intelligently shaved up, showed where the expert aimed at strength, and where he knew material could be spared. It was a case for experts. Machine-made wheels were wont to be unnecessarily heavy; and in army wheels too I have seen material left that should have been shaved away, if there had been more intelligence at headquarters. But old village wheelwrights knew better. Even I knew.

As soon as I could distinguish the heart of oak from the sap (it was not at first, for they had not taught me such accomplishments at school) I took to looking out, myself, the spokes to be used for every wheel that went from my shop, and at once the question of strength arose. At the back of the spoke was where strength was chiefly wanted; the front, "the face," did not matter half so much. In fact, a little sap was liked all up the face, because it would take a slightly better surface for painting, where painting showed. For all that it was the back of the spoke that was of chief importance. A little knot there—a little black knot no bigger than a pea— damned the whole thing. What I looked for was a length without flaw, which after being rounded up could be left at the full dimensions decided on. Nothing

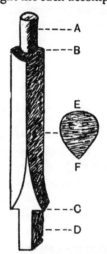

FACE-VIEW AND SECTION
OF A SPOKE

A, rounded tongue to enter felloe ; B, the knock ; C, shoulder ; D, square foot to enter stock ; E, back (heart of oak) ; F, face (sap).

might be shaved away from the back. It was heart of oak, fit to last for ever. After thirty years or so, when hard wear had worn the wheel out, the spokes were still sound, and were taken out carefully. I sold thousands of them, at a penny a piece, for ladder rounds, but the better of them were set aside to be worked up again for smaller spokes or in barrow wheels. Then they might start another career of usefulness, for another twenty years or so.

And still the oak continued good; only, the spoke could not be used again, for a reason soon to be shown.

When Cook had carried away the chosen spokes (others made wheels, but the most of that work was given to George Cook, so sure he was)—when Cook had carried the spokes to his bench and planed them true and, with compasses and bevel, marked out the "shoulders," his first job was to saw out the shoulders and cut out the "foot"—the tenon to be driven down into the nave as far as the shoulders would let it go. I think he used generally a fine tenon-saw—like a butcher's meat saw—for the whole of this work; yet in some cases, if the grain of the oak was favourable, he may have split out the foot with wide sharp chisel. I cannot remember now. Next, the foot being prepared for the nave, came the job of shaping up the parts of the spoke that would be exposed.

This was begun with axe and draw-shave, the front edge or "face" being roughly chopped-out and all the four corners deftly splintered away. A "smoothing plane" then made the sides of the spoke straight, and after that they were further cleaned up with a "jarvis"—a sort of hollow-bladed plane used for rounding spokes and for nothing else. But, down towards the shoulders of the spoke, near the nave, there were curves into which no other tool would go, and the spoke-shave came into play.

Here, I remember, was a nicety I never fathomed. Again and again I have carried a spoke to Cook, finished, for all that my eyes could see; but I think he never once let it go untouched. With a tolerant smile on his pursed lips he would take the spoke from my hands—as if recognising that I had tried; and then he would put his own spoke-shave to it, making some slight difference I never properly grasped. Yet I always believed that he knew best. There may indeed have been an element of craftsman's "swank" in his behaviour—a willingness to show that he could do better than his employer; but he never so much as hurt my feelings in this way. Moreover, he would always do just the same thing with the "turned spokes" sometimes supplied him. Heavy they were, these machine-made commodities originating from America—heavy, and clumsily finished, even to my eyes; but they seemed to offend George Cook still more, and save on emergency he unwillingly used them. He was too much of an artist in spokes.

FELLOES

After the spokes, the felloes—ash, elm, or beech—in looking out which, from the felloe-stacks, I used a "pattern," so as to get something sure to yield the required curve and the right length too. For of course felloes differed in curve according to the height (the diameter) of the wheel, and in length according to the number of spokes used.

For instance, for a front waggon wheel four feet high, felloes about two feet long would suffice if there were six of them; but if there were only five they needed to be almost six inches longer to make up the full circumference.

As may be remembered the felloes had been roughly hewn when green, then stacked away to season; but now they had to be shaped out exactly. The years that had dried them had made them very hard too,—all the better under very sharp tools, but trying to an inexpert man. Moreover they had probably become a little "cast" (twisted or warped) in the drying, so that there was always something more to be cut away. A good deal of measuring and marking therefore had to be gone through before the felloes could even be bored.

The first step was to get a plane surface to work to—an apprentice's job, a boy's job—the beginning of all things in the wheelwright's craft. It is no exaggeration to say I hated it. Probably the plane was ill-sharpened and ill-set, and anything would have gone wrong; but a resentment took hold of me against that innocent curve of the surface of the felloe under my plane. If only the disgusting thing could have been straight! The felloe lay on one side, jabbed hard against the spiked bench-iron and with its rounded top surface towards me. It looked tractable enough. Yet when I tried to plane it, too often it jumped up over the bench-iron, or proved cross-grained and would not let the plane "shoot" comfortably and smoothly from end to end. I have been persuading myself that "trying-sticks" were brought in at last, to verify the workmanship, but probably this is wrong. "Trying-sticks" were two little straight bits of wood, about seven inches long by an inch square, and painted black. If you laid them in the same direction one at each end of a newly planed surface, and bent down and squinted across them from one to the other, it was easy to see if they lay level —("true out o' wind")—and so to judge whether or no the surface they lay on was truly plane. But I think this was for surfaces farther apart than the two ends of a felloe. But however that may have been, certain it is that a planing of the "face" or front side of every felloe was essential.

By the time this was done the face was not only plane, but smooth and pale-coloured. The exact pattern could accordingly be pencilled out on it; and that done the wheelwright got to work with axe and adze, chopping down to the pencil line. The axe was for the convex outside; to get the inner line (the concave "belly") it was necessary to wedge the felloe into the felloe-horse and go at it with the adze. Cook used to work this out so neatly that the belly shone, looking fit for polishing, it was so smooth. Lastly, with the axe, the felloe was chopped down ("taken-down") to its required thickness, the fourth side of it having been marked out with a "scratch-bit"—a gauge held close against the face of the felloe and scratching into the newly-chopped "back," the newly-adzed belly. Thus finished, the felloe was a block of wood exactly squared—some three-and-a-half inches square, say, by thirty inches long—curved to be one segment of a wheel-rim. When the felloes for a new wheel had been brought to this stage they were piled up together ready, as soon as the "stock" and spokes should be ready for them.

XX

STOCKS

Of the stock (the nave or hub) I hardly dare speak, such a fine product it was, and so ignorant about it do I feel. It is true I learnt to buy stocks with confidence in my own judgment: I seasoned them, chopped them into shape, chose them at last even to satisfy Cook. Nay, he occasionally asked my opinion, if anything dubious was discovered in working. But, as I had never enough skill of hand and eye myself, I always entrusted the actual turning and mortising of stocks to a trusty man—Cook as long as he lived, and after him preferably Hole. These men, I knew, would sooner have been discharged than work badly, against their own conscience. So I left the stocks to them, only liking to look at each stock when it was brought from the lathe, and to "weight" it (poise it) in my arms and hear the wheelwright say "rare stock that." His enthusiasm was catching. I felt a glow of pride in having ministered, however humbly, to so noble a tradition. Then I left the stock again to the workman.

A lumpish cylinder in shape—eleven or twelve inches in diameter and twelve or thirteen inches from end to end—a newly-turned stock was a lovely thing—to the eyes, I thought, but more truly to sentiment, for the associations it hinted at. Elm from hedgerow or park, it spoke of open country. Well seasoned, it was a product of winter labour, of summer care in my own loft under my own hands. Long quiet afternoons it had lain there, where I could glance from the stocks across the town to the fields and the wooded hills. I had turned it over and over, had chopped the bark away, had brushed off the mildew while the quiet winter darkness had stolen through the shed, and at last I had chosen the stock for use, and put it into Cook's hands.

And now it lay, butter-coloured, smooth, slightly fragrant, soon to begin years of field-work, after much more skill—the

PLATE I

THE WHEELWRIGHT'S SHOP, FACING EAST STREET, ABOUT 1916

PLATE II

DUNG-CART 1922, BUILT ABOUT 1870
THE WHEELS AND AXLE HAVE BEEN MODERNIZED

PLATE III

PLANKS SEASONING

SAWN ASH FELLOES

A FEW ELM STOCKS

A LITTLE TIMBER STILL STORED FOR WHEELWRIGHT'S
WORK IN 1922

PLATE IV

SIDE-VIEW OF SURREY FARM WAGGON, 1919

PLATE V

FRONT OF DOUBLE-SHAFTED WAGGON, 1919

THE WHEELS HAVE BEEN MODERNIZED

PLATE VI

GEORGE COOK IN 1900

PLATE VII

WILL HAMMOND IN 1900

PLATE VIII

SIDE-VIEW OF WAGGON

skill of ancient England—had been bestowed on it, though already telling of that skill in every curve. Certainly we did not consciously remember all these matters at the time: rather we concerned ourselves with the utility this block of elm would have, with its grip for many years of the oak spokes to be driven into it by and by. But, without thinking, we felt the glamour of the strong associations; and the skilled craftsmen must have felt it more than I, because they lived in that glamour as fishes live in water. They knew, better than any other may do, the answer of the elm when the keen blade goes searching between its molecules. This was, this is, for ever out of my reach. Only, I used to get some fellow-feeling about it, looking at a newly-turned stock. I understood its parts—the shallow hollows at back and front where the blacksmith would presently put on the bonds, the sloping "nose," the clean chisel-cut of the "breast stroke." This last was cut in all round the stock to mark where the face of the spokes was to be.

So, when I had had my look, the wheel-maker—Cook or another—carried the stock to his bench, there to mark on it with straddling compasses the place for the first auger-holes, preliminary to mortising it for the spokes. A tricky job, this. One young man, I remember, marking out his stock, prepared for an odd number of spokes—eleven or thirteen; though, every felloe requiring two, the spokes were always in even numbers; which error he did not detect until he had bored his stock and spoilt it. Too big for the fire, and too cross-grained to be easily split and thrown away, it lay about for months, an eyesore to the luckless youth who had spoilt it and a plain indication that it is not quite easy to mark a stock correctly.

Likewise was it not altogether a simple thing, though the skilled man seemed to find it easy enough, to fix the wobbly stock down for working upon. It was laid across a "wheel-pit" —a narrow trench with sills, about three feet deep—where iron clamps, themselves tightly wedged into the sills, held the stock steady back and front. Then the mortices were started, with auger-holes. How easy it looked! In my childhood I had heard the keen auger biting into the elm, had delighted in the springy spiral borings taken out; but now I learnt that only a strong and able man could make them.

The holes being bored, and before the actual mortising could begin, a gauge was attached to the front end of the stock, to be a guide for the coming operations. This gauge was a slender bar of wood—almost a lath—swinging round like one hand of a clock, but extending three feet or so beyond the stock. At the outer end of it a thin sliver of whalebone projected just so far as the front of the spokes would come if they had the right "dish." Note that. The spokes would have to lean forward a little bit; and the gauge was set so that this might be attended to even in mortising the stock. Before ever a spoke was actually put in the wheelwright tested the place for it, shutting one eye and squinting down with the other to see that the front edge of the mortice was properly in line with the whalebone sticking out from the gauge. The principle was very much like a marksman's taking his aim by foresight and backsight. One mortice having been cut, the stock was levered round with an iron bar so that the opposite mortice could be cut, and thus it was done all round, splinters or borings often dropping clear, right through the stock from one side to the other into the wheel-pit. The uncut ribs of wood left between the mortices were called "meshes"—a word that will be wanted again. I do not think we shall want again the word "buzz"—the name for the strange three-cornered chisel used for cleaning out the mortices of a stock and, to the best of my belief, used for nothing else, unless for enlarging the central hole in the stock.

And now,—how dare I go on to describe that swinging drive of the wheelwright's action, fixing the spokes into the stock? Prose has no rhythm for it—no spring, no smashing blow recurrent at just the right time and place. The stock is to be imagined, ready at last, clamped down across the wheel-pit. From the front of it the gauge slants up; the dozen or fourteen spokes are near at hand, each with its tenon or "foot" numbered (in scribbled pencilling) to match the number scribbled against its own place in the stock. For although uniformity has been aimed at throughout, still every mortice has been chiselled to receive its own special spoke, lest the latter should by chance have had any small splinter broken away after all. The true wheelwright would not take that chance. He intended that every spoke should really fit tight; and there he has the spokes all numbered, to his hand.

He picks up one in one hand, and, with sledge-hammer in the other, lightly taps the spoke into its own mortice. Then he steps back, glancing behind him belike to see that the coast is clear; and, testing the distance with another light tap (a two-handed tap this time) suddenly, with a leap, he swings the sledge round full circle with both hands, and brings it down right on the top of the spoke—bang. Another blow or so, and the spoke is far enough into the mortice to be gauged. Is it leaning forward a little too much, or not quite enough? It can be corrected, with batterings properly planted on front or back of top, and accordingly the wheelwright aims his sledge, swinging it round tremendously again and again, until the spoke is indeed "driven" into the stock. It is battered over on the top, but the oak stands firm in the mortice, to stay for years.

For an hour or so, until all the spokes had been driven into a wheel, this sledge-hammer work went on, tremendous. I have seen nothing else like it. Road-menders greatly smite an iron wedge into the road they are breaking up; blacksmiths' mates use a ponderous sledge at some of their work; foresters, cleaving, make great play with beetle and wedges; but so far as I have noticed, these men (like the "Try-Your-Strength" men at a country fair) do not really know how to use sledge or beetle. They raise it up above their heads and bring it down, thump, with all the force of strong arms; but a wheelwright driving spokes, though not necessarily a very strong man, was able, with knack, to strike more powerful blows, and many of them too, in succession. With one hand close under the head he gave the sledge a great fling, then slipped the same hand down the handle, to help the other hand hold it in and guide it truly round its circle. By the time it reached the spoke the sledge had got an impetus. With the momentum of a stone from a sling, it was so to speak hurled down on its mark, terrific.

This way of driving spokes was probably very antique, and, being laborious and costly, it had died out from my shop before I had to retire myself. Hoop-tyres, superseding strakes, had indeed made such strenuous arm-work less necessary; and the lighter wheels for spring-vans and carts, besides being more rapidly worn out on the harder roads and at the quicker pace, did not otherwise need putting together so strongly. But a dung-cart or a waggon was meant to last a life-time: the wheels were heavy; "strakes" of old could not pull them together as more modern tyres did; the wheels might have to lie on their face in a meadow all the summer for "stepping" a rick-pole and then be put to their proper use again, and if they could not stand all this the wheelwright was sure to hear of it from the farmer.

So, in my first five or six years at my shop, Cook (and perhaps others) made wheels in the right provincial style—wheels to stand hard work until they fairly wore out. As I saw it practised the art must have been time-honoured indeed. Village shops had carried it on for generations. I like to think that the twelve-spoke wheel—the cart wheel—in one of the Canterbury Tales—was the work of men using the sledge as I saw George Cook using it.

XXI

"RINGING" THE WHEEL

The spokes had been battered over by the sledge—which explains why they could never be used again; for nothing less than their full size could have stood that tremendous hammering. But their full size was reduced now. Once they had been driven into the stock, they had to be "tongued" to receive the ring of felloes.

Already the day of "square tongued" spokes was nearly over when I entered the shop. True, a few had to be inserted now and again under my management, but as Cook could be trusted to do this I never learnt. There is no doubt in my mind that a square-tongued wheel was stronger than a round-tongued, at least until hoop-tyres came in; yet really the round-tongued were strong enough for modern use, and less costly—a consideration that was daily increasing in weight, when any customer might easily buy ready-made wheels (good ones too) in London. So, in my shop, round-tongued held the field. They lasted quite long enough.

With a tenon-saw the wheelwright cut in all round the tongue, where the felloe would have to "come down on the knock," that is to say, to fit down upon the spoke. The tenon-saw did the cutting; then, with chisel and mallet, the tongue was soon rounded down to the required size. Nor was this either left to chance. Another gauge—a thin slice of oak or ash, with a hole in it—was carefully tried over every tongue, to make sure that the tongue would fit the auger-hole now to be bored for it in the felloe.

At last, when all the spokes had been tongued, the unfinished wheel of "stock and spokes" was lifted from the pit and laid, face down, across a "wheel-block," or "wheel-stool." This thing (there were a number of them about the shop), old, dirty, knocked about, very strongly built and heavily made, was like a large four-legged stool framed up without any seat to it. Instead of having a seat the frame was left open, and there lay the wheel, nose downwards through the open wheel-block, with the back of the spokes towards the ceiling. On that side the tongues had been cut deeper in to form the "knock," and now the felloes were placed round on them in a ring, as nearly as possible where they would finally have to be. Then, feeling up from underneath with his pencil on either side of each spoke-tongue, the wheelwright marked on the face of every felloe whereabouts the holes would have to be bored—two holes for every felloe for the spokes to come through, besides a hole at each end for the dowel. The centre of every hole was carefully marked with yet another kind of gauge.

But I am growing far too technical and will not describe the actual boring of the felloes. It was hard work. I have seen the sweat pouring off Cook's face, as he put his inch-and-a-quarter auger through the twenty-four holes in the rim of a dung-cart wheel. Moreover, it was puzzling unless a man knew what he was at. That it had to be exact goes without saying. The root of the difficulty was that the holes were a little farther apart for the larger outside circumference of the wheel—at the back of the felloe—than they were for the inside circumference—at the belly. So, the holes had to be bored at the proper angle to fit this; yet, because they were so bored, there was trouble in putting the felloe on. Because, you see, the inside of the felloe, where the holes are nearest together, had to start going on at the outside of the wheel where the spokes are farthest apart. An ingenious implement, called a spoke-dog, enabled the wheelwright to get over this difficulty, straining two spokes together sideways until the felloe could be slipped on to them both. But this could only be done if the spokes were long enough to bend, and with very low stiff wheels this was impossible. They had to be built in quite another way from the start. I suspect this was one reason why front wheels for a waggon were not made lower. It was needful to drive all waggon spokes—not press or coax them in as for slighter wheels; but, having been driven, they were also wanted long enough for straining sideways into the felloes.

Yet another matter for the wheelwright's attention was the dowel-holes. When two felloes were finally in their place, the dowel between them was straight. Yet the dowel-holes were at an obtuse angle with one another at the earlier stage, before the felloes had been rapped down into their place. Here too, therefore, a great nicety of boring was demanded. Most important was it too, that the dowel-holes should be deep enough. A dowel too long for its holes became a peg which kept its two felloes from coming together. In such a case—it didn't often happen—the wheel was said to be "dowel-bound."

And still all was not ready. The felloes had been left square for purposes of measuring and marking; but there was a good deal of material about them that could now be spared. The draw-shave was therefore taken down again from the tool-rack, to lighten them—the draw-shave, and after it the spoke-shave. With these much was got rid of, save just where the felloes were already weakened enough by the spoke-holes.

Assuming all the boring and shaving to have been properly done (it is a good deal to assume, for it implied that all the felloes had been cut off at exactly their right length and angle for meeting) the wheelwright would now go on to ring the wheel permanently. He began gently, walking all round the still prone wheel, and persuading the felloes into their places with light tappings, with the back of his axe probably. This was more usual than the sledge—I don't know why. Whatever the reason, the axe made a fine weighty hammer, and gradually, as the felloes began to draw together, vigorous blows gave a persuasion they more and more readily yielded to. The ends of the spoke-tongues, visible at last through the felloes, were tightened then with wedges driven into them to make them fit closer. To make these wedges was boys' work. Heart of oak was their substance; a sharp axe chopped them out, the oak being held against the axe by the "heel" of the left hand, steadied against your knee. It was well to clasp the finger-knuckles up out of the way, if you didn't want to chop your fingers off or to pinch them painfully, at this operation. The felloes had to be wedged on crosswise; for if the wedge were hammered into them longitudinally it was but too likely to split the felloe—a tiresome and costly thing to do.

Once the "ring" of felloes was properly secured, the wheel could be turned over; and as soon as all the "joints" (the meetings of the felloes) had been "trued" again with the plane, the place for the tyre could be gauged all round the wheel, and the felloes reduced in width accordingly.

I don't know how this may have been done in other shops. In mine the newly-rung wheel was stood up, leaning against a post, while the man who had made it chopped all round— chopped, say, the edge of the three-and-a-half-inch felloe away to fit the two-and-a-half-inch tyre. An apprentice or a boy had to "steady" the wheel for this, holding the spokes (with perhaps a heel upon one of the lower ones) to prevent the wheel from turning round under this chop-chop-chopping at its outer rim. Lastly, the chop-marks having been smoothed away with a small plane, a little paint and putty made the new wheel ready for the tyring.

XXII

COOK

George Cook, so often mentioned in these pages, was not a very singular man in his own time, but he was of a type almost forgotten nowadays. I recall nobody like him in any English book at all. What comes to my mind in thinking of Cook is a village flavour—the flavour preserved in some of the tales of Alsace in various Erckmann-Chatrian books. His attitude was that of a very efficient if very unsophisticated provincial, keeping close to the materials of his own neighbourhood and in touch with the personal crafts of his own people. The craft in which he himself specialised had made him rather round-shouldered; he was narrow chested too and a little inclined to bronchitis. By no means a large man, and slightly bandy-legged and slightly stooping, with toes tending to turn in, he moved nimbly—you couldn't call it exactly fast—always at one quite respectable pace. His sallow face had but a few thin hairs for beard and whiskers. His speech, so quiet, was just a trifle "blobby," as if he had something in his mouth, and to be sure he often was chewing a quid. The consequent spitting—anywhere and often —was not pleasant, but otherwise it was always agreeable to be where George Cook was. I never but once saw him angry—it was over some affair in his own family which he chose to confide to me—and even then he was not loud. I think his idea was to slip through life effective and inconspicuous, like a sharp-edged tool through hard wood. It was worth while to see him on a Sunday in most respectable black. I don't know what he wore on weekdays. He took his breakfast and dinner at "The Seven Stars"; then, the day's work done, he went padding off home— it was a sort of jog-trot—to Compton. Being rather deaf, he never had a companion; but, away from the shop, he had a pipe. Smoking, it hardly needs saying, was not countenanced in the shop.

Of course my acquaintance with him was chiefly at work— at his bench or his chopping block, at the wheel-pit or the lathe or the timber stack. From the front edge of his bench a small point of steel stuck out about an eighth of an inch. Very bright it shone, because he pivoted his spokes tightly upon it when shaving them. The other end of the spoke was pressed against his waist. For this purpose he wore, strapped round him, a thick leather pad. I never knew anybody else have such a thing, but I suspect it was a part of a wheel-maker's outfit, and only partially effective. During my father's last illness a hard place on his waist, puzzling to the doctor, was explained as due to spoke-shaving, but perhaps he used no pad. In later years Cook adopted some revolving clamps for this purpose.

He was a left-handed man. Other workmen might be annoyed by apprentices or ignorant boys using their sharp axes; but you didn't do that twice with George Cook's axe—it was too dangerous a trick. Why did the confounded tool, albeit so keen-edged, seem to avoid the hard wood and aim viciously towards your thigh, or try to chop your fingers off? The reason was that in making the "shaft" for it (every good wheelwright put the ash shaft or handle to his own axe) Cook gave to his a slight bias for the left hand instead of for the right. The blade too was ground on the unaccustomed side. And though you might not have noticed these peculiarities before, you soon were scared into learning something about them if you foolishly tried to use the axe. Cook smiled. Besides his axe, of course he put in the shaft for his adze and handles for his hammers. He made his own mallets and gauges, and the "pegs" for his chisels. Truly it would not have been easy to put him out with an edged tool. I have seen him filing a sharper "nose" to an auger. It needed a sharp auger for some of his work. When he was boring inch-and-a-quarter holes in a set of dung-cart felloes the sweat would pour in streams from his pale face; but he used to look round with a deprecating smile, as who should say, "I'm sorry, but it can't be helped." He had a little grease-box—that too hand-made—hanging amongst the row of chisels over his bench. But, come to think of it, every bench had this. A big auger-hole in a shaped-out block of tough beech served the purpose admirably. You could thrust your finger (I wonder why I preferred the middle finger?) into the grease-pot close at hand and easily take out grease for anointing both sides of your saw or the face of your plane.

Cook was, as I have said, deaf, and if you wanted to attract his attention when his back was turned it was useless to call to him. The best plan was to toss a little chip either to touch him or to arrest his sight. I laughed to myself once to see him and Will Hammond—far more deaf even than Cook—searching for something in a heap of felloe-patterns. Probably the blacksmith wanted a pattern for strakes. At any rate it was odd to see these two with their heads together making some sort of friendly conversation by involuntary signs, since neither could have heard the other's mutterings. When Cook wanted a felloe-pattern for himself, he did not hunt long for a ready-made one. It was easier to him to strike out a new one that should be exactly what he required. But it must be said that no mere pattern, newly made out of thin board, equalled the felloes he afterwards got out in accordance with it. When he had finished with a felloe, the belly of it (the inner curve) hewn out with his adze, was as smooth, to the exact dimensions too, as if it had been polished.

So much for his skill as a craftsman. But when he got home he became, rather, a villager, accomplished in genial rustic arts. The hamlet of Compton was a little nook of heath and scrubby oaks, tucked away warm and secluded between Culverlands and Waverley woods, an outlying end, I think, of Farnham Common. No high-road even now has found it. You get to it by narrow tracks of carts, up and down bosky hillocks, and I fancy the place is less populous to-day than it was forty years ago—which isn't saying much. It was probably a haunt of squatters, like its more out-at-elbows neighbour, The Bourne (Bettesworth's home), a mile away. Here dwelt Cook with his big family, in a little brick cottage, his mother (a widow then) living with him. Probably she was the owner of the cottage, and of the tiny hop-kiln adjoining it.

The hop-kiln, when I saw it, chiefly interested me as the quiet scene of George Cook's annual labours. Every autumn, namely in September, he used to tell me he should be away from the shop for about a week, drying his (or perhaps he said his mother's) hops. I wondered chiefly at his having the staying power to do this—for it was an unsleeping sort of job. Seeing it was Cook I did not so much wonder at his ability; yet it was by no means every working man in Farnham who had the sense —the judgment—to dry hops, even when the hop trade was at its best and everybody looked upon a good dryer with a sort of friendly admiration. George Cook's turn at it was probably a holiday for him. I like to think of him in that little quiet kiln with the pungent scent of the hops all about him—their golden dust looking like the September sunshine grown solid. To be there at home, with your pipe whenever you wanted, and no wearisome walking—it was a pleasant change from making wheels to order. Here, in the kiln, a man was his own master. The hops alone had any claim on him. If his arduous duty to them would allow—and Cook would enjoy it the better for its being arduous—he might trot up the ladder to the upper floor whenever he liked; and there, with the sleepy-scented hops on the floor behind him, he could stand at the open doorway and see over the little hamlet—the tiny hop-ground, his garden, the autumn woods—could watch the neighbours and his own family down there in the pleasant light, and feel himself a man of importance amongst them, forgetting his daily wage-earning. An acceptable break in his long year's work this week must have made for him.

Of his garden I remember nothing. But I can surmise that the seasonal interests of it were his all the year round. Did he keep a pig, I wonder? That there was a donkey—of course with stable, hay, and all manner of country accessories—I do happen to know, for his mother's donkey-cart was sometimes mended in the old shop.

But of all his country crafts the most real part to me was the making of elderberry wine. I surmised his gardening and his keeping of donkey and pigs; I heard of his hop-drying; but of the elderberry wine I had personal knowledge.

It was like this. One winter Cook was ill for weeks with some eye trouble that would not yield to the treatment of the club doctor and in the end had to be treated at Moorfields Hospital. During that time I used to go to his cottage about once a week to make enquiries. This was after work was done. The walk out of Farnham up the hill into the night, then down the steeper hill under the pitchy darkness of Culverlands trees into the all but unknown murk of Compton—this mile and a half or so which was Cook's daily portion when he was in health —found its goal when at last the cottage door was opened and, momentarily dazzled, I was let in from the night to the little warm-lit living room. Of all this, however, little or no recollection remains. Save for the light I cannot recover any memory of the room or its inmates. I only remember that I was expected to drink, and therefore did drink, about three parts of a tumblerful of hot elderberry wine. It was "the thing" to do for keeping out the cold, and it did keep out the cold. The Cooks evidently looked upon it as the natural reward after my walk and a proper preparation for the return. Two or three times this must have happened, and I surmise that the winter nights were cold as well as dark—that the ruts in the road were frozen hard under one's feet, and so on. But the point now is this elderberry wine. It gives a provincial air. Anything less suggestive of the London suburbs can hardly be imagined. It means that the Cooks knew how to live in a country hamlet. Where a city dweller would be helpless this family profited by centuries of tradition, and they were keeping old England going ("old" England, not modern England) when they made their elderberry wine and warmed some of it up for a friend on a cold winter night.

I cannot remember when Cook left Compton and came to live in Farnham. It seemed a good thing for him; good to be able to get to and from his work without that long hill. For the hilly walk used to set him coughing convulsively and for a long time, and during a fit of coughing the water would stream from his eyes. I was glad for him to be spared this exhaustion morning and night. Now, there were but three or four minutes of level street between his home and his work.

But who shall judge the cost of this change—from woodlands to the neighbourhood of gas-works, from old English rusticity to the state of the proletariat of the eighteen-nineties? I suppose that Cook's mother had died and that her little property had to be shared amongst her several sons and daughters; but anyhow it was a come-down for Cook, not financially only, when he had to leave Compton. I begin to think it was a come-down for me too, little though I dreamt of such a thing at the time. My intercourse with him underwent a profound though unnoticed change. Precisely where he got to in Farnham I never learnt. There was no need for me to go to see him. When at last, after many years, he took to his bed and died, I not only left him alone: I didn't even go to his funeral. It's true I was myself down with bronchitis at that time; but the fact remains —and I am not proud of it—that I had unawares allowed a gulf to widen between George Cook and myself.

I did not know it at the time. I always chatted with him for a minute or two every day. I never failed to sympathise with his winter desire for the return of cuckoo-time, or to laugh at his assumed dismalness (so characteristic of an ageing villager) before any cheerful prospect. Thus if, in mid December, I happened to remark "We shall soon have Christmas here," then he, assenting, was sure to add gloomily, "Whoever lives to see it!" whereat we smiled as if we liked one another. Yet, for all this, we were no longer on the old terms. I was not in touch, through him, with the quiet dignified country life of England and I was more of a capitalist. Each of us had slipped a little nearer to the ignominious class division of these present times— I to the employer's side, he to the disregarded workman's. The mutual respect was decaying. Nor yet might Cook, for his part, view his own life with the earlier satisfaction. From being one of a community of rustics, he was becoming more and more a mechanic—a cog in an industrial machine. Those were not yet the days of "Unrest." The stealthy changes which were destined, after thirty years, to oust the old skill altogether seemed to Cook, if he discerned them at all, due to his advancing years. If life was meaner, less interesting, than of old, was it not chiefly because he had been born too soon? He would have said so. He remained an opinionated Conservative and read *The Standard* every day.

TYRING

XXIII

GETTiNG READY

THE new wheel being finished and painted and puttied (a most important matter this last as will be shown) blacksmiths took it in hand for a time. Two jobs they had to do to it: first, to put on the tyre; next, to fit and fix the small iron bonds on the stock, one behind and one in front of the spokes. Note that these were what a wheelwright called "bonds." Customers, I know, sometimes used that name for tyres, but they sounded ignorant to me.

A great business was this tyring—if possible deferred, for economy of fuel, until a number of tyres could be put on in a batch, being "hotted up" in one fire. A new wheel—say a five-foot waggon wheel—required of course a new tyre; and to look out the iron bar to be used was the very first part of the performance. The new bar (new bars were about sixteen feet long. Two-and-a-half inches wide and three-quarters of an inch thick were common dimensions for a waggon tyre), the new bar was laid on the ground, where the blacksmith trundled the wheel carefully along it, so as to get the exact length. Chalk marks setting this out were best verified by a second trundling, for it would not do to have any mistake. As soon as the proper length was ascertained the bar was cut off to the chalk mark. By the antiquated method in my old shop this was a job for two strong men. The bar was slanted up on to the anvil, across the new chalk mark on it the smith placed a special "tool" (short cold-chisel held with twisted withe or iron rod for handle) and the smith's helper—usually a strong-armed young man—smote down on the chisel two or three resounding blows with a sledge-hammer. Then the bar was turned over, to be partly cut through on the other side also. At last, being nearly asunder already, it was broken off by the smith with two or three blows with his hand-hammer. The short piece of superfluous bar was now a "bar-end," to be stacked with other waste pieces like it and sold

by weight by and by at half price. (Other refuse from the blacksmith's work was but "scrap," and not so valuable.)

"Scarfing" or "scarfing down" was the next operation. Each
end of the bar was flattened out under the sledge-hammer, the
smith himself always directing this, although his mate, strong-
armed, actually wielded the sledge. Of course the end of the
iron had to be heated for scarfing down; and while it was still
hot a hole was punched through each scarf. Then, one end
having been bent a little under ponderous sledge-blows, the bar
could be inserted into the tyre-bender. By winding a handle on
each side of this implement two men could get the tyre-bar bent
into circle, but the smith was not one of these two. His part,
more exacting, was to guide the bar through the bender, watching
especially two points. First, unless bent with care, the iron
might have a spiral twist, which it was very needful to avoid.
Otherwise the wheel likewise would presently twist inside the
tyre, and there was no doing anything with a twisted wheel. It
could by no means be made to run true on its axle. Therefore,
in first bending the tyre, the smith above all things tried to keep
it properly directed through the bender, swerving neither to
right hand nor to left. Across its diameter from side to side the
tyre must be in one plane, "true out o' wind," all round.

The other point was to bend the bar approximately into a
complete circle, bringing one scarfed end fully round to meet
the other. As the bending progressed the smith could judge
how it was going. By straining the bending bar up or down
(sometimes a lot of strength was wanted—the man would leap
from the ground so as to get his whole weight into the pull) the
two scarfs were got near enough together. At last, there stood
the half-finished tyre; a loop erect in the air resting on the rollers
of the tyre-bender. The blacksmith steadied it on one side, until
his mate could take the other side, skipping round from the
handle of the bender he had been turning. Then the two lifted
the tyre to the ground—ninety pounds of iron or so, according
to the wheel it was meant for.

And now for the "shutting"—the welding. But first, to keep
the two scarfs together, a nail was thrust through the holes that

had been punched in them. In memory I still see the men straining with strong shoulders, still hear them panting, still watch them doggedly hammering or levering, to bring two obstinate scarfs clicking into place, so that the smith may knock the nail in. But at last the nail can be hammered through and clinched over on the anvil. The tyre may be put into the fire for shutting now.

Yet there must be no hurry, for consider the smith's problem. At each stage the demands on his skill have increased until, now, a little error of his may spoil the wheel, in which case he will have an indignant wheel-maker to reckon with, to say nothing of other troubles. For observe, the tyre is to be put on hot, so as, when cold, its shrinking will tighten the wheel together. I sometimes thought its name came from that; it was to tie the wheel in an irresistible or rather an unshakeable clutch. Immense strength the contracting iron would have—I have seen thick oak spokes come over bent as no load could ever bend them, in the grip of a tyre too tight. On the other hand, if not tight enough a tyre would not pull the wheel together and would soon come off. A quarter or a half-inch more or less in the circumference might make or mar the wheel. It was therefore expected of a good tyring smith to know all the different possibilities in scores of different instances, and to get the right one. To get it. To intend it was not enough. The tyre could not be tried on first to see how it would fit. It had to be right within half-an-inch when it was once for all put on, red-hot.

So the smith went to work with due deliberation. Long use indeed had made my old friend Will Hammond look nonchalant enough at tyring; yet he was always watchful, careful. Most unusual was it for him to have a misfit with a tyre. A hook at the end of a chain hung just above the outer edge of his forge, where sundry tongs stood up in the water-trough, and in this hook rested one edge of the tyre. The opposite side lay across the hearth, right in the glow of the fire. There, in short, were the two scarfed ends, now to be shut together. The nail had tied them together temporarily; but the problem was to weld them, expanded as they were with intense heat, so that, when cold, the tyre should be of the right circumference, neither more nor less.

On these occasions I used to like to slip round to Will Hammond's left side, take the lever of the bellows out of his hand, and blow the fire, while Will kept it going with little tiny shovelfuls of coal (half a handful at a time) put on and patted down over the heating iron. Here, if anywhere, it was possible to chat to old Will, for here his impenetrable deafness seemed to give way a little, affording rare opportunity of friendly conversation; and to be on affectionate terms with such a man was reward enough, so lonely as he was too. So I stood blowing the bellows for him, carrying on some sort of shouting chatter into his least deaf ear (his hair close to my nose now and then smelt of soap) and watching how he worked his miracles.

The very act of blowing the bellows needed some practice, I found. In order to keep the heat in the iron regular the air blown up through the "tue-iron" must not fail for a moment. On the other hand, to blow too hard was to blow the smith's coal[1] unprofitably away. What was wanted was a steady blast that would die down when the iron was at last lifted on to the anvil. Then, there should be no more than a quiet flicker in the erst roaring fire.

The blacksmith never left his fire alone. Staring into it, in constant watch for "the heat"—that moment of moments when the iron could be properly hammered—staring, watching, he was for ever fidgeting about with it. Now, it seemed to be flaring too freely, and he sprinkled water on it with the little stubby heath broom kept in the trough at his right hand. Now he worried at the coal with his small sharp-pointed poker, bright of handle. Sometimes he would (with frown of great annoyance) poke out from the very heart of the fire a blazing mass of what looked to me like coal, and push it scornfully away over the further edge of the hearth, to fall on to the growing heap of clinkers there; for in fact this was but molten "dirt," not good

---

[1] Tanfield coal at that date. The coal-merchant smiled when I ordered "Tandsticker." But one word was as good as the other for me, and anyhow I got the right coal.

coal. If such a piece of clinker found its way between the two
ends of iron to be welded together, Will grew almost frantic
until he had poked it out, lest it should spoil the "shut." This
sort of thing went on amidst Will's talk of his parsnips or potatoes
—how, digging some "taters" after a drought, he had got
nothing bigger than "nuts and warnuts"; or of the grape-vine
over his father's cottage in Frensham village; or of a blacksmith
neighbour working in another shop; or of—any other country
chatter that came uppermost.

Then, in the midst of it, he would signal to his helper—the
smith at another forge or perhaps one of the wheelwrights—
and the said helper promptly got into position with the sledge.

For the moment was come. Old Will had got his heat.
Indeed, flaming sparks were whirling up the chimney; a pinch
of sand had been thrown into the fire to keep the iron from
"burning"; unaccustomed eyes like mine could not look into
the intolerable brightness; the iron was melting. One more
push down then of the bellows lever, and I too had to hasten
out, to help lift the tyre on the anvil and to help hold it there
while able men "shut" one side of it. I was not quite an able
man myself—too feeble of arm and too fumbling. Moreover, as
employer, I could not afford to be too obviously a laughing-
stock. Besides, a third man—or boy—was really often needed,
with heavy tyres. I was that man—or boy. So I saw the tyre-
shutting, and was of some slight use too.

The second half of the shut required another heat. Accordingly the tyre, turned over, was lifted back into the fire, the
bellows were blown again, the whole process was gone over a
second time. But, after the "striker," panting a little it may be,
at last put down his sledge (a chinking of the hand-hammer on
the anvil was the signal to him to leave off, as a lighter chinking
had kept time for him all along) old Will still continued, hammering out the bruises or "squats" left by the sledge. So he
worked up the edges of the new tyre until it matched the rest
of the bar.

And even so he had not quite finished. Before the new tyre
—welded up at last into an uninterrupted loop—could be lifted

down, all springy, on to the floor, it had to be measured, as also
had the wheel it was meant for.

Blacksmiths kept a special implement for this purpose—a
"traveller" or "tyre-runner." The traveller was a thin circular
disk of iron, six or seven inches
across, which the smith would hold
out, waist-high, at right angles to
himself, and run round wheel and
tyre in turn. Wheel first. The wheel
was laid up, face-downwards, where

TRAVELLER

Will could walk all round it, gravely chalking the "traveller"
where it came round again to the starting point. This was
probably done twice over, to make sure. Meanwhile the helpers
looked on silently, too fascinated by the interest of the job to joke,
though we liked joking. There were one or two questions I might
have asked, had Will been less deaf. As it was I never quite knew
how the circulations of the traveller were counted, if at all.
Having gone all round the outer circumference of the felloes, Will
then turned to the tyre, where it lay across from anvil to forge.
Now, it was the inside circumference to be measured. Will
accordingly, lifting his leather apron, straddled over, long-legged,
to the inner side of the tyre, and solemnly ran the traveller round
that also, usually twice as before. If then it showed the required
circumference, all was well. About an inch and five-eighths,
I think, was the "tightness" of a new tyre for a hind-wheel for
a waggon. The circumference of the iron had to be that much
less than the wood. The tyre that passed this examination now
needed only drilling for the nail-holes, and was otherwise ready
to be put on to the wheel.

XXIV

PUTTING-ON

Hoop-tyres, I have said before, were a comparatively new invention, and had not even yet, in 1884, quite superseded strakes. By that time however they were the usual thing. Wheels were made somewhat differently for them. In the mode of putting them on improvements were still being carried out.

Already the more primitive methods of tyring had been given up. I remember seeing, as a boy, the ring of fire built up round the tyres on the ground; remember too how my father in dry weather syringed water on to the tarred weather-boards of surrounding sheds to prevent any spark from the too near fire setting light to them. But there had been changes in these matters before I began to work at the shop. Especially the open fire on the ground had been replaced by an upright brick oven —"the furnace"—a yard or two farther from the sheds, and nothing like so dangerous to them. It opened upon the yard, and had two cast-iron half-doors. Outside ran the public lane, where wayfarers might feel the brick-work of the furnace warm if wheels were being tyred.

Apart from its greater safety I am not sure that the furnace had any advantages over the old form of fire on the ground. Inconveniences there were, at any rate. Imagine a sort of oven tall enough for a man to stand upright in, and deep enough, from front to back, for him to lie at length in, yet not more than twelve or fourteen inches wide, if as much as that. Here, a pair of waggon tyres, but no more, could stand up side by side. A little room beside them was wanted for fresh firing to be thrown in now and then; a little room, for inserting the long-handled "dog" that gripped a tyre which needed turning round. For this the furnace-man in the yard jerked open from afar the top half-door—immediately a scorching heat came out—and desperately struggled with his tyre until the lower curve of it, red-hot, had been turned up out of the fire to be replaced by the upper curves, only black as yet; but however careless of being scorched was the furnace-man, he could not get the tyres equally hot all round, as in the old-fashioned flat fires. On the other hand, if they were too hot, heavy tyres standing were liable to sink down with their own weight into a long and unmanageable ellipse. They would have been better on the ground. Moreover, at the best only two tyres could be heated at one time. Without doubt a flat fire would have been an advantage in each of these respects. But the upright brick furnace perhaps economised heat. The first pair of tyres might take half-an-hour or more to get hot enough for putting on. They could be set-in on the newly-lit fire just before eight o'clock breakfast. The men, coming back at half-past eight, would soon find them fit to put on. A second pair would get hot more quickly; and before long tyres might be put in and pulled out again as fast as the wheels for them could be got ready.

To be got ready to have its tyre put on, a wheel had to be screwed down on to the tyring platform—a circular iron platform, "true out o' wind" no doubt, cemented down to the ground conveniently near to the tyre-furnace. Big enough for the biggest wheel, and about an inch and a quarter thick, this platform had a hole in the middle to admit the wheel-hub, and out of the very centre of this hole rose an iron bar, to go up through the hub, which had to be threaded on to it. A screw arrangement, atop of this central bar, enabled a workman to draw down and tighten the hub, while all the rim of the wheel lay outspread on the surrounding platform. So the wheel was fixed face-downwards for the operation, screwed tight.

Close at hand, with a supply of watering-cans around them, stood two, or perhaps three, barrels of water for cooling ("cold-ing") the tyre as soon as it was properly on the wheel. Rain-water-butts they were, taking the drip from the adjacent sheds. In my boyhood I had delighted to mess about with them; had invented the name "hammerhead," for the little wriggling red larvae with which they were infested. In after years I found that, in a spell of dry weather, when there were many tyres, the water-butts had to be draped with wet sacks to prevent them

from falling to pieces, unless they could be kept filled with water
from the pump at the dwelling-house next the shop. A tiresome
job this for apprentices or labourers, seeing that the pump was
thirty yards away, downhill past some steps and round several
corners. Still, water was wanted for tyres—was wanted most
often in hot weather. And if the conditions of getting it were
those of a mediaeval village—well, there might be worse things
than working in the middle-ages, though it was not too profitable.

Now to go back to the "hotting" of the tyres in the furnace.
This job my father had been wont to take on himself, but during
his illness and after his death Will Hammond took it on—as far
as I know without dispute. (I find it very wonderful, the way
these men worked together for the good of the business, with
little but their own amiable good sense to tell them what to do.)
The fuel was waste wood from the saw-pits or from waggons or
carts under repair. A few old dry boards from the bottom of a
dung-cart, tossed in whole atop of the tyres, soon filled the
furnace with flame and hurried up the work accordingly.

Looking round therefore to see that all was ready—that the
sundry dogs and sledges lay at hand near the water-cans round
the tyring platform—Will summoned helpers. Though I was
not man enough to take my father's place, I liked to be present
even as "boy." There were two other men besides Will—the
chief of them the wheelwright whose wheel was to be done.
He, after giving another turn, perhaps, to the screw that held
the wheel down, took his place nearest the furnace doors; then,
armed with tyring dogs, the three of us watched, expectant,
where Will Hammond was unlatching even the lower door of
the furnace.

And now the heat came out—you could hardly face it—and
with the heat one tyre, red-hot or nearly so. (Sometimes both
tyres came, tangled up with half-burnt and flaring wood; but
that meant trouble and shouting.) With a clever movement of
Will's strong wrist, aided by a pull from the wheelwright's dog,
the tyre was thrown over (face-side down) on to the ground,
where little bits of dust and wood rubbish it fell on burst out into
sparks or instant flame. But no time for mischief of that sort

was given. Hooking our dogs over the tyre the three of us lifted it and ran with it to the wheel. As soon as a proper place could be found (for the nail-holes drilled in it had to come over the middles, not the joints, of the felloes) one section of the tyre was dropped over the rim, and the rest of it was pulled and sledge-hammered to the wheel, and at last hammered home. Often I had to hold it down with the sledge on one side, to keep it from jumping up there while being hammered down on the opposite side. For, though expanded by the heat, a tyre was even then none too large; and we had anxious, impatient, gasping moments, until it had gone over the felloes all round and been sledge-hammered near the matter into its destined place. Before that could be, the dry timber the wheel was built of was bursting into flame wherever the hot iron touched it. Smoke that half choked you, half blinded you, rose in blue and tingling clouds. There was a call for water. You seized a watering-can; poured the water hissing and bubbling on to the tyre, going round as far as you could, then hurried to the water-butt for another canful. Old Will, having shovelled back into the furnace any glowing coals that had been dragged out and shut the cast-iron doors again, came hobbling up (he had a game leg) to give any help he might. The wheelwright and the other man went round "setting" the felloe-joints into proper place; another can of water was put round, and then—

Then one began to see why the wheel had been screwed down, face-downwards. Remember, it had been built with a "dish"—a hollowness in front, a convexity at back. But now the quickly tightening tyre—tightening as the water cooled it —had pulled the wheel over still more "dish," as you could see. As the screw on the middle was loosened, the stock, set free from that pressure, rose up, an inch or more. How much, was an important matter. Will Hammond squinted across the wheel, the wheelwright squinted across it, each desirous of seeing how far his own judgment, his own endeavours, had been well applied.

But I am forgetting. Before this scrutiny the wheel had to be lifted up off the platform, and, as the tyre was still hottish as well as heavy, the lifting had to be done gingerly. The best way was for two to do it on opposite sides, balancing one another. As soon as the central screw-bar was cleared, one of the two set down his side of the wheel on to the ground; and now the other man held it up, slanting. Then he drew it upright, for the scrutiny above mentioned, and after a moment trundled it away to the shoeing-hole. This was a narrow pit, about five feet long, kept full of water and designed for this sort of purpose. But it took a fairly strong and sure man to "run" a wheel into it. Some knack at least was called for. A newly-tyred wheel might easily weigh a hundred and fifty pounds; its tyre, on the way to the shoeing-hole, was still too blistering hot to be touched; the man ran behind it, with the convex side to his right (or else he had sundry weird difficulties with it); yet just at the last he had to get to the front of it, as it ran down into the hole and set the water boiling there. Knack, as I say, was involved in doing all this easily, and afterwards in "swinging" the wheel, as it stood up in the shoeing-hole, with its back against a low post there. The said post had holes bored through it. A stiff iron bar, thrust through the stock of the wheel and then into one of these same holes, made it possible to lift the wheel and keep it swinging round and round until the tyre was cool; and others could do this. But perhaps I had been kept at school too long to learn these knacks myself; for apprentice boys seemed to have none of the reluctance that withheld me from trying. While it was still swinging, the careful wheelwright looked all round his handiwork, hammering the felloe-joints into final place, before the tyre got any colder. When this also was done, he on one side and another on the opposite side gripped each a spoke; the wheel was lifted up out of the shoeing-hole, and now, tyred at last, was ready to be finished off.

But what was that click it gave as often as not, when it was bumped on to the ground? A series of clicks, of which this was the last, a succession of sounds like the snap of a toy pistol, had been coming from the wheel as the water was poured on it from the first. I liked to hear these noises. They were the sound of spokes going home into their mortices, dowels into their dowel-holes.

They told that the tyre was doing its work. More than ablest workman could do with sledge and wedges, this shrinking hoop of iron was pulling the wheel together all round, and would not be gainsaid. If there was no further "give" in tenon or dowel, then the terrible tyre would bend the oak spokes themselves, and the dozen three-inch spokes that had been so straight were now bowed forward as if with an incipient spinal curvature. To obviate disasters of this kind—there were several sorts of them—the wheelwright was careful to leave a slight space between his felloes, for the tyre to pull up. Therefore the new wheel was left "open-jointed." But after the tyre had been cooled the felloe-joints were as tight together as if they had grown so. It was their getting so that largely accounted for that snapping sound.

Proof of what had happened could be seen. It has been said that the wheel was painted before being tyred. Putty (which needs paint, or it will not cling) had been pushed into all the joints and all the shakes in the wood to keep any water from getting in; but now the pressure of the tyre had squeezed most of it back again.

It was especially worth noticing how the seams of putty stood up on the stock from end to end. Sunshakes, longitudinal, were in my view the mark of a good stock. My father, it was credibly told me, had been wont to say that a stock might safely be in two halves, longitudinally, if only it could be worked up; for the spokes, pressed down by the tyre, would not fail to hold it together. And now the truth of this was plain enough. Forced in towards the centre by the shrinking tyre, the spokes had jammed up the stock and closed the shakes that had gaped open for years. Truly, a longitudinal crack never mattered. It was only when a crack appeared across the meshes that a stock had to be given up. The tyre would not tighten it that way; the best place for it was the fire. But tyring would effectually close up any split running through the stock from back to front.

XXV

"BOXING-ON"

Seeing how much closer the tyre had now drawn the stock of the wheel together, it would have been, plainly, useless to fix the stock-bonds before that was done. True, they might be put on provisionally; yet they were likely, in that case, to loosen with the same contraction of stock that forced the putty back from the shakes; and then the blacksmith had to tighten them again. A stock-bond was put on hot, driven down into place—even burning its way in sometimes—and at last fastened with three "sprigs"—three tiny iron pegs specially made to drive into the elm and clench neatly over the iron bond. Apart from this, the wheelwright took charge of his wheel again, when it had been tyred.

His first care was to "clean it off." Where the tightening tyre had splintered the edges of the felloes the splinters needed to be chiselled cleanly away. Moreover, the face (front) of the felloes was everywhere blackened with smoke, which (for the painter's sake) was now scraped off. Broken glass was used for this. It did not cut too deep into the felloes.

All this was, as it were, by the way. The cleaning-off wanted doing, the tyre wanted nailing, where it had been drilled all round. (Nails, indeed, would not hold it on when it got loose by and by; yet they might keep the tyre from being jerked aside before it quite needed contracting again. And seeing that this use was likely to come some months later, when all the present surfaces of the tyre had been worn away, the nails were tapering, so that they still were as tight in the tyre when it wore down thin as now, when it was new.) But all this, as I was saying, was by the way—an incident between the tyring and the boxing. "Boxing" a wheel, or "boxing it on," meant wedging into the stock that cast-iron "box" which was to run on the axle; inserting, if you like, the central iron socket into the wood-work. When a wheel, with this "box" fixed into it, was slipped on to the projecting "arm" or axle-end, it became part of the cart. The cart (or waggon) at last had a wheel to run on.

Not an easy job was this boxing. It began with chiselling or gouging out the whole of the middle of the stock. A tool called a "router" was used for this in after years, but I think not in those more distant days I am dealing with now. Rather, the central auger-hole was enlarged with the buzz. A wide gouge then shaped the hole roughly, and finally it was made a little too large for the box, which could so be shifted to one side or to the other of it.

For, as the wheel, with this box in it, would have to pivot round on the axle-arm, it was most important to have the pivoting true. It would never do to have the wheel wobbling from side to side. Presumably it would have to keep in the deep ruts of a country lane; and how could it do that if the box was out of place? Or how, again, could the upper edge of the wheel be prevented from rubbing into the cart, if the revolving box sent it periodically straddling out at the ground? Plainly, the box must be tested before it was fixed; it must be put in loose first, and only tightened, wedged up on this side or that, according as trial directed.

Very ingenious and pleasing was the "swinging" of a wheel for this purpose. The axle-arm was provisionally screwed on to the workman's bench, high enough to let the wheel lifted on to it swing round and round clear of the ground. Then, so as just to touch the tyre with one corner, a small block of wood was placed on the ground, and the wheel was spun round to see what would happen. Now the block was knocked away; now the wheel swung away from it altogether; and any such case was a hint for a wedge to be put in, the wheelwright knew where.

The wedges (hand-chopped, out of heart of oak) were not themselves allowed to touch the box. Truly, that brittle cast-iron might easily have snapped, if jarred too closely by such a sledge-hammering as the wedges were subjected to. A place having been started by a broad iron wedge (knocked in and then knocked out again) the oak wedge was driven into the elm itself, splitting it open slightly. (There was no danger of splitting dry

elm too far.) The iron stock-bond prevented the stock from
opening outwards at all; only by spreading inwards, towards the
cast-iron box, could the elm make way for this oaken wedge.
But this was exactly what was wanted. Until the box was fixed
immovable, in its right place, wedge after wedge was driven in;
and when at last the wedges came to be chiselled off they fitted
so tight that no division could be seen between them and the
stock; a difference between oak grain and elm grain alone showed
where they were. In that tight grip the box lay embedded in the
stock, ready to bear the pressure of tons without moving. Con-
siderable knack, besides experience, went to chopping off the
wedges so that they did not splinter or tear. And, at last, a
spoke-shave put on the end of the stock gave it the handsome
appearance of inlay-work.

Such, in main outline, was the art of "boxing-on" a wheel,
at least in my shop, and probably in any decent country shop.
Highly technical details might be added to this description. The
box must neither stand out from the back of the stock too far,
nor be let in too deep; but, itself wearing close upon the shoulder
of the axle-arm, it must also allow of the wheel coming up
almost, yet not quite, to touch the end of the axle-bed. On this
point the carter might have much to say by and by, and it was
the wheelwright's duty to anticipate him, providing "false-
boxes," or "dirt-irons," or "dirt-boards" to keep rubbish from
accumulating behind the wheel—rubbish of gravel, or stable-
dung, or whatever load was most to be expected.

Provision had to be made also, at the other end—the front
end—of the stock for the lynch-pin, and sundry washers and
collars. I will not go into these particulars. It would take too
long to tell even how, last thing of all, a "stopper" was fitted
into a slot—a "stopper-hole"—to allow of the lynch-pin being
taken out; and how the stopper itself was secured by a "stopper-
clasp" and staples, made by the blacksmith. Consider all this
done. There was not much in it, but it would be intricate and
tedious to explain. Let it be imagined that the new wheel is
really finished at last. From forest, from mine, its materials
have been prepared and put together by numberless forms of

skill; and now it is all but ready to be used for some special part of the age-old effort of colonising England. Yet a little more skill must be spent on it first—a little more experience, before it can be fit for that high task. After boxing, a wheel still had to be "hung" on the axle; and no mean ability was involved in doing that properly, although the man that did it might very well have had no schooling[1].

XXVI

EXBEDS

"Hanging the wheels," for waggon or dung-cart, was not so simple a job as it may have looked. Of course in the main idea it was straightforward enough. To put two wheels on an axle, with shafts attached to the axle so that a horse could draw the whole along, and with a receptacle or "body" for a load mounted up on the axle between the wheels—oh, anybody might do that. But in detail these so simple-looking problems were not a little tricky. The "exbed," or axle-bed, in my old shop was the answer that English villagers had been working out for generations to meet quite a number of difficulties. When, by and by, it was hoped to simplify the matter by using an iron axle right through, after all it was found that the product from Birmingham or Wolverhampton had to be corrected and added to by more countrified devices.

I am not referring now to those pieces of ironmongery which sought to substitute even cast-iron hubs for the ancient elm stocks of former wheels. It was amusing, indeed, to witness Cook's exasperation if he had to attend to one of these, breaking his chisels against the iron wedge that would neither release nor yet tighten a faulty spoke; or to observe the blacksmith's depre-

[1] One of the ablest, most intelligent, men in my shop could not read or write. He was versed in village lore; had begun at seven years old to earn his living by minding cows on a common, and had picked up the rudiments of his trade in a country smithy.

cating endeavour to make up with washers for the hopeless
deficiency of ill-fitting cast-iron. I do not refer to these because
the all-iron axle that went with these makeshift wheels was never,
from the first, treated as sufficient. An axle-bed of sorts was
always fitted to it, as if the veriest tyro saw the advantage of that.

Advantage, or advantages rather, for there were more than
one. Whoever missed other points could hardly fail to grasp at
once the need of raising the cart or waggon-body well above
the rims of the wheels; and this meant that an all-iron axle was
not enough by itself. In fact, even the wooden axle-bed, which
was some four inches higher, was not enough. Blocks for a
cart, risers for a waggon, were always added atop of the exbed.
So, if the load (as hay or stable-dung) happened to flop out beyond
the top edges of the body, it did not drag down on the wheels
and "skid" them. This was one sufficient reason for preferring
a wooden axle-bed. It was so obviously desirable to keep the
load well up out of the way of the wheels.

Another advantage, plain enough to those familiar with the
materials, was the greater rigidity of the wood. It is true, after
many years a five-and-a-half inch square axle-bed would bend
down slightly in the middle—if it was good beech, too tough to
break. But an iron axle was far worse. And any displacement
in the axle made the wheels run badly, wore them out sooner
therefore, and wore the horse out sooner. But no horse would
have been able to move at all an iron axle strong enough not to
bend (without other adjustments unmeet for ancient farmwork),
and no country lane, no harvest-field or meadow, could have
borne the weight of it.

So, the country workman was left, in his little shop, to solve
in his own way and with his own materials various intricate
problems connected with "hanging" the wheels of dung-cart
or waggon. It's true, some slight accommodation had been
made, when I went to the shop, though I am not sure that it
was altogether an improvement. Be that as it may, "wooden
axles" were all but obsolete. The "arms" which the wheels
now ran on were hardened iron, but had to be bedded in wooden
casings—for this reason called axle-beds or "exbeds." A waggon-

arm was about two feet long, one half of it (fitted with the box spoken of in the last chapter) being rounded and tapering to serve as spindle for the wheel, while the other half (the "tail") was flattened down to be let in, or "bedded in" to the wooden exbed. Arms like this, with lynch-pin, box and all, were bought in pairs, ready for use.

Not ready for use at all was the exbed they were to be let into. Standing out an inch or so on either side of the cart, exbeds were from four to five feet long and about five-and-a-half inches square; but they needed planing, if not sawing, to exact size and squareness, before the arms could be bedded in them.

A job to break a young apprentice's heart planing-up an exbed was, and it was often given to an apprentice to do, because it could be tested and was good practice for him in the use of his tools. So, the youth laid it on his bench, and then—

Then he found first that it lay awkwardly above the usual reach of his unaccustomed muscles. Next, if he had hoped to do like a skilled workman, and "shoot" his plane from end to end and take off delicate thin shavings, he was likelier to find his plane jumping, trying to pinch his finger against the exbed, and nibbling off little half-inch flakes of wood instead of the desired shaving. Then would the plane get choked between blade and back-iron, or between blade and wood; or it would gaily take off the beech on one side only; or perhaps it would insist on "writing its name," leaving, that is, a tiny bead standing up all along the timber, left by a minute gag in the blade. And ever and anon, the "square" put on to try the work, or may be the two trying-sticks hopefully laid across it one at each end, would disclose faults such as would set Cook hatefully smiling with his compassionate smile, and could be accepted by no workman.

However, the exbed did eventually get square enough and plane enough to pass muster; and then began a work far too delicate for any young apprentice, bedding the arms, namely, for the wheels to run as wheels should. Bedding them so that knowing persons, hearing the cart on the road by and by, might admire the skill that had hung the wheels and note whose shop they came from.

For "rattling o'er the stony street" was not the only sound of wheeled traffic. Poets might find romance there and hints of battle, but the perennial life of a peaceful countryside—the skill of mankind with materials, the prehistoric mastery over horses —was audible in another sound which obscure carters, obscure wheelwrights, knew well though poets might miss it. In an earlier chapter it has been explained how the stepping of the horse in the shafts made the cart into a sort of battering-ram, forever thumping into the wheels, this side and then that, left, right, near, off, as long as the horse kept going. It has been shown too how wheels had to be made with a "dish," to meet this difficulty. It has now to be shown how the same circumstance affected the bedding of the arms, giving rise incidentally to the sound for which wheelwrights listened gloatingly.

The sound itself may first have a word. Wheels, if one thinks of it, had several voices. That horrid shriek they sometimes kept up—that piercing scream as of agony which would make even Will Hammond smile, being perhaps the only sound he ever did hear—told probably, though not certainly, of a lazy carter's neglect to grease the wheels. Verily it proclaimed his shame cruelly far. But the sound I am talking of now, the sound we liked to hear, was a continuous click, clack, about twice as fast as the footfalls of a horse and regular as the ticking of a clock. It was the sound of the cart battering into the wheels.

Now look back to the axle-bed again. Even in placing it tentatively across the cart ("offering" it) care was exercised, just as care was exercised in deciding to put the better wheel of a pair on the near side. Now, the exbed had its "near" and "off" allotted to it, as it was laid across the cart to be marked off. Then the arms had to be "centred" (the centre found for them) on the exbed, their outlines pencilled, and their "beds" chiselled out to fit.

But here was where experience was wanted. The arms, when fixed, ought not to be exactly at right-angles with the cart; and therefore might not be bedded into the exbed exactly straight. They had to point to the ground a little and forward a little. The wheelwright carefully arranged for these things. His chalk line was again and again stretched taut along the arms; his compasses, between chalk line and arm, told him when the exact angle was reached. Measurement he had none; but his eyes knew.

His first care—that of giving the arms a slight set downwards —was required by the dish of the wheels. You see, the spokes leant outwards slightly from the stock, which was all very well until they turned towards the ground and came under the weight of the load. But, just at that one point each spoke in turn had to carry all one side of the loaded cart—thirteen or fourteen

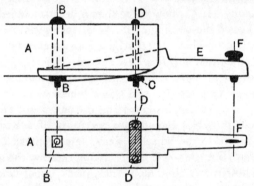

SIDE-VIEW AND UNDER-SIDE OF ARM BEDDED AND CLIPPED
INTO AXLE-BED (EXBED)

A, exbed; B, tail-pin and nut; C, clip; D, clip-pin and nut; E, arm;
F, lynch-pin.

hundredweight, say: and the weight, pressed on it over and over again, could not long be sustained if the spoke slanted. Just at that one point therefore "the upright spoke" (as we called it) was most necessary for the life of the wheel. Accordingly the arm was so bedded in the "ex" that at every revolution of the wheel the downward spoke would come perpendicular to the ground. Of course the upper rim opposite to it leant over away from the cart all the more, as if the wheel was coming off. There was the lynch-pin, however, to prevent such a disaster, and something more than the lynch-pin. The wheel had "foreway."

To secure foreway the arms were given, at bedding, a slight angle forwards, so that the wheels on them had a tendency to draw themselves inwards at every turn. It was not much. There was no rule or scale of foreway known in my shop; but wheel-wrights of great experience could get the right effect by exercising their judgment on it—a judgment centuries old perhaps, passed down the generations by village tradition. And so it was that every wheel, on every waggon or cart, had another motion, besides going round and round. In addition to that, the wheel was always sliding to and fro on its well-greased axle-arm—now driven "click" against the lynch-pin; and next second trying once more (thanks to "foreway") to pass the shoulder—"clack" —on the opposite end of the arm, only to be sent back, "click," to the lynch-pin again. That sound was more continuous and inevitable, if less noticeable, than the scrunching rattle of the tyre on the road. Our prehistoric forefathers may have heard it, when the Tribes were wandering out of Asia.

It behoved the wheelwright to take heed for one other point in bedding a pair of arms: the wheels must "take the routs." In other words the "upright spokes" must bring the rims to the permitted distance apart—no more and no less. True, as years went on and farm-yard cart-tracks were mended, this mattered less and less, so that probably many a younger wheel-wright never heard of such a thing at all. Yet, if it could be ignored in the case of two-wheeled implements—carts and water-barrels—the old rule still had some force in regard to four-wheels—waggons and timber-carriages. With all these a wheelwright must be careful still to bed his arms so that the hind wheels should "range" with the front wheels—should "follow" them or "cut the same track"—in other words, should be just as wide at the ground as the front wheels and, in fact, as every other pair of wheels in the neighbourhood.

Shall I tell how the arms were finally fixed in the exbed (and how that was fixed to the body) with clips and clip-pins, to say nothing of tail-pins? It isn't interesting enough, perhaps, though a principle governed all these details. More interesting is it to note how the exbed, ready at last, was lightly shaved-up with the draw-shave wherever possible, yet might hardly be perceptibly weakened in that way, so important was every fibre of it for strength. But this subject also has been sufficiently discussed in an earlier chapter.

XXVII

BEVELLED TYRES

The usual way of wheel-making having been described, some important variations of· it must be noticed. The "dish" of a wheel gave rise to several difficulties, which amounted to very little in the case of wheels no wider than ordinary waggon wheels, but began to assert themselves in wider wheels, such as dung-cart wheels. The dung-cart, having to go over soft fields often miry from winter frost or rain, was so much in danger of sinking into the ground that it required wide tyres—four-and-a-half or five inches perhaps—twice as wide as waggon wheels, which were more likely to be taken out in dry summer weather, for haymaking or harvesting.

But at this increased width it became plain that the rim of a dished wheel should be bevelled. It had to have a slightly smaller diameter at the front edge than at the other edge four or five inches farther back. Leaning forward away from the cart, towards the ground, it had to be proportionally nearer down to the ground, in front. If in wheels of two-and-a-half inches wide or so this need had not been very noticeable, at greater widths it might not be ignored. The wide rim, stooping forward so much, was liable to run on its edge as it were a-tiptoe. It needed to have its front bevelled-down, ready for the tyre, in such wise that the whole width of the rim, tyre and all, and not just its sharp outer edge, should be pressed on to the ground.

To the best of my belief (but memory goes dim here) the wheel-maker arranged for this, not before knocking-on his felloes, but after the whole ring of them had been wedged on.

However that may have been, when the dung-cart wheel reached the blacksmith's hands its wide rim of felloes had been pared down in front, with axe and plane, to a bevelled shape, only three-and-a-quarter inches or so deep—the same rim of felloes, at back, being about half-an-inch thicker. This meant that the wheel had two diameters—say four feet six inches on the front side and nearly an inch more at the back.

To make his tyre bevelled to fit this wood-work was the black-smith's duty. He worked from the smaller, the front, circumference, shutting his tyre to that dimension. But, once he had got his "shut," the back edge had to be enlarged—"drawn" as we said—to suit the larger dimension. The method looked simple, though it meant hard work. The tyre, say a hundred-weight of iron, was held upright on the anvil; on the inside of it the edge to be drawn was hammered out to the required size. That was all. But it was a three-man job. First the smith—Will Hammond usually—held exactly in place a rod-tool—a "fuller" it was called—to be hammered down with sledge-hammer into the as yet untouched iron. This went on all round the tyre, until all the inside of it, at back, was crinkled or corrugated into hollows, as if a man's knuckles had been pressed in there. The effect was to lengthen the back circumference sufficiently. It was the smith's "mate," with his strong arms, who wielded the sledge. The only part I ever took was to help hold up the tyre. It was inglorious; but at least I got the fullest benefit of the deafening hammer strokes, until my head rang with the noise. A skilful hammerman could sometimes dispense with the fuller, using the blunt "pane," or thin edge, of the sledge direct.

As a result of this bevelling of the wheel and of the tyre all sorts of changes followed. For no slight disasters punished the blunder, if by and by it were attempted to put the front of the tyre—the smaller circumference—over the larger circumference at the back. That happened several times in my experience, as it easily might do. The smith had only to put the tyre the wrong way about in the furnace; or, pulling it out red-hot, to throw it on the ground the same way up as a waggon tyre,

and all the king's horses and all the king's men would have been
too few and too feeble to put it on the wheel. Or again, if a
wide tyre was dropped too many inches over the rim at one side
before it was got over the other side, then too—if it could be got
on at all—there was much trouble and a badly burnt wheel.

Concerning which difficulties and our various dodges for
avoiding them; and how the wheel had to be laid down face
upwards instead of face downwards on the platform, with special
supports under every felloe-joint and special spikes tapped into
the rim to keep the tyre from dropping over too far—concerning
all these matters I was proposing to write at large. For I think
I enjoyed all this work: delighted in the pungent smoke, the
clouds of sudden steam; laughed if, in frosty weather, lumps of
ice instead of water had to be tipped from the water-cans hissing
and skittering away from the hot iron, the soon-blazing wood-
work. I enjoyed it all; sympathised with the errand boys who
used to steal in from the street to watch; and have liked now
recalling the whole operation, and yet—And yet, as it comes
back again into my memory, I am disturbed by a feeling of
something wrong about it, something clumsy.

What was the matter? I think, this. We were not following
any ancient tradition, any well-proved skill, with these bevelled
tyres. That Cook and Hammond fumbled I am far from saying.
They knew what they were at and went through every detail of
this work with perfect assurance of getting the intended result.
But the details had probably been of their own or my father's
contrivance—new dodges to meet new difficulties.

For it was not so very long before my time that hoop-tyres
had been newly introduced instead of strakes; not so long since
they had been heated in a flat fire on the ground. And while apt
devices had been adopted for this in the case of ordinary wheels,
the best way of putting on bevelled tyres had not yet been hit
upon, or at any rate had not yet become general and gained the
smooth validity of ancient traditional skill. The contrast thus
afforded was great. In watching Cook putting a wheel together
I was watching practically the skill of England, the experience
of ages; but to watch the bevelling and subsequent putting on

of a wide tyre was to watch only a makeshift operation lately
hit upon in my own little shop. The inventors of it, to be sure,
were able and indomitable men, but they were self-taught too.
They had not the picked experience of ages behind their methods,
which, I think were different in other shops. In a word, these
skilled men were but uninstructed amateurs at this particular
job. I do not wonder that the details of it strike me as clumsy
now I come to remember them. They were a crude replacement
of an older method, when wheels were not tyred but shod.

SMITHING AND SUNDRIES

XXVIII

SHOEING: SQUARE TONGUES

I USED to take a silly pride, which I am now at a loss to explain, in the thought that mine was not a shoeing smithy—nothing so countrified as that. But now, in memory, everything done in the smith's shop strikes me as having had close reference to the English countryside, and I am sorry that the smiths taught me nothing whatever about shoeing horses. Will Hammond knew; he had made and put on horse-shoes, forging out the nails for them, just as he sometimes made pilts and nails for his own boots. And I have little doubt that his junior, my friend George Porter[1], knew all about it. But they had no opportunity to teach me. Shoeing horses was as much beneath my notice as shoeing oxen would have been, if I had even heard of that obsolete part of country industry.

Yet I was not at all ashamed of shoeing wheels. Indeed, I took it for an old-fashioned way of tyring them, though that was an error. The intention of shoeing a wheel was just the same as that of shoeing horse, or ox or donkey, namely to provide an iron shield against the too hard wear of road or land. It turned out that as good a protection for wheels was afforded by hoop-tyres as by "strakes," but the hoop-tyre was put on rather to tie or pull the wheel timbers closely together. If it also shod the felloes, still its main purpose was to save the wheel from being shaken to pieces. The tyre, in fact, was the answer which the skilled wheelwright had found to the problems set by vibration and of sun-heat. But the shoe, the strake, was an answer to the problems set by stones and dust wearing against timber. The ash, the elm, might not have come home safe from a single day's work on the farm, without shoes to guard the wheel-rims across the fields. This I knew without properly grasping it. I thought (and still think) tyres were a vast improvement on the more primitive strakes; but the essential difference between the

[1] "Porter" is what we always called him, but properly his name is Turner.

two was dark to me. Lest it should still be dark to any reader, let me explain. A tyre was a continuous band, like a hoop, put right round a wheel. A strake was an iron shoe, nailed across one joint only, where two felloes met. Each joint had its strake. If there were six felloes, there were six joints and six strakes. But the strakes were never joined. They did not even quite meet.

Shoeing was a much more antiquated affair than tyring. I know that Arthur Young, travelling in Gloucester in 1767, makes reference to waggon-tyres, but it is easier to believe that he used a word carelessly than that anything but strakes was put on to farm-wheels at that day. The tradition of shoeing, though dying, was not quite dead in Surrey more than a century later. To remind me of it, there was the word "shoeing," often used erroneously in my shop for "tyring." There was "the shoeing-hole" spoken of in the last chapter—a carefully preserved puddle, with which (dirty though it was) I often played as a little boy, and into which I once stepped, over my boot-top. Wheels, I was to learn, had "soles" for shoes or strakes. The "strake chimney" might not be demolished when the tyre-furnace was built. It was still too often wanted, though we had none too much room in the cramped yard. In short, though hoop-tyres were everywhere superseding them, strakes continued to claim attention in my shop in 1884 and long afterwards.

They claimed attention, in the first place, from Cook or other wheel-makers—nay, from the very sawyers, or from the sawyers' employer at any rate, cutting out felloes from the green timber. For the felloes were longer for a straked wheel than for a hoop-tyre, there being fewer of them to make up the rim. In a waggon, for instance, instead of seven felloes for each hind wheel (as with a hoop-tyre) there were only six if strakes were to be used, while for the front wheels there were but five. It meant proportionately longer timber; and of course provision had to be made for these greater felloe-lengths, when the trees were being sawn up in the winter.

But this was not the only difference. In the newer way of making a wheel, more than half the dish was produced by the shrinkage of the hoop-tyre, pulling the wheel over more and more concave. As strakes did not do this to any great extent, and dish was very important, it had to be secured when the stock was being mortised. From the start the wheel was made more hollow. It was useless to depend on the strakes. The wheelwright himself must drive his spokes with the required slant right away.

Nor was this all. As I have previously explained, the contraction of the hoop-tyre (I have seen the word spelt tyer) drew all the wood-work of the wheel together with a matchless tightness. Sledge-hammers and wedges could not do half so well. But as the strakes were not to be expected to give such aid, the

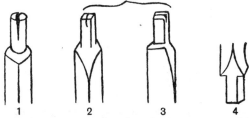

1, 2, 3, top ends or tongues of spokes, for inserting into felloes. The notch is to be spread open (thereby tightening the spoke) with a wedge driven in after the felloe has been put on. 1, round tongue; 2, square tongue, front; 3, square tongue, side. 4, foot of spoke (the tenon which holds it in the stock).

wheelwright was at pains to put his wheel together more strongly then than was thought necessary afterwards. Afterwards, in the days of hoop-tyres, it was enough if the spokes were simply rounded off into pegs or "tongues" for inserting into the felloes. I have told how little snapping noises, like pistol-shots, made music to my ears as a tyre cooled. Sometimes those noises told, there is no doubt, of some obstinate felloe going down, at last, where sledges would not drive it, on a round-tongued spoke. This, however, was less likely to happen with strakes. Therefore, to avoid any looseness or "give" in the wood-work, the wheelwright preparing for strakes was not contented with two round spoke-holes in his felloes. He chiselled-out mortices in them, and then tenoned his spokes into the mortices, as exact as in cabinet work. About these "square-tongued" spokes there were mysteries which I never fathomed. Happily for me then (but I wish I knew now) Cook knew the angles for planing off the tenons, the way to "true them up"—knew all sorts of details in fact—things for eyes and hands to learn, rather than for reason; and my eyes and hands were already too old. Moreover, the opportunities for me to learn were comparatively few. Soon, with strakes, square-tongued spokes too gave way to cheaper work; indeed I am of opinion that the wheelwrights' craft began to decline when square tongues went out of fashion. But they were always too costly, which is one reason why, to reduce their number, the felloes had been fewer.

XXIX

SHOEING: STRAKES

From first to last—from the preparation to the nailing-on— the work of shoeing a wheel with strakes was singular and noteworthy. To begin with the preparation—the strakes were cut off cold from the iron bars, with sledge-hammer and "hard-chisel." I don't know how they were measured. For one front waggon wheel, with five joints, only five strakes were wanted; but a pair of wide dung-cart wheels, with double row of strakes, took twenty-four—plenty of sledge work. Having been cut off, the strakes needed bending approximately to the turn of the wheel, and also they required punching. I do not remember any bending—how it was done (but I fancy strakes were hammered into curve when slightly hot, on the blacksmith's anvil) or whether they were bent before or after punching, but I know that the punching was laborious work for a smith. Strakes had about ten nail-holes in them—five near each end; not punched evenly, lest the nails through them should presently split the wood beneath, but dotted about at the blacksmith's pleasure though always irregularly.

In readiness for being punched the end of the strake was made at least red-hot. And then came hurry to get as much of the work done as possible without having to heat the iron again. Anyhow it was a two-man job, what with blowing-up the fire, lifting the iron (fifteen pounds or more) into proper place on the anvil, and driving the punching "tool" quickly through the three-quarters of an inch or so of glowing metal. So hot the expanse of iron was, even Will Hammond could hardly bear his fingers near enough to place the punch. He held his little finger away like a fine lady holding a teacup: he blew on his finger-nails to assuage for a moment the intolerable heat, or he plunged his whole hand into the water-trough at the front edge of his hearth. But whatever he did in this way was done rapidly, as if to lose no time. The one urgent thing was to make full use of the "heat," scorched fingers or no scorched fingers. It occurs to me to wonder What can have been the earnest expression of his faithful eyes, in these moments? I never saw. Black-haired and sweating, he bent over the anvil, while his hammer-hand rose and fell strenuously. I saw how his shirt grew moist, heard his genial laugh as he turned back to his fire again to resume, belike, some gossip about his "taters—like a ball of flour"; but I suppose only the anvil and the hot iron were ever truly in position to see a blacksmith's face when he was hammering his hardest.

As strenuous, as rapid, perhaps even more continuous (it allowed no intervals for gossip) was the making of the nails—ten for each strake and a few over, a few to spare in case presently a hurried man should drop one into the shoeing-hole. This nail-making was again a two-man job, to save time. While the smith was forging a nail at the end of an iron rod (about as long as a walking-stick) it behoved his "mate" at the bellows to see that another rod would be hot for him as soon as he was ready to turn round to the fire and take it. If the mate knew his job—knew how to manage the fire—the smith thus lost no time from his hammering; but I do not think I ever was so clever at the bellows as all that. A strake-nail was about as long as a sardine and a little thicker, but it was square-cornered and forged out to a thin end, wedge-shaped. A big thick head it had, battered over, and for half-an-inch or so under the head it was made tapering, to fit into the holes that had been punched, also tapering, in the strake. The idea was that, as the strake wore thin, still the tapering nail might hold tight in the iron.

While the nails were a-making the wheelwright had to take a hand again, fitting the newly-punched strakes and carefully marking their destined places on the wheel, so that the right one should be taken, and by the right end too, when at last it had to be nailed on to the wheel. Most important it was to get the exact place then, because every felloe had to be bored, beforehand, for those big strake-nails to enter. There was no other way of driving them into the hard timber; they would have been too big and blunt. Below every one of the holes in the iron therefore a corresponding place for a nail in the felloe was wanted. Accordingly, as I say, the wheelwright tried-on and chalk-marked every strake, and bored its nail-holes in the rim of wood, against the critical time, soon to come now, for shoeing the wheel.

One other preparation too was wanted. Somebody, probably the blacksmith, put the "Samson" ready for use, oiling its two nuts if need be, and "running them down" (namely, refitting them) on its strong arms. The Samson was a stiff parallelogram of iron specially contrived for use in shoeing. It was about as long, and half as wide, as a sheet of *The Times*. Welded square to one of its ends stretched two long arms fitted with heavy nuts; which nuts, screwed down or up, tightened or loosened a ponderous movable cross-piece—a sort of shackle from arm to arm—at the other end. This well-named implement was always

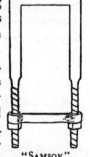

"SAMSON"

wanted for putting on strakes. By the way, I never saw a new Samson. The one we used, and could not yet do without even in 1900, had probably lain knocking about in my yard, to be handled by successive generations, for a century or more.

And now take a look at the oven, where the strakes were at last "hotted" for shoeing. This oven—the "strake chimney"—

was a sort of brick fireplace as close as three or four yards to the shoeing-hole. You may see the like in new houses, before the grate is put in; an opening without a range. It had a wide chimney some ten feet high. In this opening—a substantial wood fire being laid—the strakes were stacked, with great care as to the proper order for taking them out and as to the right end to work to. I do not remember ever seeing the strakes stacked, but as they lay one atop of the other it is plain that the next one to be pulled out would have to be also the one that must go uppermost next on the wheel, and no other would do instead.

Before the cooking was done the wheelwright trundled his wheel into the shoeing-hole, where he "hung" it, nearly upright, to the low post at the back of the hole, steadying it with a stout iron bar thrust through the central opening of the wheel. The front of the wheel faced him; a section of its rim lay hidden in the dirty water of the shoeing-hole; at top of all was the joint of the two felloes across which strake No. 1 was to be nailed. The wheelwright tapped these felloes again smartly with his sledge to get them properly close together; he also tapped one nail into the rim to be a guide for placing the strake in the great hurry by and by. The new nails, in two buckets of water, were set down near the wheel; the Samson, with a spare sledge perhaps, was laid handy; a helper was called out, with another sledge; he, and the wheelwright also—shirt sleeves up of course— picked each a handful of nails from the bucket of water at his side, spat into his hands, and with raised sledge stood ready; the blacksmith grunted "Now"—and Now it was, and no mistake!

At double-quick time the smith hooked out a red-hot strake, seized it with his tongs by the middle, hurried it across the wheel-joint to the place marked by the one tapped-in nail, and held it down while the wheelwright banged in a nail. Forthwith the other man, at the other end, striking down the iron all along to fit the rim, got in his nail; flames and choking wood smoke leapt up; the men, burning their fingers and wrists, dipped their hands hastily into the pail of water, smote in their other nails— whack, whack, bang, bang—with deft sledge work, the smith caught up the spare sledge to help, somebody exclaimed fiercely "He's burnin'!" as the flames shot up higher; the coughing wheelwright puffed the smoke aside to see that all was right, then (lest "he," the wheel, should burn too much) pulled the now fastened strake round into the shoeing-hole, where the water began to pobble and boil with the sudden heat, and clouds of white steam mixed with the blue wood smoke. The men stood back panting for a minute's rest, and watched the heaving turmoil in the water.

But only for a minute. Before the water was quiet, each was stooping for another handful of nails from the bucket, spitting on his hands for gripping the sledge better, watching where the smith was already hooking out a second strake. And then the same thing again—crackle of burning wood, hiss of water, rising of steam and smoke, all to the loud clatter of sledge blows. This for a minute, followed once more by the sudden pobbling noise of boiling water, as strake number two was pulled round into the shoeing-hole.

Two or three things are to be noticed now. First, observe that the strakes cannot be put on in their final sequence, one, two, three, four and so on. As number one is turned right round into the water, the one that comes opposite to it—number three or number four—is the next to go on, and not number two. I did not hear of any formula for this rotation, but, if there was such a thing, it would have helped the smith when stacking the oven.

Another thing to note was that in the first strake, if in no others, one nail—only one—was driven in firmly yet not driven home. In all the turmoil and hurry, the wheelwright was mindful to leave this one nail standing up an inch or so. His reason appeared as soon as the time came for putting on the Samson. Hooked in, at one end, round a spoke, the Samson (with its nuts) was at the other end hooked over the projecting nail—under the nail-head perhaps. Once fixed safely there it was gradually screwed up—this nut and then that—until the intervening felloe-joint could squeeze together no closer. So it was done with every joint round the wheel; and this was the best tightening that could be effected with strakes. Of course hoop-tyres did the work far better and at less cost; the Samson pulled the wheels far less dishing. This was why they had been built more hollow at the start. Still, there was not much left for mortal man to tighten after Samson had pulled the joints together.

One pleasant memory of my boyhood clings to the thought of the old strake chimney. After a shoeing, when the wood cinders glowed almost too dazzling to look at, a rack of church-warden pipes was brought from my grandfather's house adjoining the yard and set down in the heart of the fire. When it was lifted out again the pipes were almost transparent with great heat; but cooling, they looked like new ones, chalk-white, with the last speck of nicotine burned from the bowl, the last stain of red sealing-wax from the mouthpiece. That was a fascinating sight for a boy. But when, following my father, I took my grandfather's place, churchwarden pipes were gone out of fashion, and the strake chimney was comparatively rarely used, even for its legitimate ends.

XXX

THE NEW IRON AGE

In the slow transition from village or provincial industry to city or cosmopolitan industry, one sees a change comparable to the geologic changes that are still altering the face of the earth; a change like them unnoticed, yet like them irresistible and cumulatively immense. Already, during the eighties and nineties of last century, work was growing less interesting to the work-man, although far more sure in its results. Whereas heretofore the villager (a provincial craftsman, say) had been grappling adventurously and as a colonist pioneer with the materials of his own neighbourhood—the timber, the clay, the wool—other materials to supersede the old ones were now arriving from multitudinous wage-earners in touch with no neighbourhood at all, but in the pay of capitalists. So the face of the country was being changed bit by bit. Incidentally, occasion was arising for the "Unrest" of the present day. Village life was dying out; intelligent interest in the country-side was being lost; the class-war was disturbing erstwhile quiet communities; yet nobody saw what was happening. What we saw was some apparently trivial thing, such as the incoming of tin pails instead of wooden buckets. Iron girders had hardly yet begun to oust oak beams from buildings; corrugated iron sheets were but just beginning to take the place of tiles or thatch. If an outhouse was boarded up with planed deal match-boarding from Norway instead of with "feather-edged" weather-boarding cut out locally by sawyers one knew, who was to imagine what an upheaval was implied in this sort of thing, accumulating for generations all over Europe? Seen in detail the changes seemed so trumpery and, in most cases, such real improvements. That they were upsetting old forms of skill—producing a population of wage-slaves in place of a nation of self-supporting workmen—occurred to nobody.

Although in my old shop the flood of changes was not yet— the flood which at last has all but overwhelmed the ancient handicraft—various smaller changes had begun to trickle in, as early as 1884 and the three or four following years. I think I bought no new paint-pots from the local pottery. The old ones, having been "burnt out" often enough (you started fire in a paint-pot with a wisp of shavings from the wood shop, after which the old dry paint burnt by itself—and smelt to Heaven— —leaving the glazed earthenware tolerably clean) the old paint-pots, not renewed, were replaced by paint tins, improvised from "empties" that had come from the manufacturer full of some special red or green. You couldn't burn out these tins so well— they fell to pieces if the solder melted—but why trouble? More and more came in their place—products perhaps of man's work, but more likely of machine work, made for nothing more dignified than the dust-hole.

And not the smaller quantities of paints alone arrived in

"tins." "Drums" of white lead, of "Venetian," of "Driers" came, instead of the barrels in which these materials were formerly packed. The wood-worker who made barrels was going, if the tin-worker was coming. From that industry, at any rate, old skill was "getting the push."

And the wood-worker was going, or at any rate his ancient provincial skill was falling obsolete, not only as to the utensils and materials I bought for my shop but likewise as to the things made there. Ploughs (I had heard of my grandfather standing in Farnham market with a sample plough every week) almost ceased coming for repairs in 1884. A few new plough-beams were put in from my stock of timber; I was responsible (as employer) for a few new curved "stilts" or handles. For a year or two I still stocked ploughshares, turnfurrows and other castings from the Reading Ironworks for the wooden ploughs my father had been wont to supply. A carrier named David Budden, I remember—a man with anxious-looking clean-shaven face and black shiny gaiters—used to bring the castings by road, the ploughshares being in half-dozens tied together with string or with wire. These I found it worth while to keep in stock for a time. But after a few years the Reading Ironworks closed down; their trade, so far as I knew, was done with. Wooden ploughs had gone out of use—had been driven out of the market by cast-iron ploughs, painted a pale bright blue.

The history of harrows and of "drags" (similar to harrows but heavier implements) is much the same. In fact, iron harrows came into vogue a year or two earlier than iron ploughs. I learnt but little about the wooden kind of harrows, though I fancy two or three pairs were made in my time. I knew that their larger and curved timbers were called "larrows," these being mortised on to thin slats or keys, and I knew how harrows were hooked by the corner, two together, to a draught bar called a whippance. Oak was the stuff harrows were made of—heart of oak; and besides that the wrought-iron attachments for them—the "copses," the loops, put on hot—were ingenious, the "tines" themselves, I knew, sometimes needed "lining" with fresh steel, being worn down by much dragging through the soil. But, although I understood that there was a mystery about placing the tines and letting them into the larrows, the opportunity for making it out never came to me. Cast-iron harrows —bright blue like the iron ploughs—shifted all that sort of work from old shops like mine to foundries. I do not know whether such interest went with the making of them as Cook and Hammond had enjoyed in making the wooden ones.

Wooden hames (or haims)—well, there had once been a demand for them in my shop. Cook knew how to make them; Hammond could go through all the detail involved in ironing them up. Moreover, we had a "pattern" of their shape—a thin lath of delicate curves, brown with age; proof enough, in itself, that of old the making of them had been a common task for skilful wheelwrights. More—I remember not only marking-out an ash butt to be sawed into future hame-planks, I even lined-out, by the pattern, and perhaps I helped saw, the stuff for a new pair of hames. The very toughest ash butt was good enough for them, and might give approximately the right turn—if the tree had been cut off low enough to contain an inch or two ot the curve upwards from the roots. Indeed, nothing less would suffice, so delicate and slender were the curving hames. Such loving work was put into the pair I have mentioned—they had so much shaving, forging, filing—that the cost of them, to me, exceeded the traditional price which was all I could charge the farmer they were made for. I resented, not openly, his grumbling at the cost, not knowing, then, that that grumbling too was traditional. But of course I could not have competed against the midland factories, with their steel or brass hames. The work was easily standardised; localised skill in it was unnecessary, and, so far as I can see, the ready-made article was really better than I could produce. None the less, it was well for workmen like Cook and Hammond that they were not dependent for a living on the demand for hames; for the demand passed them wholly by and addressed itself to machinery and machine-workers.

Yet another branch of the wood-workers' living was captured away from them, when wooden axles were driven out by case-hardened iron arms. This too, in my little shop, had already come to pass just before my time, though the last remains of the older method gave me an inkling of what it had been. And here again I think the change probably resulted in a better product, though it gave a quietus to one more form of skill and favoured machinery at man's expense. The workmen in my shop, to be sure, always maintained that the old five-inch wooden axles "ran" better—more easily and smoothly—than the new two-and-a-half-inch iron arms; and I always agreed. But really I have no knowledge that it was so; and I do know that to provide a good standard iron arm and box was easier than to make and fit an ancient wooden axle; and, probably, being so much less cumbersome, the iron allowed of some saving in weight and therefore in horse-flesh.

It[1] would be difficult in these days to find even the timber, or the experience that could season the timber, for a wooden axle for a waggon or dung-cart, to say nothing of the huge wheel-stocks required for it. A quartered butt of beech, not "biscuity" but hard as bone, near eight feet long too by six inches square—this is what must have been used for many thousands of axles, less than half a century ago. How it was shaped up with proper foreway and under-set for dished wheels, or how iron "clouts" (with "clout-nails") were carefully fitted into it to take the wear—is all but gone from my memory, as indeed it was hardly worth storing there, when iron arms from Birmingham were already making the old wood-work obsolete. But there are, none the less, a number of things I should like to know about the history of wooden axles.

I should like to know, for instance, when they too were innovations, and what preceded them; or rather, from what origins, and by what stages of improvement, the art of making wooden axles had been evolved and had become a widespread tradition[2].

For, when one reads of the folk-wandering of the prehistoric tribes, and learns how some of the tribes migrated, say from

[1] Note G, p. 208.
[2] I saw one, placed on the top of a stile, in the Isle of Wight; one in the yard of a village smithy near Guildford. Several dung-carts in a farm-yard near Rye had wooden axles. They are still in use near Worthing.

western Asia all across Europe—whole nations at a time—in waggons, then it is a puzzle what those waggons could have been like. What wheels could they have had; and, still more, what axles? Were they wooden axles, at all like that one that was put on to Mr Allden's dung-cart—fitted to the strake-tyred wheels —in my old shop in 1884? If it is hard to think that the barbarian axle-trees were at all like that, I find it even harder to conceive in what essentials they can have been different and the waggons yet hold together through far travels and the wheels run round. Some construction equally durable they must have had and yet—

Everything about a wooden axle and its wheels seemed to imply a long-settled population. How could nomadic tribes have accumulated, I will not say the experience, but even the material required? It was not any timber that would serve or even any beech; but to get the right stuff involved throwing and "opening" a tree at the right season, and on the right soil too. Did the wandering barbarians cart a sawpit along with them? or a stock of seasoning timber, or a stock of it seasoned? Did they take benches, wheel-pits, the requisite axes and chisels and handsaws? Or, if not, how did the wandering tribes come trailing over Europe? or how many thousand years did they spend upon the migration, building villages, gathering traditions of handicraft, seeming to settle down, and then off again?

Such things of course I shall never know. Yet I cannot help suspecting that some of that sort of life was still going on as late as when Mr Allden's cart came to my shop for a new wooden axle in 1884; and that about that time the ancient iron age was waking up to new encroachments destined to be more momentous to mankind even than its prehistoric arrival had been.

XXXI

ORDINARY IRON-WORK

In the general run, through hundreds of details of the wheel-wright's craft, iron and wood were not so much competitive as mutually helpful. Either seemed content merely to eke out the other's deficiencies. The hardness of the iron for small things and the comparative lightness of the wood for large things, made a blend that had stood for ages. There can be no doubt that wood-work came first. It had seen stone followed by bronze, and that by iron; and as yet iron still held rather a subordinate place. Thus it shod the wheels, provided hard axles, furnished many a "pin," or "copse," or "link," or "eye," yet was hardly in any case indispensable. The latch[1] of the front door in my shop was a wooden one. In some ways iron imitated wood-work, notably in aiming, everywhere, at the utmost lightness consistent with strength. Wherever a three-quarter rod might do, if reduced to half-an-inch at the other end, the blacksmith would "draw it down" with patient hammering, or perhaps would "shut" a thin piece on to a thicker piece, welding the two so that you could not see where they joined.

This shutting of iron (there were other uses for the word[2]) was a process worth watching. The two pieces to be "shut" were first of all thickened or "upset" at the ends to be joined. The way to do this was to heat the end in the fire and then hammer it back or stub it against the anvil until the iron was swollen just there. Each swollen tip was then "scarfed down," or hammered thin and fitted or stuck into the other; and then, with further heatings, the two pieces were welded into one another. Under this treatment the reason for the initial

---

[1] Note H, p. 208.
[2] Besides such familiar uses as shutting a door, shutting-up shop, etc., carters talked of shutting-in a horse between the shafts, or shutting it out. In west Surrey we said shet instead of shut, talking so of shet-links, shetlicks and so on.

upsetting became clear; for the hammering thinned it down again, and the swell of the upsetting was lost in any good shut.

"Drawing-down" just mentioned—the opposite process to "upsetting"—was the counterpart, in smithing, to "shaving" in wood-work. Its object was to reduce the weight; and how much that meant could sometimes be seen, when some job or other brought to the shop had been "ironed-up" by a blacksmith unfamiliar with the wheelwrights' traditions. Such products always looked heavy and clumsy. The stock-bonds had not been "chamfered off" (by hammering down thin) at the edges; the "eyes" (never "barrelled") had been left square at the neck;

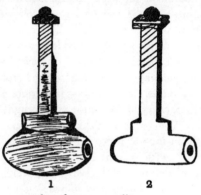

1   2

1, barrel eye; 2, ordinary eye.

nowhere had opportunity been taken to "draw-down" a thick piece of iron to thinner dimensions. This omission looked almost nauseating at times. Why, oh why? I used to wonder, had not this or that "strap" been hammered to a more acceptable thinness. "Straps" were attachments, narrow flanges, standing out from a piece of iron-work and containing nail-holes or screw-holes so that the iron-work could be fastened to an adjacent piece of wood. If the "strap" would but hold, the thinner it was the better; and the end of it at least might be as pointed and thin as a willow-leaf. But smiths not brought up to wheelwright traditions naturally did not understand the details of this work, and left their straps none the stronger for being so thick and heavy

and ugly. It must be owned, however, that one other consideration may have swayed them. "Drawing-down," as it occupied
time and therefore cost money, was losing favour under increasing
competition. Carters could not complain as of old if their horses
had overmuch weight to pull, for employers stood too much
aloof to be easily approached. Class differences carried them
farther and farther away from the men who used their horses or
built their carts.

There was one survival in the smith's shop which seemed to
have come down from some far-off generation when
"time" did not matter so much, some era when a
blacksmith might go dreamily to work caring not
for usefulness at all, but for what he thought pretty.
I am thinking of the pattern that Will Hammond
used to make, with file and punch, on certain flat
inches of waggon iron-work, of cart iron-work. He
spent hours at it. Where he learnt the tradition I do
not know. He never deviated from it, or neglected
it, or originated any part of it. He put it on to his
"staves" because it was the thing to do, and had
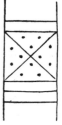

DESIGN ON
IRON-WORK

been the thing time-out-of-mind, seeing that an hour more or
less didn't matter. With file and dot-punch he worked away, in
the temper to be contentedly humming over his vice, marking-out
his simple and ancient decoration. A design very like it (you
could hardly be less ornate) may often be seen stamped in
leather across the toes of a pair of boots, where likewise it may
be of prehistoric date.

At a period a little before my time smiths had indulged in one
other form of decoration. But I will leave strouter-sockets, and
the simple, and I think quite unnecessary, bead forged round
them, for the next chapter. Here I must digress to question,
but not to explain, how the blacksmiths' tools originated. They
were not like wheelwrights' tools. The edged tools for the wood-
workers were within the skill of local manufacture. It is true,
the men in my shop generally bought them from the Birmingham traveller, who used to go round the shops for orders after
he had booked any I might have to give for axles, springs, chain,

files, and so on. From the same source the wheelwrights got their hand-saws, their "twisty-bitts," and ratchet braces. I could name one family in a near village who had specialised in wood-men's axes, chisels, plane-irons. This family had some secret process and enjoyed a high reputation amongst workmen all round the neighbourhood for the excellence of the tools they made. So much for the woodmen's tools.

But I never heard that the blacksmiths' tools came from any-where nearer than the Midlands. Certainly the smiths in my shop could make their own punches and drills—an old screw-driver furnished the hard material they wanted. They also forged out their hard-chisels for cutting iron; their own tongs and pincers too. But their other implements came—just as did their anvils, their vices, the "tue-irons" for their forges, their shoeing-platforms—from the Midlands, product of no such village skill as theirs. The blacksmiths' "stocks" for cutting the "thread" or "worm" round a bolt; his corresponding taps and dies for "tapping" the nut, and then again all his array of files and rasps; told of a knowledge of iron and a form of skill not to be learnt at ironing-up dung-carts and waggons, or at shoeing horses or wheels. So too with the large "mandrils"—those large hollow castings, like a huge sugar-loaf—on which the stock-bonds were hammered, or the smaller mandrils for shaping up whippance irons. Will Hammond and smiths of his sort could not do without these implements but knew nothing of their source. I do not know whence the blacksmiths got those numerous "bolsters"—those little hardened impressions (like the marks of fossils) of "collars" and shoulders and so on, into which they beat (and thereby shaped) their bits of iron-work, but I have a vague idea that they did indeed make these for themselves. Yet how? It is a mystery, like the making of a file. As behind that, so behind the making of a "bolster," stands a shadowy antiquity of many generations of blacksmiths.

A thing the smiths in my shop could have made, but nothing like cheaply enough, was chain. How were self-respecting men to compete against the women chain-makers of Cradley Heath? Will Hammond and his colleague didn't try. I bought chain

for them—used to chop off for them myself the lengths they
wanted for tailboards, "drug-bats," "roller-scotches," and so on.
A ridge-tie was that twisted "back-band" chain which hung a
pair of shafts over a horse's back, opposite to the leather "belly-
band." Sometimes my men would shut a few links on to a
chain I furnished to them; sometimes they would supply a
waggoner or a timber-carter with a "shut-link" in case of
emergency. A "shut-link" (pronounced shet-link) was really
not shut at all. It was a link that could be opened, as a split
key-ring, and then be closed together again. With a shut-link a
handy carter, if a chain snapped, could join the two pieces
again, provided, of course, that the blacksmith had properly
"nealed" the link—left it pliable, that is to say. With the
exceptions mentioned, and putting on a tie-chain (with dog and
ring) to hold the hind wheels of a waggon if there was danger
of running away, smiths in my shop had not much to do with
chains. The day-long chink-chink of their hammers, the occasional explosive bang when some special forging was effected
in oil, meant waggon-irons, cart-irons, shaft-irons, in plentiful
variety.

Always there was a call for some form of skill that had been
perfecting, I daresay, in rural smithies for centuries. One
evidence of the co-operation between wood and iron was the
intercourse all day between the two shops. Now a woodman
would journey to the smithy to get an armful of iron-work; now
it would be a smith, going to where the new waggon was
a-building, to take exact measurements for his "stays and copses."
Sometimes, hearing a noise of running, I would look up from
writing my ledger in the office, and see a man scurrying back to
the body-shop from the smithy with a red-hot rod in his hand.
It was a "burner" he was taking, to clear out some hole left too
ragged by his auger. Next minute the shop filled with a cloud
of yellow-blue smoke as the burner was thrust up and down in
the auger-hole, but then white steam promptly followed as
water was tipped over the hole, and the quenched burner was
hurried outside the shop, to be leant on end safely on the ground
there.

To this sort of accompaniment the blacksmiths' hammers were chinking all day. Now and then the men were interrupted for tyring or for shoeing; now and then harrow-tines, or a pickaxe, or a garden-fork, needed "laying" or lining with fresh steel, or the tines even needed replacing altogether. Excepting for light through the open half-door, or from the window over the bench and vice, the smithy was kept pretty dark. Will Hammond preferred it so. If the skylight did admit a splash of sunshine, as it sometimes tried to do on summer noons, he was prompt to veil it with an old sack he kept nailed for that purpose to the sooty rafters. The sunshine, he said, put his fire out; and very likely it did affect the look of the "heat," so all-important to a blacksmith.

However that may have been, the old smithy preserved a decent darkness, showing up strongly the roaring fires, the glow of sparkling iron. And in this gloom the smiths passed their days of interesting variety, making or mending the unnumbered irons for waggons or carts. Of some of these they kept a small stock made up, such as "stays and copses" for bodies, "rings and gudgeons" for barrow wheels, eyes for tailboards, and shutlock-hooks to hang the tailboards on. "Fore-irons" for shafts were in constant demand, and the smiths liked always to have two or three sets by them. In a spare half-hour they would start making them—"long-staples," and tug-hooks and quilers (probably coilers) and drayels and "ring-and-starts"—to say nothing of hookcapping-irons and keying-irons and galling plates and prop-stick loops and ferules and key-stick cranks. It was truly a world of strange words for a novice in the old smithy; afterwards it began to be a question rather, in what far-off reign had English rustics first used those terms?—or was it, perhaps, before reigns were thought of?

One thing was plain enough. However ancient the traditions of the smithy might be they were still vigorously alive. Not once or twice only, but over and over again, some careful carter asked for this or that slight modification, to suit a special horse, a special bit of hilly road, or what not. Whenever a new drug-bat (skid-pan) was wanted, or a new roller-chain, one of the smiths not only put on the bat or shut the link to connect the chain, but he had to go out to the waiting waggon, to test the lengths of chain, and make sure that the new work was really what was needed.

XXXII

THE IRON AGE MOVING ON

But quiet though it was—looking almost stagnant if seen daily—an encroachment of iron-work upon wood-work was continually going on, and probably had been going on for a very long time. In three directions, at any rate, I beheld it. During say the sixteen years between 1884 and 1900 iron ousted wood in my shop in regard to bumpers, rave-ends and strouters.

Bumpers were blocks of wood fastened to the back of a tip-cart so as to touch the ground and keep the rest of the body raised a little off it when the cart was tipped. In dung-carts the same effect had been achieved by the main timbers themselves, the tail-ends of which, called "pummels," projected some ten or twelve inches behind the rest of the body and took the shock (the "bump") when the cart was tipped for the load of swedes, say, to be shot out on to the barn floor. But the construction of ordinary carts for general purposes—for sand or gravel, for coal, bavins, clover, or hundreds of other things—did not result in "pummels." Instead of pummels, and not part of the main framing like them but an addition, a sort of after-thought, bumpers were notched and bolted, one each side, to the main timbers. About three inches square, they projected some eight or ten inches beyond the cart, and were very effective in keeping its more delicate workmanship from smashing down on to the ground every time the cart tipped. Bumpers were shod with a stout plate of iron bent round them.

So carts were built, I think, during the eighties. But by the end of the century the wooden bumper was out of date. Loops of iron (usually square iron), called "tipping-irons," were now the fashion. As a matter of fact they were not nearly so good a protection for the cart as bumpers had been; but then, carts were anyhow beginning to shake to pieces, or to wear out more quickly, in the more hustling times and on the harder roads.

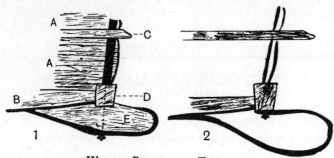

1, WOODEN BUMPER.   2, TIPPING-IRON
A, side-board ; B, main side ; C, rave ; D, hind shutlock ; E, bumper.

Bumpers instead of tipping-irons would not have saved them. And the latter were less costly to make, and also looked lighter. Any contractor who cared more about public esteem than about truly efficient carting preferred the lighter-looking iron-work to the rather clumsy-looking wood. And in fact the tipping-iron, with its rather beautiful curves, answered quite well. I willingly admit that much.

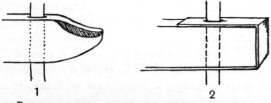

1, RAVE-END, SHAVED.   2, RAVE-END, SHEATHED IN IRON

In rave-ends a truly valuable improvement was made when the once slender end was cut off square and sheathed in thin iron hooping.

It was railway work that almost necessitated this change. Of old the ends of cart-raves had but required shaving-up lightly with a draw-shave, just for the sake of reducing the weight and finishing neatly. But, by and by, carts began to wait on railways, with loads to be transferred to railway trucks; and then trouble began. Backing his cart close up to the truck the carter found that his delicate raves snapped like matches, or at least battered in and split. The tough ash could not stand being backed against the truck by a backing horse. What was the remedy? It was simplicity itself. The raves had to be cut off at their full thickness and wrapped in iron. I do not think waggon-raves ever received this treatment, although waggons were framed up in just the same way as "raved-carts," as we called them. Waggons were not so often used for railway-station work, or so often left to the tender mercies of inexperienced horse-drivers.

The use of iron in place of wood for strouters was rather a bad step backwards, although it became almost universal. Truly it was a saving of artisan's time, and therefore of money, to the buyer of the cart or waggon, and it gave him a somewhat lighter looking vehicle. The public, seeing it, might praise the owner of this smart up-to-date tackle.

But, in point of fact, waggons and carts lost in strength considerably, and gained little if anything in lightness, by the substitution of one material for the other. The iron strouter was none too efficient for its purpose, and in two respects was an actual source of weakness—bad weakness too.

What was the purpose of strouters? Their use was to act as a sort of buttresses to the body. Raved-cart, dung-cart, farm-waggon, whichever it might be, was open at the top. It had been built up from the bottom timbers in more or less delicate skeleton frame-work for holding loads. At the front-end, near the horse, this frame-work was held together by the "head" or heads, across from one side to the other. But there was nothing of this sort at the other end, the "tail." There, the "tailboard" was made to let down or to take right away, and there was great need of some contrivance to keep the side-frames from "spreading." They were as unstable as two sides of a packing-case would be if one of its ends were knocked out.

Such a box was the empty cart. The end was left out. The load, and the act of loading, emphasised the consequent weakness. Whether the carter was chucking roots into his dung-cart, or shovelling sand into his raved-cart, or pitching corn-sheaves into his waggon, or stacking sacks of flour in it, or netting-over a load of sheep—whatever the work, still it tended to push the frame-work out and to cause "spreading."

Nor was this quite all. In most of these vehicles provision was made for widening the load, above the wheel level. Thanks to "out-raves" and rave-boards, the bulkier loads—hay, corn, straw, manure—could be piled high and wide, and yet not touch the wheels. Only, of course, every pound of load a-top increased the strain on the frame-work, and made it more and more needful to correct the tendency of the vehicle to "spread."

The wheelwright's answer to this problem was, strouters. To a certain extent, it is true, yet to a very small extent, "hind-staves" had served the same end. I strongly suspect that wooden stays and wooden brackets had once held the place even of these, but in my time a hind-staff in iron had been well developed and had no rivals.

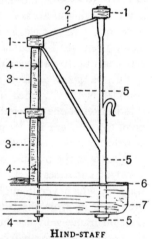

HIND-STAFF

1, section of ash rave; 2, iron copse; 3, ends of side-boards; 4, running pin; 5, hind-staff; 6, shutlock plate; 7, ash shutlock.

Yet this, at the best, was very insufficient. On farm-waggons it was insufficient even with two of them aside. A four-horse waggon was nearly three times as long as any cart, and required, as I have explained before, to be kept narrow at the waist for the sake of turning or "locking." But, seeing that the waist tried to bulge outwards, especially with the pressure of the load (three or four tons perhaps) inside, while also the frame-work spread at the tail as badly as in any two-wheel cart, the waggon was "stayed" with iron staves at the middle as well as at the tail.

As I have just said, however, something more was needed.

On either side of the middle staff every waggon had six or seven feet of raves, only too liable to sag outwards or "spread." To prevent this the waggon was buttressed by strouters—two before the middle bar and two behind it.

An iron strouter was a neat bit of blacksmithing, forged from round iron, and thicker at the bottom than at the top. It formed a good stay for the outer rave—the "outrave" as we called it—and it had an attractive air of lightness and strength. But it

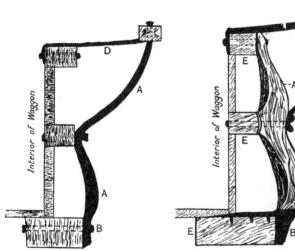

Iron Strouter (A—A) fastened with bolt (B) to main "side" of waggon or cart. It forms a stay for the outrave and supports the copse (D).

Wooden Strouter (A—A) in iron socket B, with iron stay C and iron copse D, fastened to timbers shown in section E, E, E, E.

rested all its support on the bolt which held it at the bottom, and this same bolt weakened the main timber with a hole right through it. Higher up the iron strouter was fastened with another bolt through the middle rave, and was a source of weakness there too, while it gave no support at all to the upper rave. The uses of a buttress were in fact all but gone from it.

The wooden strouter, which it superseded, had none of these disadvantages, only it looked a little more clumsy and cost more labour to put in. A bolt did indeed hold it—one small bolt through that top rave which the iron strouter failed to support at all, and this was, I think, a defect. I judge by the number of times in which I have seen a rave broken at that bolt-hole. But at least the strouter buttressed the waggon all the way up and not at expense of any weakness to the main "side." The socket it was driven into was but nailed on to the top of the main side, but it gave a firm support to the whole of the strouter, not piercing it anywhere, but clutching it all together as in the hollow of your hand. The lower end of the iron stay was secured to the strouter not by any bolt. A coach-screw (what we called a "nut-head") was enough. A nut-head did not make any dangerous hole through the bottom rave.

After hames, wooden strouters were the most strikingly beautiful things the wheelwright made. There may have been more delicacy in a well-shaved spoke, yet not for eyes so inexpert as mine. It seemed impossible not to admire strouters. Large and full they rose from their sockets, gracefully they tapered off to a fine slenderness at the top. They were like an excellent growth—like some living thing—so shapely. Every curve was lightened with bold shaving; the iron-work screwed to the middle of them was comfortable to see.

I never was quite man enough with the tools to finish a strouter myself, but many a one I have begun, chopping it into a peg at the lower end for driving down into the iron socket. It was driven down with a heavyish hand-hammer, and if little splinters from it curled away against the iron so much the better, for that meant that the wood would fit the iron tightly. Ash was the material—the middle of a broken cart shaft. All old shafts were carefully saved, to be cut into strouters. One was sure of a good straight grain, and tough too, out of a shaft.

When the thick piece of ash had been driven properly down into the socket, its upper part pressing inwards slightly against the two raves—the raves it was to buttress—their position was pencilled on to the strouter before it was knocked out again. (The strouter-socket, having the shape of a split flower pot, made it as easy to knock the strouter up as it had been laborious to drive it down.) Then the wheelwright went to work upon it once more with his axe. So the shape was roughly chopped out, to be finished with smoothing-plane and draw-shave.

The material for the iron-work of an old-fashioned strouter was almost as inexpensive as the wood-work. As sections of old shafts had been used for that, so, for the sockets, old cart tyres were chosen. When the old-iron merchant (sort of rag-and-bone man to our trade) came to clear away the waste—the old tyres, the bar-ends, the scrap, the cast— Will Hammond was careful to reserve a few tyres of just the needful size, for strouter-sockets. A set or two of sockets could be forged up at any odd time and kept in readiness—lest a call for them should come when the smith was busy at something else. The fashion of "beading" a strouter-socket, pretty though it looked, was already obsolete before my time, but the undecorated strouter-socket, forged out from a piece of an old tyre, was a nice bit of workmanship.

WROUGHT-IRON STROUTER-SOCKET, ready for nailing on to the main side of waggon or cart. The beading extending round the back from the two straps was a decoration omitted in later work.

The "straps" were turned at right angles to the socket itself and punched for nailing down to the wood-work (they were nailed on hot, for the better fitting), and at the base of the socket was a small hole for nailing the strouter when it had been hammered down into its place for the last time.

Dung-carts, though framed-up in their stiffer way, were still liable to spread, and had to have one strouter each side therefore. In its simpler style the dung-cart strouter was a most graceful thing, sweeping up from the socket in one curve to the top rail, there being no intervening rave. It was shaved-up out of ash, just as in the other case.

XXXIII

WILL HAMMOND[1]

The first and last thing to be noticed about "Old Will" the blacksmith was his deafness. If it had been absolute we should have approached him habitually in some different way and forgotten his affliction, but as he could, sometimes, just hear, so we always treated him as if he were normal and we were at once and all the time "up against" his trouble. He was only not absolutely deaf. There were some things he did hear, faintly; so that it was always worth while to try if he could hear what was said to him, or rather, shouted at him. His fellow-workmen alleged that, at his club "feast" (Will was a Forester) the place to find him was near the big drum, because there he was sure of enjoying the pleasure of hearing something for once. And, it is true, the experience of hearing did rejoice him. I remember finding him in the street one dinner-time chuckling and all smiles, because a cart was passing with an ungreased wheel. Will had actually heard its piercing shriek. And still, after many years, that glowing summer afternoon comes back to my memory because it was enriched by his smile.

His terrible deprivation, of many years standing, was something like a solitary confinement in its cruel effects on him. Most tender-hearted of men, he had not for very long heard an affectionate voice—for I do not think affection travels on a screaming shout, and it was in a screaming shout that even his wife and daughters had to speak to him. Of course, he by no means kept pace with the affairs of the day, nor could any new ideas about his work be conveyed to him. What he had learnt in his village boyhood he knew, and there it stopped.

For instance, passing a "male fern" in my garden, he turned to me solemnly to ask "Snake vairn?" using the old Surrey country talk, and so throughout. He rarely got a new idea. In his later years—during the Boer War—the nearest he could get

[1] Note K, p. 210.

to the name of Kruger was "Kroozer—or some sech name."
Though he lived for years in a Farnham alley, he failed to
pick up any of the manner even of a little country town. He
was all rustic. In hot weather he went slouching through the
streets (he had a "wound" in his leg) like a harvester, coat over
shoulder, shirt unbuttoned, short black pipe in mouth. At his
work, with his leather "apern," he was still a village man. I
heard weird country superstitions from him about horse-shoeing.
A faulty nail, which had had to be withdrawn from a hoof,
needed to be kept bright (in his pocket was the best place), lest,
going rusty, it should magically injure the horse's hoof. What
he didn't know about strakes and strake-nails was not worth
knowing; or about harrow-tines, or ironing-up wooden hames,
or clouts for wooden axles—all of them rustic things.

Certainly he was of the remote country—buried under old-
world notions—a follower of the crafts of Anglo-Saxon colonists
before the Conquest. Frensham ("Fruns'm") was his birth-
place, hard by Churt ("Cheert," as he called it) in the Surrey
wilds, below Hindhead. His father had been a husbandman in
that village, had fallen down dead while crossing the meadows
there—and that, Will thought, foretold what his own ending
would be. In the same cottage where he had been born his
mother kept the home together for his brother—now another
husbandman, as deaf as Will himself. Several times I saw the
mother—a black-haired and very handsome woman even at
that age; and several times I heard of the grape-vine on the
cottage walls. But the only wine I ever knew Will produce was
"elder-wine," though I think he sometimes spoke of "pa'snip-
wine."

He probably helped on the land until he was sixteen years old.
At that age he was apprenticed in my grandfather's Frensham
shop—managed in those days by my father's brother Richard.
For him Will seems to have conceived a strong liking, as I
realised long afterwards. On his death-bed, wandering in his
wits, the deaf old man spoke to me under the impression that I was
my own uncle, spoke friendly and happily, as if at some long-ago
village festival. To my own father he looked up with something

like veneration. Once (I was looking him up in his cottage in the alley) he narrated to me at great length how "the only row" he "ever had with 'n" was when my father—already failing for his last illness—insisted on "striking" at the anvil, to help Will making strake-nails. Will, seeing him distressed, urged him, as master, to take an easier place, namely at the bellows. But my father would none of it; answered only with masterful reproof. When at last he went away, the job being done, Will said sorrowfully to the other blacksmith, "There's our guv'nor bin and done for his-self."

There is reason to surmise that he had a taste for ritual, for ceremony—as so lofty-souled a man might well have. A sort of air—"swank" if you like—which he sometimes put into his hammering gives good ground for that surmise. He would frown, look important, take pains to show that he was being a good smith. To be sure, I used to regard this ostentation as a sort of sign-language, because talk was of so little use to him. But if so, it was in part a sign of his own feelings in need of dignified expression. The consciousness that this was so saved me from thinking the over-acting quite absurd. He could hammer with a silly air of importance and yet not look silly—only rather tragic. For did it not all mean that the man was very lonely, very hungry for that fellowship he would have found in ceremony if his infirmity had not shut him out from all ceremony?

From all—or all but all. One hour in the year there was when he could let himself go, and he did it with a gusto. It was on Christmas Eve. Whatever the day of the week it was the custom in my shop—perhaps my grandfather had introduced it there, perhaps my father—to have "a bit of a clear up" before shutting-up at sunset for Christmas. The woodmen scraped together their shavings, the yard was made tidy, and Will Hammond especially spread himself at sprinkling and sweeping the smithy. He was an unprofitably long time at the task, but by four o'clock, when the bell rang, his old shop was neat, orderly, spick-and-span, as if ready for the Prince of Peace himself to look in during the coming holiday. What Will thought about it all I do not know; yet if looks go for anything—if there was any meaning in the happy chirp of his voice .when we wished each other "A Merry Christmas"—he was feeling very blissful. Charles Dickens would have beheld him with great affection and esteem.

XXXIV

"JOBBING"

Those who had been duly apprenticed were wont to say, in my shop, that a man learnt more as an "Improver," in the first twelve months after his apprenticeship was over, than in all the six or seven years of "serving his time." Although there may have been some swank about this, I think there was some truth too. It was not only that an improver was liable to be discharged, and had to try at last to work well, if he had never tried before. This was what the skilled men chiefly meant, and it was true. A youth, turning from apprentice to improver, must now prove his worth or "get the sack." But more than this: experienced judgment was called for in many jobs that an apprentice could hardly be trusted to do, and this the elder men understood. The case was probably the same in other trades. A watch-maker assured me that, while it was comparatively easy for a youth at a technical school to learn how to make a new watch, the test of a true workman was at the repairing bench. Certainly this applied to wheelwrights. A machine could turn out a wheel—of sorts—but to mend one required, in many cases, long experience. Because this was so, I learnt to dislike employing either an old pensioner from the army or a young boy from a technical class. The soldier (besides being usually out of the habit of steady work) could not bring any experience of his own to bear and was afraid to move without orders. The army had killed his initiative. The boy, on the other hand, with no experience at all, was wont to think he already knew enough. He would not be told, and he was too vain to learn the lessons constantly coming from repairs.

From repairs, in fact, came the teaching which kept the wheelwrights' art strongly alive. A lad might learn from older workmen all about the tradition—all that antiquity had to teach —but at repairs he found out what was needful for the current day; what this road required, and that hill; what would satisfy Farmer So-and-So's temper, or suit his pocket; what the farmer's carter favoured or his team wanted. While "new-work" was largely controlled by proven theories and by well-tried fashions, on the other hand repairs called for ingenuity, adaptiveness, readiness to make shift. It wasn't quite enough to know how to do this or that; you needed also to know something about why, and to be ready to think of alternative dodges for improvising a temporary effect, if for any reason the time-honoured methods known to an apprentice could not be adopted.

You had to be prepared to cope with queer and inconvenient accidents—if a horse ran away and snapped a shaft, or turned a cart over, or if a tyre came off a wheel. Sometimes a message would come that a waggon-axle had broken asunder out at Where-is-it, a mile away, or Farmer What's-his-Name would send asking for a man because a dung-cart wheel was jammed and would not go round. In such cases, and their variety was legion, an apprentice would have been helpless. Nor would it do to send an army pensioner too timid to do the smallest detail without instructions. What was wanted was an experienced man, sure of himself and well versed in the use of odd apparatus and handy tackle for emergencies.

Such a man going to "pick-up" a break-down—a waggon on the road, say, with a wheel run off—would know what to take with him—a screw-jack, a "chopping-block" or two, several levers, an old wheel, perhaps a handful of oak wedges, one or two sledge-hammers—for it might well be that all these things would be wanted. And, reaching the break-down, he would know how to lever it to the road-side out of the way of other traffic, and how to scotch-up one side of it safely while he worked on the other side. With none of the conveniences of the shop at hand, he could improvise a bench, a vice. The road was his "wheel-block." A stone might serve a useful turn.

Perhaps the trouble was a cart brought to the shop with a wheel that wanted greasing, that squeaked hideously and seemed likely to catch fire with friction, yet refused to be taken off the arm. "Coomed-up" the wheelwright would say, possibly instead of gummed-up, but certainly meaning that the old grease, which should have been periodically cleaned away (any old sack would have served), had hardened into solid obstruction round the lynch-pin, or the collar, or the washers. Then the skilled man knew perfectly well how to turn the cart over, how to get his sledge-hammer to work without smashing the wheel, and, when he had got the wheel off, how to burn the old grease away from the axle-arm without spoiling the "temper" of the case-hardened iron.

Sometimes, in an ignorant attempt to correct "too much foreway," a carter had got the stock of a wheel so saturated with grease that the oak wedges no longer held and the cast-iron box, grown loose, had worn away too large a hole through the centre of the wheel. It fell to the wheelwright, then, first to fill up the superfluous space round the box; next, so to drive in new wedges that they would hold in spite of the grease; and, lastly, to find out what had been the origin of the mischief and to put it right. The employer had many other things to see to and could not always give personal attention to every one of these details. An experienced and self-reliant man was wanted.

While problems like these just instanced were common enough, other repairs, arising out of normal wear and tear, were part of the daily routine of the shop. This or that piece of iron-work, or of wood-work, had fairly worn out, or had been damaged and needed replacing. This it was especially that kept the ancient traditions still young and vigorous. For here the workman— whose apprenticeship had but brought him into contact with a skilled senior—came into contact with the forces of weather, of sun and rain and frost, of road-grit and horse-strength—the frictions and strains and stresses which are the inexorable law-givers to all crafts, in all time.

Day after day the work from this source—"jobbing-work" —came to the shop. Often the yard was crowded with carts and waggons brought in for some slight attention; though, to be sure, in bad winter weather whole days would go by when nothing—not so much as a wheelbarrow—came, and I began to wonder what to set the men at. In the first year or two this didn't matter so much. There were spokes to be dressed, felloes "turned out" by the sawyers to be shaped; the woodmen had enough to do. In after years the purchase of ready-shaped timber made winter a difficult season to get through, as no "short time" had ever been worked in my shop. The farmers never helped me out, in those circumstances. Truly exasperating it was. Sometimes I knew of a certain cart wanting a new wheel, a certain waggon with the boards worn out, a pair of shafts that would need a new "bolt" (cross-bar) before they could be used next spring. I knew where these things stood in their sheds, getting covered with dust, and I would suggest to their owners to let me have them now, in a slack time. Yet I don't remember ever getting any work that way[1]

But, by and by, when spring brought a change of weather and the shop was busy and the yard full, when the farmer wanted his wheel, or his waggon, or his decrepit shafts urgently by next day, then would come peremptory messages, unreasonable demands, to get the job done forthwith or it would be taken away to some other shop. Yet not seldom it happened that, after a job had actually been taken out of its proper turn and the owner notified, it would be left in the yard in the way for a week or two. In summer weather, though, there was not much time for grieving about such things. Every hour brought its fresh job, or saw some old one fetched away. Now and then some member of the staff, acting for me while I was myself busy, would make an inconvenient promise. Then he became unduly urgent about the job he had taken in, wanting to attend to it first. Or he had some favourite customer, or another had tipped him, or he had a fancy for doing this tailboard, that splinter-bar, rather than the wheel I wanted him to repair next. These, however, were but problems of management. They did not affect the problems of wear and tear, which taught more than the apprentice could be shown.

[1] See also p. 43 and Note L, p. 210.

These were so various—each illustrating some detail in the craft—it is hard to choose amongst them. Much might be told about repairs to shafts. Hardly a day passed without some of this. For instance, when a horse was being "shut-in" (backwards, of course) it was only too liable to set a heavy hind hoof on the fore end of a shaft and cause it to "spring." The only thing to do then was to splice the shaft. As this involved taking out the iron-work the opportunity was seized of mending it in the blacksmith's fire before it was put back. Did the hooks want lining? Would the ridge-tie serve another turn, or were its links getting so thin as to make a new ridge-tie necessary? Nothing but experience could instruct one on these matters. It was useful experience again—it taught a lot about shafts—to watch Will Hammond with his tongs, winding and nailing a red-hot "wroppin-cleat" as he called it—a narrow band of hooping—round each end of a splice. He knew, if you didn't, just where the strength was wanted.

Shafts had to be spliced, sometimes, not because of any break but because, lasting too long, they had actually worn sharp at the points from being dropped down on to the ground so often. It was enough to make you shudder to see a horse shut-in to shafts like that. He had but to stumble sideways and the ash would pierce his shoulder like a sharpened stake. But, though humanity counselled splicing, there were several details to consider. Perhaps it would suffice just to saw off the dangerous end and round-up the stump a little? In no case must the shaft be made so long or so short as to wear into the horse-collar; a consideration that showed why new shafts and shaft-planks were sawed out to a certain length. At the same time it became clear why just that curve was chosen for them. The shafts, having approached the horse's shoulders and collar conveniently close, were better turned away again slightly, just at the very end.

Whenever a farm-waggon was brought in for general overhaul and painting quite a number of fittings unattached to the main structure needed looking to. To say nothing of the extra pair of shafts, with "false splinter-bar" for hanging double shafts (for two horses side by side), a well appointed waggon would have two detachable "ladders"—for extending its fifteen feet or so to, say, twenty feet. This spelt hay-making, or corn or straw-carting; and often the ladders proved to need a new "key" or cross-piece. A split ash pole would do; it didn't matter about being very straight, so long as it could be slender and light, yet tough. The waggon also had a drug-bat and chain (for skidding the wheel when going down hill) and a roller-scotch (we never called it anything but plain roller) for up hill. Scotch and skid were alike fitted for the near hind-wheel; that being the wheel handiest for the waggoner, walking that side of his horses.

The repairs to "rollers" are singularly pleasant to remember, so suggestive are they of summer and country roads. The roller was a little cylinder of elm—about eight inches long by three

Dog-stick, to be hooked behind a cart (2 wheels) axle when going up hill, so that, in the event of a stoppage, the fork at the end may immediately stick into the road and prevent the cart from running back.

inches in diameter—hanging at the back of a waggon so as to be let down as a scotch for the hind-wheel, going up hill. Whenever the horses wanted to stop for a rest, there was the roller ready to keep the load from running backwards, for it followed the hind-wheel at not more than three or four inches away. Carts (two-wheeled vehicles) never used this apparatus. Cart-drivers would pick up a stone by the road-side to serve the same purpose; or sometimes (not often) a "dog-stick" was supplied to them, to hook on to the cart axle-bed when going up hill, and drag along, prong-like, behind. When the horse stopped the dog-stick immediately dug back into the road-surface—which must have been bad for the road if helpful to the horse.

But the waggon, or any heavy four-wheel, had a roller, swinging down from the hind axle, out of the way when not in use. At the bottom of the hill the roller was easily unhooked on one side and brought round (to be hooked then, on a swivel, to the front of the stock) so as to trundle along on the ground, close behind the near-wheel. It trundled on an iron spindle, this

spindle being attached to two light "roller-cheeks," and each of
them to a slender chain about three feet long each side. The elm
core was itself cased in three iron bonds.

And you saw why, when it came to repairs. You felt as if
you were on a dusty road then.
For road-dust lay in the wheel-
track which the roller so closely
followed; hot summer road-dust
rose in clouds from the horse-
hoofs and smothered the roller.
No doubt there was sometimes
mud, yet that was not what you
thought of when you saw the
roller, or at any rate what I remember now. It must have been
dust—the dry soft powder of hot
weather—that had polished the

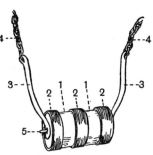

ROLLER-SCOTCH

1, elm roller; 2, iron bonds;
3, cheeks; 4, chains; 5, spindle.

bonds bright and thin, and worn away the elm between them and
made the spindle shine.

And then, as you looked at the chain and the cheeks, with
the holes worn so big and the iron so thin (surely the blacksmith
would have to "cut and shut" those cheeks?), in fancy you were
aware of the going of the waggon, the step of the horses along
the lonely and interminable country roads. For those links,
those cheek-ends worn so thin, told of the dangling roller,
swing-swing, mile after mile. Of course my fancy is foolish. Often
the roller must have swung so on a starlight night or a rainy
winter morning; but then, I never saw it so. What I did sometimes see was a farm-waggon trailing along in the dust with
summer light glinting on the dry roller-irons, as the roller (with
a bucket beside it) swayed and swung on the hind exbed.

XXXV

"CUTTING AND SHUTTING"

Other things being equal, summer was better than winter for making and tyring a wheel. No matter how well-seasoned the timbers were, still they shrunk in dry summer air and swelled out again in winter rains. In the long days the stock of the wheel shrivelled a little, the shakes along it (there were always shakes in a really good stock) visibly opened wider, and the fibres of the elm could therefore be pressed tighter together when at last the tyre was shrunk on; so that then was the time for putting-on the stock-bonds. There was less fear of their shaking loose in years to come, if they were properly fixed in summer.

Men who used carts knew something about the advantages of a little moisture for tightening wheels. Not for the horse's sake alone was it that carters would drive through a road-side pond, or choose to ford a stream rather than go over a bridge beside the ford. The wheels were better for the wetting. Very careful countryfolk—with but one cart to cherish perhaps, and that a donkey-cart—would keep a wet sack over the wheel on the sunny side for the same reason that made me, when the sun was most blazing, throw wet sacks over the water-butts in my yard, the object in my case being to keep the staves from shrinking and falling apart.

But, while water-butts might be filled or at any rate could be kept covered all day, wheels could not be so protected. For hours at a time they might have to travel, in full sunshine, over scorching roads, when the tyres grew so hot you couldn't bear your hand on them; and at such times it was a pity if the wheelwright did not learn a thing or two about wheels hardly to be picked up otherwise.

One obvious thing was that the tyres were getting loose. Before ever your eyes saw the wheels your ears might have heard that something was wrong. Though I never pretended to be able, like some of the men in the shop, to distinguish certainly what state a tyre was in by listening to a smart hammer blow on it, I did, in the course of years, learn to discern in a second the curious jangling noise on the road of a loose tyre. Yards away I knew it. It never deceived me. It was almost as sure a sign that summer had come as to hear strawberries hawked about the town. As sure as May set in hot, the wheels everywhere began their queer scrunching yet ringing chackle. They could no more help it than I could help hearing it and interpreting it as "tyre loose."

What to do, then, was a question for experience to decide; or it should have been. Some owners, it is true, were sure enough of themselves to give definite orders, which was about as wise as it would be to tell a doctor what medicine he should give you if you felt an illness coming. The experienced wheelwright was in fact a professional and most people were prudent enough to be advised by him when a tyre was loose.

The symptoms that guided him were not few. As the tyre had ceased to tie the wheel together, everything—stock-bonds, spokes, felloes—was slackening in its place, was beginning to fret and chafe against the thing nearest, and would soon do serious mischief unless checked. Look at the spokes. Drawing, each one, a hair's breadth out of the supporting stock, and each trying, as it were, at every revolution, to hold up the whole load without dependence on its neighbours, the spokes were, one and all, a little o'erparted. Looking closely, you could see where, in here and there one, a tiny crack was showing at the back, just where the spoke is thinned-down for mortising into the stock. This was conceivably a sign that the tyre had been put on over-tight months ago, when the wheel was new (but the spokes were likelier to bend, then, than to begin breaking); or it may have shown that the wheel had got out of gear in running; but what-ever the cause, there at last, at the back of spoke after spoke, was a minute black fissure you could hardly get a hair into, yet sure sign that the wheel was going wrong. A tightening of the tyre might suffice if the disease were dealt with in time; otherwise it would be necessary to take the wheel to pieces far enough to renew some of the spokes, or even to stiffen it by putting in every other one new.

The drawing-out of spokes when the rim had been taken off was an engaging piece of work. The wheel, thrown face-downwards across a wheel-block, lay at about the level of the workman's knees. His axe was the tool he used for taking out the spokes, whichever of two courses he chose. The simpler way was to chop a deep notch in the back of the spoke (heart of oak, you know) so as to give him something to hammer at, after which he turned the axe over in his hands and used it as a sledge for driving the spoke out of the mortised stock. But that was a wasteful thing to do with spokes, for the notch spoilt too much of the heart, and usually the spoke was worth getting out whole. For this, a stiff iron ring—oblong in shape—was slipped over it and tightened with an oak wedge. Then the man fell to work on the wedge, smiting it (away from the stock) heavily with the back of his axe. Something had to give way. And since the wedge was heart of oak, and did but grow tighter in the iron ring the more it was smitten, there was no alternative but for the spoke to draw out bodily (ring and wedge and all) from the mortice that had held it so long.

Now and then (not often) a drawn-out spoke was found to have been enlarged with a thin piece added to the foot to make it fit its mortice. Such a discovery told tales. Too plainly some beginner had made that wheel. Too plainly he had cut his mortice too big, or the foot of the spoke too small, and had been obliged to tack on a tiny addition. These additions, to make tenons fit mortices too large for them, were sardonically called "prentices" by the smiling seniors.

Spokes went wrong also at the other end, namely in the rounded "tongue" which fitted, like a peg, into the felloe or wooden rim. Sometimes the tongue snapped right off, leaving the spoke quite loose at that end. And, as it was not always expedient to take the wheel to pieces, the spoke was then fixed to the felloe with small iron hold-fasts, called "dogs," one at each side. This served for a time, but at best it was but a poor makeshift. If anyhow possible it was better to put in a new spoke.

But almost always the real mischief was in the felloes. Neither would the spokes have shifted, nor the iron tyre itself have loosened, if the wooden rim had never moved. But that could not be. Ash, elm, beech—the felloes, whatever they were, now were covered with mud, now dried up with dust; this minute almost shrivelling under the sun-hot tyre; the next, swelling in the sudden water of the ford. In short, from one cause or another, the fibres of the timber of felloes were constantly on the move, until at last the felloes began to wear against the very tyre which should have tied the wheel tight and shod it. Meanwhile, the tyre itself, not wearing much inside from its friction with the wood-work, was constantly getting thinner on the outside, where it touched the road. From three-quarters of an inch thick a waggon-tyre wore down to three-eighths; but by then it was time to call in the expert, for tyre and felloes too were chafing each other badly.

The very first thing of all was to take the wheel off. This meant blocking up the axle, if it was a waggon wheel involved, taking care to trig the other wheels lest the waggon should try to run away meanwhile minus a wheel. In case of a two-wheel, the cart might be propped up or turned right over. But in every case the object was the same, namely, to swing the faulty wheel free of the ground, so that, after its lynch-pin had been knocked out, it could be "run" to the blacksmith's. If both wheels had to come off, care was taken to mark them, "near" and "off," so as to replace them on the right side by and by.

A strong lad could do all this. But, now, an experienced blacksmith was wanted, to "cut" the tyre off. Finding out where it had been "shut" when new, he held his rod-chisel firmly there, for the lad to smite down on it with a sledge-hammer until suddenly the old shut sprang right asunder. This was what we called "cutting." Pedants might talk of "shrink-ing" a tyre; that was the aim. But the blacksmith named the process when he said "cut and shet," and the cutting was done as I have described. It was not, indeed, invariably necessary. Sometimes a tyre hung so loose that it dropped off. Sometimes —but this alternative must wait. Take it that in ninety-nine cases out of a hundred the loose tyre had to be cut. Even then it required freeing from the rim. The wheel, which had lain prone on the anvil for the sledge-hammer work, was now dropped bump, to the ground; and the tyre (still hanging by the nails) was levered away from the rim with two iron bars which the lad held, one in each hand. Then he knocked out the old nails, chalked tyre and wheel so as to know which tyre belonged to which wheel, and stood them up ready for expert inspection.

Inspection was likely to discover some curious things that had been happening. The wood-work, though protected by the tyre, had been wearing away under it. Yet not evenly. The felloes, with the grain of the wood lying more or less parallel to the tyre, had lost a little more than the spokes which came through them

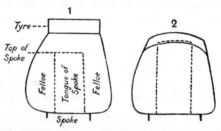

1, Section of new wheel-rim with new tyre; 2, section of worn wheel-rim with old tyre, chafing upon tongue of spoke.

and met the tyre "end on." This was one odd thing. The spoke-ends were inclined to protrude.

Another odd thing was that the wear of the felloes was by no means level all across, from front to back. On the contrary, the whole rim was rounded now. It rose up in the middle in the shape of a halfpenny bun, and, what was most remarkable, the tyre had hollowed over to fit it. Its original flatness had disappeared.

What was the explanation? Though I never could be quite sure, I think what happened was that dust had found its way in from the outside, and, as fast as the wood wore away, the iron bent down over it. Whatever the cause, this was the effect. While the wood grew rounded, the tyre tended to grow hollow. Sometimes it was too hollow to be got on again, and, willy nilly, the customer had to be put to the expense of a brand-new tyre. But sometimes it was not so bad as that. It only wanted shutting up again where it had been cut, but, of course, tighter than before.

Just here, the process being identical with that for shutting a new tyre, the "traveller" (described on p. 122) came into use again. And first, the outside circumference round the rim of the wheel had to be ascertained; yet even this could not be done until that roundness caused by the dust had been chopped away to make the felloes level again, as when new, and the protruding spokes cut out.

This operation, called "soling down" the wheel (in preparation for putting on its shoe), was for the skilled wheelwright. Taking an old axe (for grit in the felloes might have spoilt the edge of his own sharper tool) he leant the wheel against a post, and then (with a boy—or me perhaps—to steady the wheel with hands and foot) he chopped the rim level all round. He also gouged out the ends of the spokes, lest they should protrude too much against the inside of the tyre, and thereby keep it away from the sole. Further, the felloe-joints needed looking to and perhaps opening half-an-inch or so, lest presently they should close up before the cooling tyre had forced all the spokes back into place. When all this had been prepared, and not until then, the smith could measure round the wheel so as to shut up the tyre to proper tightness. It will be easily seen that, in the course of years, a wheel-rim thus dust-worn and chopped away grew very shallow. It looked wizened, like the jaws of a toothless old man. In these circumstances felloes all round were wanted, strong enough to carry a load.

So far, I have assumed that wear and tear left the rim otherwise sound and strong. In fact, however, that was not often the case. Felloes were always getting into the wars, always being broken, or losing their curve under an over-load, or splitting at the joint. The commonest trouble with them was a crack just at their weakest part, namely where they had been bored for the spokes. For this there was no remedy but to put in a new felloe; and not seldom all the felloes had to be renewed, for one reason or another. The wheel, as we said, wanted a new "ring." If this was seen betimes, the trouble of cutting off the tyre was spared, for the wheelwright split out the doomed felloes and the tyre dropped away. Usually however it had to be cut asunder afterwards, for shutting up again at the proper size for the new "ring" of felloes now put on. In the rather rare case of a tyre being too tight for the wheel instead of too loose, it could be "drawn" (stretched) slightly with a "fuller." The fuller was a rod-tool for holding on the inside of a red-hot tyre and corrugating it (under sledge-hammer strokes) until the necessary circumference of tyre had been obtained.

Many more things might be told about the flaws, the diseases of wheels and about the experience and skill involved in curing them. Yet this is not a handbook for mending wheels. No monograph after all could teach that art. It was for the hands and eyes to learn first in years of apprenticeship; and then for the judgment to follow up, summer after summer. In my own case judgment had so much exercise during so many years as almost to supply the perception that no youthful training had given. Yet not quite. There were some mysteries about wheels I have never fathomed to this day, and now the old art is dying out.

As I have said just above, summer was the time for repairing wheels—they were brought jangling to the shop by the score in dry weather. That too was the season for most other repairs— when boards twisted and all shakes tried to open wider to the heat of the sun. Yet one accident there was which I do not remember happening at all save in very cold weather. Twice or three times, if not more, intense frost caused cart-axles to snap like glass; and I think once or twice a hop-ground digger, impatient to believe the frozen ground soft enough for his work, brought his "spud" and waited by my smithy fire while his friend the blacksmith repaired a snapped tine.

And more than once or twice, in cold weather, a shy tapping called me to my office door, to find some little boy there with a penny and "Please sir can I have my hoop mended?" He was directed to the blacksmith's shop where they knew how to shut up a hoop.

XXXVI

SUNDRY IMPLEMENTS

An order once reached me, I cannot remember from whom it came, for a new nib or neb; so I walked to Moor Park or a farm near it, to measure one of these implements I knew to be in that neighbourhood. When I reached the foreman—a stranger to me—and asked if I might look at his nib, a comical peppery expression went over his face, as if he felt he was being insulted; and then I became rather painfully aware that he had a big and fiery nose. I promptly reassured him. What I wished to see was his "timber-bob" or "pair of wheels."

A neb was, in fact, a pair of wheels and not much else, chiefly used for shifting a heavy "stick" or butt of timber out of an awkward place into a handier one. I had a smallish one in my timber-yard, for the sawyers; but its dimensions were no guide to follow. Its wheels for one thing were not more than five feet two high, and comparatively slight, whereas, on most nebs, the wheels, if not higher in diameter, were wider of tyre than was needed in the fairly solid soil of my yard. I wanted to be sure, for I had no spokes and felloes for wide and high wheels, and perhaps no arms strong enough for heavy wheels to run on.

For of course "a pair of wheels" had to run on "arms." In old days these were of wood, cut out of one piece of beech or oak, solid with the axle between them; but in my time they were of case-hardened iron, bedded into a short connecting "exbed." On top this exbed or axle was strengthened and heightened by a "riser" of elm or beech; and this was about all, excepting shafts or a pole for hauling the contrivance along when the tree had been slung up between the wheels.

The principle of loading was simple and ingenious. The neb was pushed back to the middle of the tree, straddling over it with one wheel on each side. There, its shafts being lifted towards the sky, the riser atop of the axle lay back almost on the tree. So, a stout chain round the tree easily reached the riser and was hooked on to it. But when the skyward-pointing shafts were pulled down again for hauling, they brought the riser upright and the tree rose with it, clear of the ground. Two or three strong men could generally do this. You see, the length of the shafts gave a good leverage.

As even six-foot wheels would not otherwise have taken more than a three-foot tree in between them, more room was obtained by curving up the axle or exbed. A tree too big even for that could hardly have been got home to a saw-pit at all; at any rate it would have been more profitable to dig a saw-pit under it and cut it up where it lay. This is what my father once did with an elm at Tilford. No neb would have spanned it: no timber-carriage could have got it to Farnham. It was for smaller trees than this that the neb was useful.

As it was chiefly on large estates that nebs were wanted, the demand for them was not great. Timber-carriages were a little more plentiful. Besides the farmer who carted my little lots for me, several builders kept timber-carriages of their own, as did also one or two timber-merchants. Repairs fairly often came my way therefore, but when a new pole was wanted the owner would often furnish the material himself—in pine, perhaps—as I had no ash or oak big enough, long enough, straight enough; and it was by no means worth my while to prepare stock for so infrequent a need.

Excepting for its much heavier dimensions, a timber-carriage was not very different from a waggon with the body taken off. Two or three small ones were built at the shop in my time, but I never had much to do with a big one, with its massive wheels. The pillars (pillows?) on which the load rested were lined, on top, with stout iron bars, notched all along to give a purchase for levers when it came to pushing the trees off.

Amongst other implements out of the common but occasion-ally made in my shop, wheelbarrows especially designed for a washing factory may be just mentioned. They were built wholly of oak, to be more resistant of wet; and no paint was allowed on them. Again, a firm of horse-slaughterers now and then wanted a new "knacker's cart." There was nothing special about building these carts save to imitate an older one, by whom designed I do not know. Perhaps the oldest thing about a knacker's cart was the smell of it, which however was supplied from the slaughtering factory. I don't think it was this piece of antiquity that (in after years) caused King Edward's (or perhaps it was King George's) swift motor-car to go at a walking pace past my old shop. An English knacker's cart had halted in the street and I was measuring for new wheels for it when the King of England passed, on some incognito military errand from Aldershot. Did he ever smell such a smell before, I wonder? Did he know that feature of his country?

Now and then we had to mend a water-barrel—a barrel on cart wheels—for some sheepfold probably. Not that we knew anything of barrels themselves; but if an existing barrel needed a new hopper, or new hoops for fastening it to the framework, or new boards for a man to stand on at the sides—if anything like this was wanted, to whom should the barrel be sent save the local wheelwright? He had the elm board for the hopper, the iron for the hoops; he employed a wood-worker, a smith; he could look to the wheels, or splice the shafts; certainly the wheelwright was the man. So, water-barrels came to me for attention. Though I forget the details, I often remember—as one of my first and pleasantest jobs at the shop—pottering about a water-barrel along with a skilled man (my friend now), fitting a new hopper, I think. It is a pleasant memory—the colour of the boards, the warm August afternoon, the sound of hammering— my own hammering—thundering along the sleepy street; the intercourse, still at that time so strange to me, with the good-tempered confidence of a skilled workman.

Just because we, in my father's shop, were skilful in wood and iron, men cunning at other crafts looked to us for the sort of help we specialised in. It was not solely for wheels and farm-work that the local wheelwright's experience was called in. A baker came to me to make him a new peel; for who else was so likely to have the long tough ash he wanted, or to be able to get it cut out and planed and shaved? Similarly, I was called upon to supply a potato-mill. The elm boards, and the beech for the drum, well-seasoned, lay in my shed: the wheelwright and the blacksmith had the tools and the skill to embody in wood and iron my customer's idea. Or, to come to an end, now and then I supplied a new beatle, or beetle, for a customer wanting to split wood.

A beetle (pronounced bittle, to rhyme to spittle), with a set of wedges, was the recognised tool for cleaving any timber, whether straight-grained oak for spokes or a cross-grained and crooked stamm of any tree for firewood. Fascinating work this was, by the way. With the wedges cleaving down between the clinging fibres—as he let out the wood-scent, listened to the tearing splitting sounds—the workman found his way into a part of our environment—felt the laws of woodland vitality—not otherwise visited or suspected. No professional person ever dreamt of that strange world; no sawyer even got there. Intellect might hear of it; but the senses alone can know, and none may tell, what the world is like down there in the grain of the oak butt, the fir-tree stamm. A man must explore it for himself, with his wedges, watching what happens as he drives them down.

As the wedges explain the sort of beetle I sometimes supplied, they must be described. The number I used myself was four: three of iron and one of oak. Of the former, two were each about as big as three matchboxes put end to end, a trifle thicker, perhaps, at the top, but of course drawn down "to nothing" at the other end. The third iron wedge—thinner, shorter, rather wider, something like a small axe-blade in fact—was rather for cleaving spokes than for general use, and need not be further considered. Of the other two already described, one was driven into the timber until level with it; and then, if need be, its fellow was put in beside it, thus doubling the opening. If, even so, the block remained obstinate and would not fall asunder, it was time to put in the oak wedge, longer than either of the others and thicker than the two of them together.

Even this oak wedge involved more experience than might be thought. I used to chop a wedge for myself with an axe, from a chosen bit of oak; but when, years afterwards, my sawyer tried to saw one on his saw-bench, I found that he did not know what oak to choose. The saw had never taught him what was to be learnt with axe and chopping-block. Moreover, he sawed the wedge too finely thin, so that the end snapped off. A properly chopped oak wedge never snapped, though it sometimes split. The sap of the stuff that was being cleft—which, if green oak for spokes, stained the wedge an inky blue—seemed to get polished sometimes, so that when you would drive the wedge farther in it sprang out into the air, pinched out by the clinging fibres. If the wedge was chalked at such times, there was less danger of its jumping and hitting you in the eye. Or it might be rubbed in the dusty ground.

But now, to return to the beetle—seeing that the two iron wedges might want driving far down into the block, it would never do to have them smashed and ragged at the top. To obviate this, they were made originally slightly rounded just there where the blow fell on them. But even so the iron soon battered down, if a sledge-hammer was used on it. Yet the weight, if not the hardness, of a sledge was wanted; and this the beetle gave. A beetle was really a heavy and long-handled wooden mallet, substitute for a sledge-hammer.

The head of it was a cylinder eight or nine inches long by about five inches through. At the exact half-way the cylinder was pierced by an ash handle, small enough at one end to go easily through the head, but at the other end so big that, after getting tighter and tighter, at last it would not go in any farther. The advantage was soon apparent to the workman. The more he swung the beetle the tighter it became. Yet, to make assurance doubly sure, a small wedge was also inserted, to keep the head from flying off. A nasty thing, this. It happened once in my experience; when the head of a badly-made beetle went whirling up into the air. As I was not present, but only heard of the mishap afterwards, I did not have to run.

It was not everybody who knew how to make a beetle-head, simple though it looked. To prevent it from splitting a strong iron ring was hammered over each end tight enough not to fly off easily, yet not so tight as not to be slowly forced back towards the middle. For, with continually banging down upon the iron wedges, the wooden beetle-head was slowly wearing back upon its own rings—battering over them and forcing them back too. Therefore it had to be of an equal tightness all along, or even a shade tighter the farther it wore back; and yet if the head was too big, too tight, in the middle, so that the rings could drive back no farther, then by and by one of them would come off altogether.

The idea was to choose for the beetle-head such wood as would batter back over the ring and not splinter wholly away. The best for this purpose, they said, was the timber of an apple-tree; but I never tried it. Beech was a good substitute—though not such beech, ill-seasoned, as was all that could be obtained recently. That was about as tough as a biscuit. The worst wood for a beetle was elm, which was too cross-grained to curl back over the iron rings.

THE OLD ORDER CHANGING

XXXVII. *Prices*

XXXVII

PRICES

It has been already explained how, having no other guidance, I priced the work to my customers by my father's and my grandfather's charges, making schedules of figures from an old ledger. This plan was only not quite disastrous because, as also has been explained, there was in fact a local traditional price for new work and new parts, which nobody dared to exceed. This much was painfully proved to me long afterwards. A certain standard cart, I ascertained, was being sold throughout the neighbourhood at less than cost price. Accordingly I tried to get sundry rivals to join me in raising the price. One of these however made the project known to a good customer of mine and succeeded in getting that customer's work away from me. This was one of the many occasions when I should have welcomed pressure from a strong Trade Union, to compel other employers to make the changes I could not introduce alone.

My father had probably known for years how unprofitable some of the trade was. New work, he used to say, did not pay. Even in his time, and under his able management, it was only worth doing at all for the sake of keeping the staff together and getting the "jobbing"—the repairs; for, as there could be no standard in them, it was still possible to make a profit at jobbing. On the subject of profits other tradesmen in the district were as ignorant and simple as myself. Although Farnham fancied itself a little town, its business was being conducted in the spirit of the village—almost indeed of the mediaeval manor. Men worked to oblige one another. Aldershot was almost as bad; Alton was if possible worse; and the most conservative village in the whole neighbourhood set the rate to which my own trade lived down. I doubt if there was a tradesman in the district—I am sure there was no wheelwright—who really knew what his output cost, or what his profits were, or if he was making money or losing it on any particular job. In later years, after the habit of giving estimates had become common (as it was unknown in 1884), I several times lost work to rivals who, I found out, were working for less than the mere iron and timber were to cost them. They never knew. Nor did they know if on to-morrow's estimate they were to make a fabulous profit. Well on into the present century these matters, in my trade, were settled by guess-work, not by calculation. We knew nothing, thought nothing, of how much we ought to have. But it was very needful to know how much our customer would pay.

This strange way of conducting business had possibly worked out well enough, say in Queen Anne's time when the shop was founded. In the course of generations errors would get corrected and a reasonable charge standardised. Neighbours, with little or no competition, would find out the fair prices of things and not dream of departing from them. Even in my grandfather's day the traditional prices would often hold good. Then, there were no "overhead" expenses—rates, fire-insurance, railway carriage, office charges, and so on—to compare with those of the present century. The wages left the employer a good margin. Thus, my grandfather paid but 17s. a week where my father paid 24s. Materials cost less[1].

But by the time I dropped into the business many changes had begun. Some of the old work was growing obsolete, unexampled work was coming into vogue all round. Not only was it that "The Iron Age" (as already pointed out) was on the move again, after years of quiescence. Better roads, and imported foodstuffs too, broke up the old farm-life on which my shop had waited. Instead of waggons, vans to run twice as fast were wanted, and their springs and brakes and lighter wheels revolutionised the industry my men had taught me. At the same time the break-down of village industries was introducing changes which were reflected in my shop in the shape of butchers' carts and bread-carts—unknown of old—and in brewers' drays and in millers' vans, not to mention vehicles for bricks and other building materials.

While novelties were pouring in upon the trade from one

[1] Note M, p. 211.

side, on the other side an unexampled competition began to be felt, keeping the prices still low. Things were not as in the pre-railway days. Now, discontented customers would buy "steam wheels" from London. Lighter wheels than any that could be made in my shop—wheels imported ready-made from America—had to be kept in stock along with the ancient sort of naves and felloes. But the prices were effectually kept down also by competition of another sort, or rather of a very ancient sort. Dorset villages, Wiltshire villages, entered into the rivalry. Thanks to their lower wages and rents, and their far less costly timber, places one had never heard of were able to supply local farmers at so cheap a rate that it was worth the farmers' while to ignore, or to sacrifice, the advantage of vehicles made locally with a view to local conditions. The circle of my competitors widened out by hundreds of miles.

In all these circumstances it is not wonderful that the price of wheelwright's work by no means kept pace with the cost of it. To tell the truth, the figures in my shop in 1884 (as extracted by myself from the old books) were not much in excess of those which Arthur Young found current in the southern counties in 1767[1]. For a waggon the price had risen from about £21 then, to £29 or £30 in my father's time; but carts, which at the later date were but £12 or less, had averaged as much as £10 even a century earlier.

Conceivably a man in so small a way of business as to do much of his work himself—and this must have been the case with many a village wheelwright—could make both ends meet even at these prices, even in 1884; and this the more if he got "job-bing" work to keep him going and to confuse his calculations. I knew one man who threw up a situation he had held for years in a rival's shop—probably under the impression that it was a profitable thing to be an employer even without capital; and began building new carts for a pound or so less than the local price. I am fairly certain that he kept no accounts to show him how much less his profits amounted to now than his weekly wages had been of old. Perhaps he never would have known

[1] *Six Weeks' Tour*, etc., 3rd edition, *passim*.

this had there been plenty of repairs for him to do; but as it was, he had to close-down within twelve months, being too honest a man to profit by bankruptcy.

In these circumstances it is not surprising that I began at last to feel a need of some change or other. It is true, I knew nothing about "Costing." Methods for that were not devised until years later; but, in the simpler things, I did after four or five years—say in 1889—know well enough that some of the work was not paying its way—was even being done at a loss. Yet too often I saw work going elsewhere which I felt ought to have come to me. And one thing, if not certain, was probable: under my ignorant management the men had grown not so much lazy as leisurely. I knew this but too well; but I did not know how to mend the matter. Too early, indeed, I had realised how impossible it would be to carry out any of the Ruskinian notions, any of the fantastic dreams of profit-sharing, with which I had started. The men in the shop, eaten up with petty jealousies, would not have made any ideals work at all. But to discharge them was not to be thought of. How could I even find fault with those who had taught me what little I knew of the trade and who could but be only too well aware how little that was? Moreover, they were my friends. Business was troublesome enough even on the best of terms, but I could not have found the heart to go on with it all at the cost of the friction which must have come if I had begun trying to "speed-up" my friends and instructors. Meanwhile, none the less, the trade these friends of mine depended on for a living was slipping away, partly by their own fault.

What was to be done? How long I thought it over is more than I can at all tell now; but eventually—probably in 1889—I set up machinery: a gas-engine, with saws, lathe, drill and grind-stone. And this device, if it saved the situation, was (as was long afterwards plain) the beginning of the end of the old style of business, though it did just bridge over the transition to the motor-trade of the present time.

I suppose it did save the situation. At any rate there was no need for dismissals, and after a year or two there was trade enough—of the more modern kind—to justify my engaging a foreman, whom I ultimately took into partnership. It proved a wise move from every point of view save the point of sentiment. The new head had experience and enterprise enough, without offending the men too, to develop the new commercial side—the manufacture of trade-vans and carts—when the old agricultural side of the business was dying out. Wood-work and iron-work were still on equal terms. Neither my partner nor myself realised at all that a new world (newer than ever America was to the Pilgrim Fathers) had begun even then to form all around us; we neither of us dreamt that the very iron age itself was passing away or that a time was actually near at hand when (as now) it would not be worth any young man's while to learn the ancient craft of the wheelwright or the mysteries of timber-drying. It might be that improved roads and plentiful building were changing the type of vehicles wheelwrights would have to build; but while horses remained horses and hill and valley were hill and valley, would not the old English provincial lore retain its value? We had no provocation to think otherwise, and yet:—

And yet, there in my old-fashioned shop the new machinery had almost forced its way in—the thin end of the wedge of scientific engineering. And from the first day the machines began running, the use of axes and adzes disappeared from the well-known place, the saws and saw-pit became obsolete. We forgot what chips were like. There, in that one little spot, the ancient provincial life of England was put into a back seat. It made a difference to me personally, little as I dreamt of such a thing. "The Men," though still my friends, as I fancied, became machine "hands." Unintentionally, I had made them servants waiting upon gas combustion. No longer was the power of horses the only force they had to consider. Rather, they were under the power of molecular forces. But to this day the few survivors of them do not know it. They think "Unrest" most wicked.

Yet it must be owned that the older conditions of "rest" have in fact all but dropped out of modern industry. Of course wages are higher—many a workman to-day receives a larger income than I was ever able to get as "profit" when I was an employer. But no higher wage, no income, will buy for men that satisfaction which of old—until machinery made drudges of them—streamed into their muscles all day long from close contact with iron, timber, clay, wind and wave, horse-strength. It tingled up in the niceties of touch, sight, scent. The very ears unawares received it, as when the plane went singing over the wood, or the exact chisel went tapping in (under the mallet) to the hard ash with gentle sound. But these intimacies are over. Although they have so much more leisure men can now taste little solace in life, of the sort that skilled hand-work used to yield to them. Just as the seaman to-day has to face the stoke-hole rather than the gale, and knows more of heat-waves than of sea-waves, so throughout. In what was once the wheelwright's shop, where Englishmen grew friendly with the grain of timber and with sharp tool, nowadays untrained youths wait upon machines, hardly knowing oak from ash or caring for the qualities of either. And this is but one tiny item in the immensity of changes which have overtaken labour throughout the civilised world. The products of work are, to be sure, as important as ever—what is to become of us all if the dockers will not sweat for us or the miners risk their lives? That civilisation may flourish a less-civilised working-class must work. Yet others wonder at working-class "unrest." But it remains true that in modern conditions work is nothing like so tolerable as it was say thirty years ago; partly because there is more hurry in it, but largely because machinery has separated employers from employed and has robbed the latter of the sustaining delights which materials used to afford to them. Work is less and less pleasant to do—unless, perhaps, for the engineer or the electrician.

But, leaving these large matters, I would speak of a smaller one. Is there—it is worth asking—such laughter about labour, such fun, such gamesome good temper, as cheered the long hours in my shop in 1884? Are we not taking industry too seriously to be sensible about it? Reading of "Scientific Management" I recall something quite different from that—something friendly, jolly, by no means scientific—which reached

down to my time from an older England. A mischievous spirit
itself freshened one up sometimes. One day there came, knocking
at my office-door, an innocent apprentice-boy with a message
from the wheelwright who was teaching him his trade. "Please
sir," the boy said, "Mr —— sent me to get a straight hook."
Of course I ought to have been angry with the man for wasting
time in sending the boy off on a fool's errand, and with the boy
for coming to me when he must assuredly have been sent to the
blacksmiths. But in fact I could not be angry. I sent the boy
back. "Go and tell Mr —— if he wants a straight hook to
come and ask me for it himself."

And though there cannot have been any profit in that trans-
action I have always valued the good temper it betokened all
round, as a product of industry too much overlooked in modern
times. There ought really to be a little fun in work, for the
workman's sake. And I think he will insist on it, even at the
cost of a little less Civilisation for the Employing Classes.

NOTES

NOTE A. TO PAGE 18

Taking the routs. The importance of this consideration to a farmer appears in Arthur Young's *Six Weeks' Tour through the Southern Counties*. Young says (3rd edn, 1772, p. 154), "from Gloucester to Newnham, which is twelve miles...ruts all the way; and what is remarkable, I found by them, that they build their waggons, with their wheels full three inches nearer to each other than in the eastern counties, which is surprising: a Norfolk or Suffolk waggon could not stir even in this turn-pike road."

Marshall, in his *Rural Economy of the Southern Counties*, 1798, gives a number of measurements of the width of waggon wheels "at ground" as we used to say. It is strange to note that Marshall, though he seems to have been so practical a man, did not always measure the wheels in a manner that could have satisfied wheelwrights in my shop. There, what we wanted to know and to secure was the outside measurement "over all"—anything from 5·feet 10½ inches to 5 feet 11½ inches. It was not enough to measure the felloes, which might vary. What was wanted was the width of tyres, or of strakes rather; and a "six foot stick"—a long "straight-edge"—was the instrument used, by two people, with much care. Still, Marshall's measurements are interesting, and their very diversity (as in the case given by Young) shows how little intercourse there can have been in those days between different districts of England. According to Marshall (vol. I. p. 58):

"The waggon of Kent is of the middle size....The width of its track...measures about four feet ten inches, from middle to middle of the ruts...."

(Vol. II. p. 136.) "The waggons of the Weald" (of Sussex), "as of most deep-roaded districts, are tall and large, with a wide grasp, or span, between the wheels, which are here, frequently made, with fellies, of six inches broad; narrow wheels, nevertheless, are also in use. I have measured the ruts of a broad-wheeled waggon, full six feet, from out to out; or about five feet and a half from middle to middle."

(Vol. II. p. 321.) "The Wiltshire Waggons run remarkably wide; full five feet and a half from middle to middle of the ruts; I have measured one near six feet, from out to out, far exceeding, in this respect, the waggons of most other parts of the kingdom: they are peculiarly well-adapted to a side-hill country; and are, on the whole, well suited to the country, in which they are employed."

NOTE B. TO PAGE 19

My grandfather's belief in the efficacy of wounds as an influence in training seems to have been a country tradition, not confined to wheel-wrights, or to Surrey. It occurs in the East Riding of Yorkshire, where (says the editor of Best's *Rural Economy*, in a footnote to p. 43) "the country people still firmly believe, that unless the shearer (reaper) cuts himself the first time he handles the sickle, he will never be expert at that implement."

NOTE C. TO PAGE 55

The aunt mentioned on p. 7 made the following remark apropos of her own childhood days in the twenties of the nineteenth century:

When a new waggon was finished at the shop the event was cele-brated with a wayzgoose (she probably said "waygoose"), or supper and songs, at the "Seven Stars"; at which the master and his own special intimates were present along with the four or five workmen from the shop in a sort of family party. Amongst the songs "Jockey to the Fair" was one. All joked together on level terms. One of the men was always twitted for saying "whitenin'" instead of "whiting." "Might as well call blackin' blackenin'," they told him.

At Christmas it was usual for the men to have elderberry wine in the master's best room, and that season was also the excuse for another supper, at which not only the regular men, but the sawyers too, were present. A difficulty connected with the sawyers, who were likewise invited to a supper given by a carpenter, has been spoken of in the text, as also has the neighbourly solution of it. Recalling all this the aunt said, with a laugh, "I think people used to be happier then. They weren't so stuck up. There wasn't so much difference between tne classes, but 't was more like a family."

(A correspondent writes "The word wazegoose is well known in the printing trade...as describing the annual feast of the workmen... usually a summer excursion....")

NOTE D. TO PAGE 64

The change from "long-boarding" to "cross-boarding" had already been made, in the case of two-wheeled carts, in the period (about 1880) when my brother was working in the shop, and by 1884 it had extended to waggons too.

The introduction of "deals" with their standardised thickness had made it possible to cross-board waggon or cart, without any of those irregularities incidental to the use of elm boards. Cross-boarding was, there is no doubt, cheaper; and I suspect that, even at this period, increase of all costs of production was beginning to make cheaper methods necessary wherever possible. The dates—1880 to 1884—are not without interest. Though no one knew it, "Unrest" was coming fast, even then.

NOTE E. TO PAGE 67

Mr Lunn's waggon, shown in Plate V, was built (according to H. Hole, one of the few who remain[1] of the original staff) by my father's elder brother John, about 1866. Hole has some right to an opinion. The near "side" of the waggon is indeed embellished with a "beading" from end to end, just as he says. He adds that this decoration, which he calls "oblows," was carried out with a special tool possessed by my uncle alone; and he claims to remember the making of the waggon soon after he himself was taken on as "boy" in the shop in 1865. John Sturt's latest work cannot have been of much later date than that. In my own earliest recollection of him—say 1867—he was already a helpless cripple.

Hole has a further claim to knowledge of the waggon. In 1876 (the date stands in the oldest ledger I have) he rebuilt it, from the floor upwards, with new raves and head and one shutlock. Who else should be sure of the waggon, if not the man who did all this work to it?

Yet I cannot think Lunn's waggon was the same that he saw my uncle John building in 1866. It must be far older than that. A waggon built then, in "Old Sturt's" timber, would not have wanted all new raves only ten years later. Hole must have seen John Sturt, with that unique tool, working his "oblows" on somebody else's waggon—a likely enough thing; and Mr Lunn's must have been on the road long before that date.

The square iron of the rave-stays is not so conclusive a sign of early work as could be wished. Round iron certainly superseded it long ago,. but I cannot say at what date.

It is interesting to note that this waggon came into the shop to be repaired and painted in 1920—when it was nearly seventy years old at least. It was on that occasion that this picture of it was secured.

NOTE F. TO PAGE 86

This primitive notation was especially useful amongst illiterate people, affording them a crude decimal system of counting though they might never have learnt to read and write. I have seen the tale of cartloads marked in this way on the side of carts or of railway trucks; and the following account of its use amongst Yorkshire shepherds is given by Best (p. 83):

"...on Monday the 18th of Aprill wee tolde the ewes and lambes, and delivered them to the shepheard who carryed them to field; he marked the number of them on a sticke, and wee sette them downe in our allmanacke, as wee doe alsoe them that dye betwixt one markinge time and another, as for example this marke ✚ standeth for 20, this marke X for ten, and this, which is called faggett-marke, ⦀⦀ for 5."

<hr>

[1] He has since died, August 1922.

(The mark for 20, given in the Surtees Society's publication, is but a printer's asterisk. The marks known to me, in weighing up hundred-weights of old iron, reached only to 5—a stroke scored across IIII—and then began again. See p. 86.)

NOTE G. TO PAGE 157

Mr George Turner ("Porter") still working (1921) as blacksmith where, in my time, he was junior to Will Hammond, lately mentioned that he had seen my father "line out wooden axles as fast as you could speak."

NOTE H. TO PAGE 159

FASTENINGS

The Iron Age had not made much headway for things of humble use at the time when the door-fastenings and window-fastenings of the old shop were contrived. Grandees may have indulged in locks and keys; the wheelwrights of old—my grandfather and his predecessors, with a living to earn—made shift with devices of their own. In these primitive appliances the wood-worker's ingenuity was more in evidence than the blacksmith's; iron was still but a useful handmaid to timber.

It made its chief appearance in securing the three windows that looked out on the little lane which led to the hop-ground at the back of the shop. This lane sloped up steeply past the windows, getting so high at the third window that even little boys outside had to stoop if they wanted to peer down into the shop and watch the workman at his bench below them. The windows were not made to open. Narrow panes of glass, overlapping, were puttied into the spaces—two (or was it three?) on either side of a stiff centre-post. But these windows were shuttered at night. You knelt up on the bench underneath to fasten the shutters—taking care not to put your knee on any nail or screw or sharp-edged tool.

All day long the shutters (painted "lid-colour") were swung back against the wall outside, a hasp, such as any blacksmith could have made, being driven into the wall and pivoting round to hold the shutter in place. (Passing boys—but not so often as you might think—sometimes pushed the hasp back and set the shutter swinging free, darkening the bench for the man within.) But at night the shutters were closed across the window, one being rabbeted (rebated) over the other. Then a "pin" (an iron dowel about as big as a pencil, and with a flat head) was thrust through shutters and centre-post by an apprentice outside, and "keyed" inside with a little key hanging down by four or five inches of "dog-chain."

So much for the side of the shop, with its windows which did not open, up by the lane. The front followed quite a different principle. It stood back—this front did—behind an ancient elm-tree, with some fifteen feet or so of sloping vacant space separating it from the street. And whereas the windows at the side did not open, everything in the front could be opened—the middle doors of course, and also the windows on either hand.

These front windows, when I first went to the shop, were but open spaces only closed at night with their wooden shutters. And when (as previously told) I had glass window-frames made for use by day, still I went on the old pattern: the new windows were merely glazed shutters —two on each side of the door. At night they were lifted right out and the original wooden shutters were put up instead of them. Moreover, like the shutters, the windows were lifted up from inside, one rabbeted over the other.

No bolt or hasp or pin secured them, as in the case of the side windows. The fastening in front—most effective—was a wooden bar right across the two shutters. One end of the bar was pushed into a special hole; the other end was simply dropped into and over an iron crutch driven strongly into the opposite framework. That was all; but it was enough. No bolt could have held the shutters or windows more safely. A drunken man lurching up against the place at night might have split the thin panelling, but he would not have pushed the shutters inwards. The bar, about eighteen inches up from the window-sill, held them tight.

The middle doors—the entrance from the street—could not be on this pattern, being made not to remove but to swing outwards. When open and hooked back, indeed, they partly blocked the window-space on either hand. These doors had to let a waggon pass through; the door-way they closed therefore was between six and seven feet wide. Nor was there anything they could be shut up against, when they were folded together at night. One of them had a rabbeting or filleting to secure the other, and this rabbeted one, of course, was the last to be closed. The other, meanwhile, was fastened with two home-made bolts. So far, so good. But how was the first one, when finally folded together against it, to be secured, with neither bolt nor lock and key?

The problem after all was solved easily enough. True, there was no means of unfastening the doors from the street. That had been unnecessary while the owner lived in the house next door and could get through the shop from the back. From inside accordingly the doors were fastened. Drawing them together (and thereby shutting out the street)—all the windows having been shuttered and pinned or barred in the glimmer of summer evening or the pitchy dark of winter night—the job of fastening the doors could and was after all done easily from within—easily, by the feel of it, and most safely. About half-way up, and close to them, a stiff wooden bar was lodged behind the doors. One end of it went into a socket in the door post; the other end slipped through a slot in the opposite post, then dropped into a notch prepared for it, and there lay the bar. From outside, a strong horse could hardly have broken it; from within, a little boy who knew the trick might have moved it easily.

At the middle of the bar, and on the inner side of it, was a strong staple; and over this was linked a short piece of chain hanging down from the door. So the door was pulled tight up to the bar. But, "to make assurance doubly sure," a pinule which hung down from the pole —a small pointed piece of iron no bigger than your little finger—held this link down over the staple. When you had attended to this the front of the shop was safe for the night. After this, all you had to do was to pick your way through the dark to the back door and padlock that, and the shutting-up was done.

So it must have been accomplished for over a century and a half. And I recall it now as an example of the shifts men were put to, before the iron age had got on the move again.

NOTE K. TO PAGE 172

A leather apron (mentioned by Shakespeare in *Julius Caesar*), made of chamois ("shammy") leather, was a blacksmith's protection against the sparks that flew up under his hammer.

Neat's-foot oil (not mentioned in the text) was always called for by Will Hammond when he unshipped and dragged into the daylight his bellows to be oiled. I never bought neat's-foot oil for any other purpose and to this day I am ignorant about its advantages; but Will Hammond demanded it on these occasions and I got some for him from a local saddler.

When Will's hands chapped in the winter, his remedy was to seal up the chaps with cobbler's wax.

NOTE L. TO PAGES 43, 178

The tardiness of farmers, putting off sending to the wheelwright until the last, was no new thing. As long ago as 1641 Best unawares owned to it in his *Rural Economy in Yorkshire* (Surtees Society, 1857). He says (p. 35):

"About the time that wee beginne to cutte grasse, or howsoever the weeke afore wee intende to loade hey, wee sende worde to the wright to come and see that the axle-trees and felfes of the waines bee sownde and firme, and to put on their shelvinges, and likewise to put in stowers, wheare any are wantinge."

And again (p. 46):

"It is a good way to speake to the foreman, afore yow beginne to leade (winter corn), to see the waines bee well-greased, and alsoe to have five waines made ready, that you may always have one in readinesse, for fear that some chance to miscarry or bee defecktive, and thus doing yow shall never bee in dainger of losing a good opportunity, or seekinge the implements when you shoulde use them."

Plainly the disadvantages of being dilatory were not unknown.

NOTE M. to page 198

In his *Six Weeks' Tour through the Southern Counties* (3rd edition, 1772) Arthur Young gives the following table of prices for farm tackle in various districts he passed through:

	WAGGONS £ s. d.			CARTS £ s. d.			PLOUGHS £ s. d.			HARROWS £ s. d.		
Near Bury ...	25	0	0	12	0	0	1	10	0	2	0	0
Braintree to Chelmsford ...	20	0	0	6	6	0	1	10	0		...	
Crickly Hill ...	18	0	0		...			...			...	
Lanvachers ...	9	0	0	4	0	0	0	9	0	0	14	6
Devizes to Salisbury ...	20	0	0	10	0	0	0	18	0	0	7	6
Salisbury to Bruchalk ...	20	0	0	10	0	0	0	18	0	0	7	6
Ingatestone to Chelmsford	25	0	0	12	0	0	1	10	0	2	5	0

"These prices," he says, "vary from the prices of timber, iron, and workmanship."

The low prices at Lanvachers seem to point to a survival of still earlier prices in some isolated village shop. In this connection it may be noted that in October, 1701, Lady Grisell Baillie near Edinburgh paid £48 Scots (£4 sterling) for a cart at Mellersteans.

These Scottish carts may have been what Celia Fiennes at about the same date called "Dung-potts," on which "the wheeles are fastened to the axle-tree and so turn altogether."

Young gives further the following estimate for sundry farm tackle, for stocking a new farm:

	£
One broad wheel waggon	70
Three narrow ditto ...	70
Six carts	72
Three pr. harrows ...	6
Three rollers	5

Amongst my father's papers (but I have no idea where this one came from, or who "Chales Faukner" was, or who Isaac Holloway) is the following wheelwright's bill, in which the low prices are worth noting:

1790 Mr Chales Faukner to Isaac Holloway	£	s.	d.
27 Desember for a New Duncart	1	16	0
for a ex to the Cart	0	5	6
for two doart bourds	0	0	8
for fiting the sharps	0	0	6
for a Cay stick to yᵉ Cart	0	0	4
1 January 1791 for takeing down a waggon and puting up a fram	0	1	0
for puting two stans	0	0	6

					£	s.	d.
29 for a Bitel and Handel ...	...	...	...	...	0	0	7
for a ax Handel ...	...	...	...	...	0	0	6
23 February for a waggon Sharp ...	...	...	...	0	3	0
28 for a Handel to a plough	...	...	...	...	0	1	6
for a Broad Bourd	...	...	...	...	0	1	6
12 March for a Chrow steaf	...	...	...	...	0	0	10
19 for two pear of Heams ...	...	...	...	...	0	2	4
14 Aprel for a Heam	...	...	...	...	0	0	7
29 for a peal to a plough ...	...	...	...	...	0	0	6
5 May for a pear of Cart weeles ...	...	...	...	1	14	0
20 May for a Box to a plough	...	...	...	...	0	2	0
for a Chrow steaf...	...	...	...	...	0	0	10
for a Broad Bourd	...	...	...	...	0	1	6
3 June for two Boltes	...	...	...	...	0	1	6
for two Larg wippances ...	...	...	...	...	0	1	4
for a Cay in a tail Lader	...	...	...	...	0	0	8
28 for sheathing a plough ...	...	...	...	...	0	3	0
for steaving the plough ...	...	...	...	...	0	0	6
for a Broad Bourd	...	...	...	...	0	1	6
for taking down a fram and puting up a waggon	...	0	1	0
18 July for a pear of sharps	...	...	...	...	0	6	0
17 october for a Broad bourd	...	...	...	...	0	1	6
24 Nofember for a Chaf Cuting Box	...	...	...	0	8	0
					5	19	2
ston *s.*							
One Hog W 27 at 3 pr Ston ...	...	...	...	4	1	0
					1	18	2

Seteld this bill by
Mr Isaac Holloway

GLOSSARY

ARM. The end of an axle on which the wheel runs.

AXLE-BED. The wooden case (usually of beech) for an axle.

AXLE-BLOCKS. Pieces of wood on top of an axle-bed to carry the waggon or cart at a higher level.

AXLE-TREE. The whole axle, inclusive of the arms, fashioned out of one piece of timber. (This was often called "wooden ex.")

BACK (of a felloe). The convex outer side, covered by the tyre.

BACK-BAND. A ridge-tie (q.v.).

BACK-IRON. The part of a plane screwed against the blade, to keep the shavings thin.

BAR. One of the stout cross-timbers in a dung-cart bottom. Wheel-barrows, being made on the same principle, were also framed-up with bottom bars.

BARRELLED. Shaft-eyes or other irons forged out in the shape of a barrel. The barrelling kept them strong, while it lightened them.

BAVINS. Bundles of the "sprays" or lightest branches of timber.

BEATLE or BEETLE. A heavy two-handed mallet, used with wedges for cleaving wood, where a sledge-hammer would not do.

BELLY. The inner (hollow) curved surface of a felloe.

BIT or BITT. A tool for boring wood. (See Brace and bitts.)

BODY. The part of a vehicle that receives the load.

BOLSTER. (i) A tool for fitting into a blacksmith's anvil, bearing the impression of some special shape the iron is to take.

(ii) A thick piece of timber (usually beech or elm) across under the pillars (pillows?) of a waggon, to support the body.

BOLT. (i) One of the wooden bars (there were usually two) at the back of a pair of shafts.

(ii) Bolts and nuts (once called pins) were smallish iron dowels, with head at one end, and, at the other end, a nut for tightening.

BOND. An iron ring round the stock or nave of a wheel.

BOX. (i) A pair of handles hinged together, so as to be closed on to the bottom of a pit-saw for the bottom-sawyer's use.

(ii) The hardened iron centre of a wheel, in which the arm runs.

BOXING-ON. Fitting a wheel on to its arm by letting-in and wedging the box.

BRACES. (i) Wooden pieces across right-angled corners, as between shafts and shaft-bolts. Braces lent themselves to graceful shape and much shaving.

(ii) Brace and bitts. Brace. A tool for boring. One part of it could be pressed against the waist of the workman and so held tight against the work, leaving the man both his hands free. To this part was swivelled a rotary crank, worked round and round with the right hand; a detachable boring tool or bitt being fastened into the foot of the crank.

The bitts were of three sorts:

(i) Centre-bitts, for starting holes finished by auger.

(ii) Shell-bitts. Hollow gouges.

(iii) "Twisty-bitts." Spiral tools which in course of time superseded centre-bitt and auger.

BREAST-STROKE. A line cut in while a stock was being turned, to mark the place for the front of the spokes.

BUMPER. A thick wooden end bolted to the main side or body-timber of a tip-cart, so as to take the shock and the wear of tipping. The bumper was shod with iron.

BURNER. A pointed rod of iron, heated for burning away in a hole any roughness left by the auger or bitt.

BUTTERFLY. A simple design shaved upon a piece of timber with the draw-shave.

BUZZ. A three-cornered chisel, used chiefly for clearing out the corners of mortices in a stock.

CARRIAGE. That part of a four-wheel to which the wheels are attached, forming at the same time a detachable carrier for the body. Farm-waggons had two carriages—the fore and the hind. So had timber-carriages. In vans, drays, and all "spring" vehicles the hind wheels were hung on to the body; while the fore-carriage, running on the front wheels, was the "under-carriage."

CAST. To twist or warp.

CLEAR HERSELF. A saw (always of feminine gender) was required to push out its own sawdust as it went.

CLEAT or CLETE (probably akin to clout, *infra*). A patch of iron, usually for mending broken timber, but sometimes (as in locking-cletes) put on to new timber in places likely to be worn.

CLINKER. A lump of dirt that has been pushed out, molten, from the smith's fire.

CLIP. An iron clutching the axle-arm up into the axle-bed, and fastened itself by clip-pins, these being long bolts tying the whole arrangement securely under the cart body.

CLOUT. An iron plate let into the arm of a wooden axle (on the underside) to take the wear of the box in the revolving wheel.

Lying flush with the wood, and requiring to be very smooth and exact, the clout was fastened with special countersunk nails called clout-nails.

COACH-SCREW (or nut-head). A big screw with a square head, for winding into place with a wrench instead of with a screwdriver.

COLD-CHISEL (often called hard-chisel). A chisel of specially hardened steel, for cutting cold iron.

COLLET. A special ring on an axle-arm, between the lynch-pin and the box of the wheel, to keep the push of the wheel from grinding into the lynch-pin.

COOMED-UP. Possibly gummed-up. A wheel on which the grease had gone dry and stiff was said to be coomed-up.

COPSE. (i) (for harrows, etc.) An iron turned into a loop to clutch the end of a piece of wood, so that a horse could be harnessed to it.

(ii) On the body of a cart or waggon a copse was a thin piece of iron holding the outrave at its proper distance away, the whole being held up by a stay from the strouter.

CORD-WOOD. The smaller branches of timber, stacked in "cords"; used chiefly as firewood.

COTTER-PIN. A minute split-pin, inserted through a hole close outside a nut. When its ends are then spread it cannot get out of the hole nor will it let the nut run off.

CURLY. Wavy. The surface of seasoned timber sometimes ridged up into very shallow waves and was called "curly."

CUT. The opening made by a saw.

Timber (Planks) of which a portion had been sawed away was said to be "in cut."

COPSE BOLTED TO CORNER OF HARROW. (When the whippance had been hooked into the copse, the harrow could be dragged behind a horse.)

A similar copse was used for other purposes: e.g. for attaching a drug-bat to the drug-bat chain.

DIRT-IRONS or DIRT-BOARDS. A sort of eaves standing out over the stock of a wheel from the end of the axle-bed, to keep dirt from falling down into the division between axle-bed and stock.

DISH. The convexity of a wheel on a horse-drawn vehicle.

DOATY. Affected with dry-rot.

DOG. (i) When the tongue of a spoke had snapped off in the felloe, leaving the spoke free, two small holdfasts might for an emergency hold the spoke in place again, being tacked one on each side of it. These holdfasts were called "dogs," and should not be mistaken for a Spoke-dog (*q.v.*).

(ii) Iron tools used in tyring. These were distinguished as (*a*) the furnace dog—a round bar with wooden handle for turning the tyres round in the furnace, and (*b*) stout bars of square iron for picking up a red-hot tyre pulled out of the furnace.

(iii) The Dog and Ring (not the same as Ring-dog, *q.v.*) was a special contrivance by which one end of a tie-chain having been twisted round a wheel could be easily tied into the other end.

(iv) Dog-stick. This was a stout wooden bar attached to back of the axle-bed of a two-wheel cart so as to be let down and trail under the cart going up hill, when a forked iron in the end of the dog-stick was immediately ready to dig into the road if the horse stopped or if the cart tried to run back.

DOWEL. A wooden peg, about the size and shape of a sausage, between two felloes.

DOWEL-BOUND. The state of a wheel in which the dowel-holes were not deep enough, so that the dowels kept the felloes apart instead of letting them meet.

(A wheel might be "bound" in other ways. The tyre, tightening it, ought to have forced every part up into its place. But sometimes the spokes, standing up above the felloes, prevented the tyre from tightening on the rim; and in this case the wheel was "spoke-bound." Or it was "felloe-bound," if the felloes came together in the rim before the spokes had been properly tightened into the stock.)

DRAG. A large-sized harrow.

DRAUGHT-PIN (see Pin). An iron rod for attaching the shafts of a four-wheel (waggon, timber-carriage, lorry, van, or drag) to the fore-carriage.

Sometimes there were two short draught-pins—one for each shaft. Sometimes one draught-pin spanned the whole width. In either case the draught-pin was kept from working out of its place by a split-key (*q.v.*).

DRAW-BOARD-PIN (see Pin). A wooden peg so inserted as not only to hold a tenon in a mortice but also to draw it up very tight there.

DRAW-DOWN. The blacksmiths' word for hammering a piece of iron thin.

DRAW-OUT. To extract a spoke from a stock. (Used in the same way as for a tooth.)

DRAW-SHAVE. A stout and long knife-blade, with handle at both ends, for pulling or shaving away the superfluities of timber.

DRAYEL. A strong loop of iron stapled into the outside of each shaft, near the front end, so that the chains for another horse could be hooked in.

DRUG-BAT (Drag-bat, drug-shoe, or skid-pan). A thick cast-iron shoe carried (by chain) on front of waggon or van, so that, on going down a hill, it could be let down under the near hind-wheel. So skidded, the wheel did not go round but had to be dragged forward and too great a pace was checked, while the cast-iron pan, and not the tyre that lay in it, took the wear and tear of grinding into the road.

DUMMY. A rough three-legged stool, with a long wooden bar rising from the centre. The bar was bored with holes all up, into which the workman could put his hand-lamp at any convenient height.

EXBED. The usual name for axle-bed.

FALSE-BOX. A thickish iron ring spiked to the back of a stock round the true box, and standing out so as to prevent dust or dirt from slipping into the box.

FALSE SPLINTER-BAR. If the fore-carriage, with its splinter-bar, was made for only one horse, a longer splinter-bar could be made to hang in front of it. Two horses could then be harnessed side by side. This false splinter-bar had all the fittings for double-shafts, or even for a pole and traces.

FELLOE. One of the wooden sections of the rim of a wheel.

FELLOE-BLOCK. A length of timber for cutting into one or more felloes.

FELLOE-BOUND. The condition of a wheel in which the felloes were too long, so that they tightened-up together before the spokes had gone into place. (See Dowel-bound.)

FELLOE-HORSE. A complicated implement into which a felloe could be wedged aslant on its back, while the wheelwright adzed-out the curve of its belly.

FLITCH. The half of a tree which has been sawn asunder lengthwise.

FOOT (of a spoke). The flat part or tenon mortised into the stock.

FORE-HEAVY. When a cart was badly balanced, so as to throw too much weight forward on to the horse's back, it was said to be fore-heavy.

FORE-WAY. A forward angle given to the arms of an axle, so that the wheels revolving on them were less likely to run off.

FOXY. Oak-timber is foxy hearted, when the heart of it decays into a rusty string of fibres.

FRESH. Timber not completely seasoned. Green.

FROW. Brittle. Timber (cut from a tree already ageing) was called frow, or "frow as a carrot."

FULLER. An iron tool (held in a rod) for hammering iron tyres into corrugations, so as to increase their circumference.

FUTCHELL. A coach-builder's word for the parts of a fore-carriage represented, in wheelwright's work, by hounds (*q.v.*).

GALLING-PLATES. Two small squares of iron screwed in to face one another so as to take the friction where two timbers met and might chafe. Especially was this the case where the body of a tip-cart hinged down upon the shafts. Galling-plates were therefore always fixed each side of a tip-cart, one in the body and one in the shaft, so as to meet when the former was pulled down upon the latter.

GIRT. A quarter of the circumference of a tree. In ascertaining the cubic contents of a tree, a string was passed round it and doubled, then doubled again. This (with an allowance for the thickness of the bark) gave what timber-measurers called the girt.

GREEN-TIMBER. Timber not yet dry but still containing sap. Fresh (*q.v.*).

GUDGEONS. Round irons (gagged where they would be driven into the wood) fixed into the two ends of a barrow wheel, or of a barley-roller, for spindles.

GUG. A small iron peg rivetted into the inner side of a clip so that, when the clip was tightened into its place the gug might give further security against slipping.

HAMES. Hames were set over a horse's shoulders and the shafts were hooked to them; so that it was the horse's shoulder-work that pulled the cart or waggon along. The hames being made of light timber—or latterly of steel or brass—would have chafed into the horse's skin, but for the padding afforded by the collar under them.

HEAD. The front cross-piece of waggon or cart holding the upper parts of the framework together.

1, HOOK-CAPPING IRON, ready for rivetting on to the end of a shaft;
2, ELONGATED EYE into which the hook of the capping is suspended, the eye itself being bolted into the body.

HOOK-CAPPING IRONS. (I have some dim memory that these were said to be a special invention of my father's.) Hook-cappings were fitted (and rivetted) over the back ends of shafts, each iron then ending in a stout crook for hooking into an elongated eye set under the cart body.

These irons made a substantial hinge between the body and shafts of a tip-cart.

HOPPER. A square receiver made of wood, and fastened over an opening to act as a funnel.

HORSE. Horses were almost as numerous as dogs amongst the old implements. Generally it may be said that, while the latter were chiefly notable for tenacity of hold, the former simply had to support any given object's weight. Dogs were of all shapes; but horses always were framed up on four legs.

I remember of them, and describe in their proper alphabetical place, Felloe-horse, Saw-sharpening horse, Shaft-horse, Wheel-horse.

HOUNDS. Parts of the framework of a fore-carriage.

JARVIS. A hollow plane for rounding-up the sides of spokes.

KEY. (i) A slat of wood across from one side to the other of an old-fashioned long-boarded waggon-bottom or cart-bottom. Usually oak.

(ii) A similar slat for harrow or drag, or fore-carriage.

(iii) A slender piece of wood (preferably ash) uniting the sides of fore or tail-ladder.

(iv) A thin piece of iron, about as big as a knife-blade, for dropping down through a slot in the end of an iron bar or pin, thereby preventing any side-ways movement. (See Split-key.)

(v) "To Key" a tip-cart was to put in the key-stick that kept it from tipping inopportunely.

KEYING-IRONS. Part of the apparatus for keeping a tip-cart rigid when it was not wanted to tip.

KEY-STICK. A slender piece of wood containing, at each end, an iron crank for "keying" the body of a tip-cart down on to the shafts.

KNOCK. The shoulder of a spoke on which the felloe should finally rest after being wedged into place.

LADDER. A strong though light framework for extending when desired the loading capacity of cart or waggon. These ladders were made with two stoutish side-pieces connected by two thin but tough slats or keys, and were chiefly used for hay. The fore-ladder, whether for cart or waggon, stretched out a foot or so higher than the horse's back. The tail-ladder (for waggons only) carried the load back beyond the farthest stretch of the opened tail-board.

LARROW. Larrows (four, or sometimes five) were the main timbers of harrows and of drags. The tines (q.v.) were mortised into them, and they were connected by "keys."

LAYING. Strengthening a length of iron or steel, with another piece welded into it.

LIGHTER. A thick bar of wood across the front "sides" of a dung-cart, lying just over the back ends of the shafts. One end of the lighter formed a handle for tipping the body; and through a mortice in the middle of the lighter stood up the hinged tip-stick from the shafts.

LINE. A line or "chalk-line"—a strong cord wound on a reel—was the wood-worker's instrument for marking future saw-cuts or axe-cuts on his timber.

LINE-OUT. To mark with help of a chalk line.

LINING. A blacksmith's term for adding a fresh piece to the thickness of iron or steel. Much the same as "laying" (q.v.).

LOCK. The turning of the fore-wheels, in relation to the hind-wheels.

LOCKING-CLETES. Two thick plates of iron nailed to a waggon-body to receive the wear of the tyres, just where the fore-wheels cut into the body when locking round.

LONG-HUNDRED. 120 or more of short spokes, reckoned as 100 full-length spokes.

LONG-PIN. A bolt long enough to tighten any wooden framework together which could not be otherwise conveniently mended.

LONG-STAPLE. A piece of round iron, the ends of which were pointed and turned down at right angles to be clenched through the fore-end of a shaft. Meanwhile the middle part of it (some eight inches long) stood about three-quarters of an inch above the upper side of the shaft, like a short railing. On this "staple" were strung the ridge-tie and the various hooks for harnessing the horse to the shafts.

LOW-TAILBOARD. A single piece of wood (about ten inches wide and one and a half inches thick) sometimes used across the tail of a tip-cart when the ordinary framed tailboard would have stood too high above the load.

MANDRIL. A cone of iron, on which the blacksmith could beat out any ring of iron to the dimensions required. Mandrils for stock-bonds were so large that they had to be hollow and to stand on the ground. Other mandrils could be slipped into the socket provided for such things at the end of the anvil.

MEETINGS. The average, or general cubic contents of a "parcel" of trees. If, for instance, a number of trees measured about ten cubic feet ("ten-foot cube") each, they would be "ten-foot meetin's."

MESHES. The parts of a stock left standing, between the mortices for the spokes.

MULLER and STONE. Implements used in grinding paint. The muller, in my shop, was heavy, and rounded at the top for two-handed pressure. The stone was a flat slab.

NEAL (ANNEAL). To take the brittleness from iron, so that the iron can be bent permanently without breaking.

NEB. An implement on two wheels, for moving a piece of timber. Sometimes called "A Pair of Wheels," or a "Timber-bob."

NEEDLE. A slender rod of iron, from 18 to 24 inches long, curved and having a hooked end like a button-hook; used in timber measuring for pulling the tape or string under a tree which lies too close on the ground.

NOSE. The front end of a stock or nave.

NUNTER. A small block tenoned at each end into a piece of timber, to hold the two pieces at the desired distance from one another. Often the nunter was bored longitudinally (like a cotton-reel) to shield a bolt passing through it from one timber to the other.

NUT-HEAD. A Coach-screw (q.v.).

OBLOWS. The beading worked (for ornament only) along the main "sides" of a waggon.

(This word had already gone out of use in 1884.)

OFF and ON spokes were mortised into the stock in two rows, in one row the spokes being half an inch or so farther back than those which alternated with them, in the other row.

PANE. The thin end of a hammer-head.

PILLAR. Probably pillow. Much the same as bolster (q.v.).

PIN. (The use of the word pins for bolts and nuts suggests that these were late introductions into the shop, replacing wooden predecessors.)

Where tenons were pinned into mortices, the pins were commonly chopped or chiselled out of oak. Made very slender yet tapering they were hammered in until they grew tight, when the ends of them were cleanly chiselled away. For various kinds of pin see clip (pins), draught-pin, draw-board-pin, long-pin, round-pin, tail-pin.

PINCH. Of a saw that cut too narrow a cut and worked tightly in it.

PINULE (called pinnel). Any round and pointed iron, about as big as your finger or smaller, commonly chained near to its hole so that it was always ready to be dropped in when wanted.

PLOUGH-BEAM. The backbone or main timber of a plough, to which all the other parts were attached.

PLOUGH-BOLT. A large and heavy whippance.

POLE. (i) The long beam which, in timber-carriage and farm-waggon, joined together the two under parts, viz. the fore-carriage and the hind-carriage. The fore-carriage, with its round-pin (q.v.) going down through the front end of the pole, could pivot round on it. Not so the hind-carriage, which always had to trundle along in the rear of the other, led by its pole. In waggons the pole was fixed to the hind-carriage; but in timber-carriages it was much larger and heavier, and was made to slide to greater or less length to suit the load.

(ii) In later times a pole was used (as with omnibuses) instead of double shafts, for harnessing a pair of horses side by side.

PROPSTICK. A propstick was often hung under each shaft of a two-wheeled cart, to be let down when the cart was still, so as to take the weight and relieve the horse's back.

PUMMEL. The hinder end of the main side of a dung-cart, standing out beyond the tailboard and serving as a "bumper" in tipping the cart.

QUILER. (Perhaps coiler.) One of the fore-irons on a shaft. In later years a hook strung on the long-staple did duty for it.

RACE. A pocket clasp-knife with point turned back. It was sharpened at the turn, for scratching marks on wood.

RAIL. See Tailboard Rails.

RANGE (of wheels). To keep in the same direction.

RATCHET. A boring tool, handy for working in narrow corners.

RAVE. One of the slender side-rails in the framework of waggon or van or two-wheeled cart.

RIDGE-TIE. A chain of double links twisted into one another, for casting over a horse's back to hold up the shafts. It served the opposite purpose to the leather Wantie or Belly-band, and was sometimes called Back-band.

RIMER. A square rod of steel or hardened iron, to be turned round and round inside a metal hole until its sharp corners have enlarged the hole.

RIND-GALL. A flaw in timber, discovered only when the saw disclosed bark grown over by sound wood.

RING. The complete circle of felloes round a wheel.

RING-DOG. A heavily made hook, with ring at the end, for turning over a log of timber. The "dog" bit into the timber; the "ring" was for inserting a lever.

RING and START. An iron ring, about two and a half inches in diameter, shut (loose and dangling) into a pointed iron peg. This peg, or "start," was driven into the underside of a shaft, and through the ring dangling from it the trace was threaded when the horse was harnessed.

RINGS and GUDGEONS. The rings were two broad iron ferules for the stock of a barrow wheel, to keep the stock from splitting when the gudgeons—the iron spindles—were driven in.

RING-SHAKE. A circular shake in a tree, following one of the rings of growth, and dividing the outer part of the tree from the inner part, so that the latter was liable to come out like a pith.

RISER. An additional timber bolted to the top of a pillar or exbed, so as to raise the body higher.

ROLLER (or roller-scotch). A small cylinder hung so as to trundle along behind a waggon wheel moving up hill, to be in place for scotching the wheel immediately, if for any reason the waggon stopped.

ROLLER-CHAIN. One of the light chains by which the roller was held in place.

ROLLER-CHEEK. A slender iron into which the roller was suspended, at the end of the chain.

ROSE NAIL, or CUT NAIL. A flattish nail made of wrought-iron, very useful for its toughness before wire nails were introduced.

ROUND-PIN. The stout iron pivot that held the head of a waggon down in its place, allowing the fore-carriage underneath the head, attached to the horses, to turn freely. The round-pin answered to the perch-bolt in coach-building.

ROUTER. A tool for carving out the centre of a stock in a wheel, to admit the box.

ROUTS. The same as ruts. A waggon or dung-cart was required to "take the routs," i.e. to keep to the usual ruts.

(A connection between this word and route appeared when men in my shop spoke of the route-marching of soldiers from Aldershot as rout-marching.)

RUN. (i) To split easily.

(ii) To "run" a wheel was to trundle it along by hand.

RUNG. One of the rounds or steps of a builder's ladder—usually made of an old spoke.

RUNNING-DOWN. When a nut was tight (with rust or otherwise) the blacksmith had to ease it up-and-down on its bolt. This was called "running-down."

SAMSON. An implement for drawing two felloes very tight together, in readiness for nailing a strake over the joint between them.

SAW-SET. A small wrench for straining outwards or inwards the teeth of a saw.

SAW-SHARPENING HORSE. A long four-legged stool, with pegs upright in it; slotted so that a saw could be rested in the pegs while its teeth were being filed.

SCARFING. Thinning (with the hammer) any two pieces of iron where they are to be welded together.

SCRATCH-BITT. A wooden gauge with an iron tooth for scratching, as with a sharp knife, an indelible line to be followed with axe or plane or chisel.

SCRIVER. A sharply-pointed piece of iron, with handle-end turned into a loop, to be used where a "carpenter's" (wide) pencil would not go.

SHAFT-HORSE. A cross-bar, made so as to slide up or down on an upright, so that the shafts of a two-wheeled cart could be lodged on it at any desired height.

SHAFT-IRONS. The set of irons provided for a pair of shafts, for fixing the harness. Each set of shaft-irons comprised two long staples, sundry hooks threaded on the staples, two drayels, two quilers, and two ring-and-starts.

SHARPS. The old-fashioned name for shafts.

SHOEING (to wheels). Putting on the strakes or shoes which preceded hoop-tyres.

SHOEING-HOLE. A ditch, about eight inches wide by five feet long, between sills; kept full of water for cooling tyres or strakes.

SHOOTING-BAR. The hindmost of the cross-timbers in the bottom frame of a dung-cart.

SHOULDERS. The projections making the triangular face of a spoke, preventing the spoke from being driven any farther down into the stock.

SHUT-LINK. A spare link, made like a split key-ring, for inserting into a broken chain by a carter when away from a smithy, or in any emergency.

SHUT-LOCK. (Pronounced shet-lick in West Surrey.) Either the foremost or the hindmost cross-timber in the bottom of a waggon, or of any vehicle other than a dung-cart. The function of the shut-lock was to hold the longitudinal timbers in place. (The Sussex name was Dware.)

SHUTTING. The blacksmiths' term for welding.

SIDES. The main outer timbers in the bottom framework of any vehicle, barrow or truck.

SKID-PAN. Another name for a drug-bat (q.v.).

SLABS. The outside pieces of a tree, which remain after the middle has been sawn into plank or board.

SOLE. The wooden surface of a wheel; the surface which would meet the ground were it not shod or protected by strake or tyre.

SOLING-DOWN. Preparing (by chopping) a new sole on a worn wheel, in readiness for a new tyre.

SPANNER. A wrench for nuts.

SPLINTER-BAR. The front cross-piece of a fore-carriage, containing the iron "eyes" for hanging the shafts.

SPLIT-KEY. Made by bending the two ends of a thin piece of iron together, so that they could be thrust, flatwise and together, through a slot in the end of a pin. Once through, they were separated and curled back, one each side, and prevented the pin from slipping out of its place.

SPOKE-BOUND. (See Dowel-bound.)

SPOKE-DOG. A tool for straining two spokes together after they have been driven into the stock, so that their tongues will be close enough for a felloe to be slipped over them.

SPOKE-SHAVE. The finishing tool for smoothing away any edges left by the draw-shave, after a timber has been sufficiently reduced in size. The spoke-shave was characteristically useful in curved places like the front of spokes, where a smoothing-plane could not be used.

SPREAD. Of the body of any vehicle. To bulge outwards beyond the intended width.

SPREADER. A light rod holding the trace-chains asunder, when horses are harnessed in a team.

SPRIG. One of three minute iron pegs driven into a stock against the bond and then bent over on the bond to fix it in place.

SQUARE TONGUES. Tenons cut at the ends of spokes, for mortising into the felloes.

STAMM. The part of the butt of a tree in the ground, where it curves outwards for the roots.

STANDS or STANDARDS. The upright bars in any wooden framework, *e.g.* in tailboards.

STAVES. The front-staff, middle-staff and hind-staff were iron supports built into waggon bodies or raved-cart bodies, to prevent the raves from spreading.

STICK. The trunk of a tree after it has been thrown.

STOPPER, STOPPER-CLASP, STOPPER-HOLE. To admit the lynch-pin a slot was cut through the nose of a stock so that the lynch-pin could be dropped through into the arm. The stopper-hole was kept closed by the stopper, a small block of wood exactly fitting it. And lest the stopper should fall out when the wheel turned, that too was held in place by the stopper-clasp, which was stapled to the stock itself.

STRAKE. An iron "shoe" over the junction of two felloes, stretching from centre to centre of the felloes. (An old strake, standing on its edge, would sometimes do instead of a fender in front of a narrow fireplace.)

STRAKE-CHIMNEY. The wide brick fireplace or oven for heating strakes.

STRAP. Iron hammered thin and provided with holes, for nailing or screwing to a piece of wood.

STRAP-BOLT. A useful contrivance by which a piece of wood could have, nailed to one end by a "strap," a bolt and nut (instead of a tenon) to tighten it to a cross-piece.

STROUTER. An upright support or strut for the side framework of waggon or cart.

STROUTER-SOCKET. An iron cup fixed to the bottom of waggon or cart, for holding the lower end of a wooden strouter.

SUMMER. One of the inner longitudinal timbers in the bottom framework of waggon or raved cart. The ends of the summers were held in place by the shut-locks.

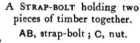

A STRAP-BOLT holding two pieces of timber together.

AB, strap-bolt ; C, nut.

SWAN-NECKS. Curved hooks fastened to the shafts of a dung-cart, for attaching the shafts to the body. In other carts, and in my shop, swan-necks were replaced by the costlier but steadier hook-capping irons.

SWEEP. The back-bar across the fore-carriage of a waggon or timber-carriage working round under the pole.

SWINGING A WHEEL. Putting it in free revolution, round and round on its axle, without touching the ground.

TAIL. (i) The hinder end of a waggon or cart.

(ii) The hinder end of an arm.

TAILBOARD RAILS. The top and bottom pieces of a tailboard frame.

TAIL-HEAVY. The opposite fault to fore-heavy. In a tail-heavy cart the tendency was to lift the horse off the ground.

TAIL-PIN. (i) The pin (fastened with a split-key) which held the tail of a waggon down to its place on the hind-carriage.

(ii) The strong bolt by which the tail of an arm was kept up in its place in an axle-bed.

TAP. (i) The screwed groove in a nut, fitting over the thread or worm of the bolt. In an "untapped nut" the groove had not yet been cut.

(ii) The tool for cutting it.

THREAD. The thin upstanding spiral on a bolt or screw.

THROW. To throw a tree was the West Surrey word for to fell it.

TIMBER-BOB. See Neb.

TINES. The long steel teeth in a harrow for scratching into the ground.

TIPPING-IRONS. Bent irons on the rear of a cart to serve as "bumpers" on the ground when the cart is tipped up.

TIP-STICK. (Sometimes of iron.) The upright bar in front of a dung-cart. It was hinged from the shafts through the lighter on the body; and, being perforated with holes, made it possible to keep the body tipped at any desired angle for crossing a field.

TONGUE. The end of a spoke prepared for inserting into a felloe.

TRAVELLER. The blacksmith's rotating disk for measuring round the circumference of wheels and of tyres.

TRUE OUT O' WIND. Without winding or twist. Plane, in the Euclidean sense.

TRYING-STICKS. Two small sticks placed at different ends of a surface not easily visible, so that it could be more plainly seen whether the surface was true out o' wind or not.

TUE-IRON. That end of the tube from the bellows which lies immediately under the fire on a blacksmith's hearth.

TURN. (i) To saw out with a curve.

(ii) To give to a pillar the requisite convexity or turn.

TWISTY-BITTS. Boring tools, made in a spiral, for fixing into a brace. (These excellent tools superseded augers, and, being new things, received in my shop a name which may have been unknown elsewhere.)

UPSET. A blacksmith's term for making an iron bar or rod bulge.

WANEY. The edge of a plank or board where the thickness diminishes or wanes to include a portion of the bark.

WAYZGOOSE. A bean-feast. (See page 206. The celebration described on that page was oftener called WETTING THE WAGGON.)

WHEEL-BLOCK or WHEEL-STOOL. A heavy four-legged framework on which a wheel could be thrown for repairing.

WHEEL-HORSE. A substantial framework to be used in making wheels that would have been too small to be made on the wheel-pit. This implement was not known in my shop when I first went there. One of the men eventually made one for the increasing number of van wheels.

WHIPPANCE or WHIPPLE-TREE. A wooden bar to be hooked on, by its centre, to a harrow, while its two ends were chained to a horse. (A stronger whippance for ploughing was called a plough-bolt.)

WOODLOUSE. A small pinch of skin, black with contained blood.

WORM. The same as Thread.

INDEX